COUNSELLING
INSIGHTS

COUNSELLING
INSIGHTS

Practical Strategies for Helping Others
with Anxiety, Trauma, Grief, and More

EDITED BY VICKI ENNS

ACHIEVE
PUBLISHING

Published by ACHIEVE Publishing
120 Sherbrook Street, Winnipeg, Manitoba R3C 2B4
www.achieve-publishing.com

ACHIEVE
PUBLISHING

Bulk discounts available. For details contact:
ACHIEVE Publishing at 204-789-2452 or info@achievecentre.com

This book is typeset in Adobe Caslon Pro and Bernino Sans.
Printed with vegetable-based inks on 100% PCW paper

ISBN: 978-1-988617-03-9 (Canadian edition)
ISBN: 978-1-988617-04-6 (US edition)
ISBN: 978-1-988617-05-3 (ebook)

Printed and bound in Canada
First edition, third printing

Book design by Ninth and May Design Co.

10 9 8 7 6 5 4 3

*For our clients, who had the courage to allow us
to witness vulnerability and grow along with you.
This book wouldn't exist without you.*

CONTENTS

viii   Foreword

x   Introduction

1   Developmental Trauma *By Vicki Enns, MMFT, RMFT*

28   Situational Trauma *By Michelle Gibson, MSW, RSW*

58   Anxiety *By AnnMarie Churchill, PhD, RSW*

86   Depression *By Sheri Coburn, MSW, RSW*

118   Self-Injury *By Trish Harper, MSW, RSW*

150   Suicidality *By Tricia Klassen, MSW, RSW*

182   Substance Use *By Amber McKenzie, MSc, CPsych*

217   LGBT2SQ+ Centred Approaches *By Marion Brown, PhD, RSW*

246   Grief *By John Koop Harder, MSW, RSW*

274   Conclusion

276   Resources

309   Glossary

317   Acknowledgements

319   Speaking and Training

FOREWORD

I have been privileged over the last 10 years to be able to get to know each of the nine contributors to this book. In addition to being counsellors, social workers, or therapists, they are also trainers with the Crisis & Trauma Resource Institute (CTRI). CTRI is a professional development training organization that provides training and resources in the areas of mental health, counselling skills, and violence prevention. Our purpose is to provide exceptional training and resources to better lives.

As the CEO of CTRI, I provide the overall direction for the development and delivery of our workshops and services. However, it is these trainers who bring the material to life wherever they teach. Each of them has a wealth of experience in helping and supporting people who are struggling with a variety of psychological, social, and situational issues. In addition to their insightful understanding of the issues they write about, these authors present information in a way that is not only helpful but also accessible to a wide range of audiences.

At CTRI, we believe that access to knowledge and skill development changes individual lives, communities, and organizations. Through this book, we are working to distribute timely, relevant, and helpful resources to our clients and society as a whole. This book was not just written for clinical counsellors, but also for the multitude of frontline helpers who work to support people who are seeking guidance. This book is a resource for social service and health care providers, educational professionals, social workers, and anyone who identifies as a care provider.

In my role at CTRI, I frequently ask people about why they've attended a specific training of ours. One common theme is that our workshop participants are looking for solutions to a problem they have encountered with someone they are helping.

This book is designed in the same way as our workshops, which provide practical and actionable strategies for helpers. Each chapter looks at a specific issue or situation that helpers commonly encounter and includes theory, examples of real-life application, and practical strategies. Throughout this book, case studies related to both youth and adults are used to illustrate concepts and strategies.

I am happy you've chosen to read this book, and I am confident that it will provide you with new insights about how to better support and help the people you work with.

Randy Grieser
CEO, Crisis & Trauma Resource Institute
Author, *The Ordinary Leader: 10 Key Insights for Building and Leading a Thriving Organization*

INTRODUCTION

Liling feels that the world can be a scary and unfair place. This constant dread keeps her holding onto suicide as an out from her depression.

Alison battles with alcohol use and is afraid of where her drinking has led her, describing the shame she feels that she cannot solve this problem on her own.

Jake has to work to manage his anxiety daily. He has come to realize how deeply scarred he is from years of absorbing homophobic slurs and dismissals.

Oki clearly recalled being forcibly removed from his home at a young age, when he was sent to live in a very remote residential school. This experience stole from him his home, his family, his traditions, his fun, and his innocence as a young boy.

These are some of the people you'll meet and the stories you'll hear in these chapters. They are ordinary people who sometimes have extraordinary challenges. As helpers, caregivers, and counsellors, we can experience both the harsh challenge of promoting change in people's lives and the tremendous privilege of being allowed into such intimate conversations. Our role, whether formal or informal, is to help alleviate suffering and foster growth. We may get caught in polarized feelings of either being driven to try to fix things and rescue people, or else we can feel helpless and ineffective. Life has a way of making change hard. Hearing from other helpers is a key way of finding balance, inspiration, and guidance to focus our efforts.

Who Should Read This Book

This book is for you if you are someone in a helping role – a counsellor, principal, parent, teacher, social worker, support worker, neighbour, family member, or anyone who is actively supporting another person who is seeking change. It is for you if you have heard statements that leave you feeling unsure or even stumped, wondering, "What is the right thing to say? How can I help? What should I do?"

VOICES OF DISTRESS

"My mom thinks I'm crazy."

"Do you know how many times I've tried to quit drinking and using cocaine this week? Seven times. Do you know how many times I've failed? Seven times."

"You can't change what happened. I'm just broken."

"I can't take it anymore, and what's the point of living anyway?"

Working with people is largely an art form. Rarely is there a clear-cut answer. Yes, research guides us, textbooks inform us, teachers and supervisors teach us models of helping, and a plethora of websites offer sound pieces of advice. These provide a necessary foundation for making informed choices when we are working with people. What you can't get from a textbook or a website, however, are the *gut* responses, the *heartfelt* resonances we feel with people, and the unexpected life lessons taught to us by the very people we are trying to help.

In my own practice of more than 20 years as a counsellor, couples and family therapist, and supervisor of trainees in a graduate counselling program, I have been humbled over and over again by the innate strength and courage of the people I support. I have spent a long time in graduate and post-graduate study, but I can confidently say I have learned the most from my clients, as they graciously let me walk with them. They have taught me what it means to persevere, to fall and get up again, and to heal. It is this collaboration that provides any kind of meaningful map for this work.

What You Will Find in This Book

At some point, all of us will feel the need to make changes in our lives, whether they're motivated by distress or discomfort, pressures from other people or events, or societal attitudes that tell us we should be different. The choppy waters of change are often very difficult to navigate without help. This book offers practical strategies and guidance for supporting people of all ages with a variety of issues, whether psychological (anxiety, trauma, depression), based on life circumstances (loss and grief, attitudes that don't affirm LGBT2SQ+ identities), or due to harmful ways of coping with these or other life stressors (self-injury, substance use, suicidality). The topics addressed in this book are diverse, and they certainly do not include all the symptoms or situations that cause people distress. But the common thread of clients feeling helpless, overwhelmed, and stuck carries across these chapters and is relevant for many other experiences not explored here.

Knowledge is always evolving. Counselling is a live, organic process that will never look exactly the same from one person to the next. However, there are common elements that guide us in the right direction, like buoys marking the way for safer passage. Every once in a while, we get a glimpse of a deeper understanding of one person's or one family's experience that can help guide us the next time we find ourselves in similar waters with someone else. It is these glimpses of understanding that inform the chapters that follow.

Throughout these chapters, you will read stories of people caught in the waves of persistent patterns of stress and vulnerability. We begin with chapters about supporting people who have survived trauma, recognizing that the high prevalence of traumatic impact underpins the development of many other mental health struggles. Beginning with a trauma-informed lens can help you consider the intermingling of concerns that are so often part of what people are dealing with.

You will also encounter recurring themes, such as building authentic relationships as an essential foundation for helping others, seeing the whole person and not just their problems, and recognizing the inherent strengths within every person that allow their resilience to emerge and make them more whole.

Each chapter begins with an introduction to the psychological issue or situation at hand. The authors then explore some case applications, including both youth and adults, to illustrate potential impacts of the issue and the helping process in a *real-world* scenario. Each chapter puts an emphasis on how to apply the ideas in order to inform how to *be* with other people, and *ways to offer support*. Authors share their learning from research, counselling experiences, and the unique wisdom of the people they have encountered.

VOICES FURTHER ALONG THE JOURNEY

"Life is okay now. It's okay today."

"Laughter, described as a long-absent friend, began to visit her more and more."

"I have more confidence and a stronger sense of identity."

"I am strong, and I am good."

Each author is unique in his or her own voice, style of writing, and approach to the helping process. This diversity is part of the richness of this book and is a way for helpers from different backgrounds and experiences to see themselves and their clients in these pages. Additional resources, related to and mentioned in the subsequent chapters, are provided at the back of the book. These resources are designed to be used by readers in a wide variety of helping roles.

A Note About the Case Applications

Although each story is informed by the experiences of real people, all actual names and identifying details have been changed. Case applications are composites of accumulated stories or completely fictionalized to protect the privacy of actual people. Any resemblance to any particular individual is purely coincidental. In the spirit of respect and gratitude, we authors and editors offer thanks for all the teachings we have received as helpers of others.

Core Beliefs

The broader context informing all the chapters in this book are the core beliefs held by the Crisis & Trauma Resource Institute (CTRI), where each author works as a trainer. These guiding principles inform how we all approach our work with people:

Trauma-Informed Approach

We recognize the prevalence of trauma in our world and how pervasive its impact can be on all people. In any service delivery, this requires the promotion of a sense of safety, trust, and choice for individuals and an approach of compassion and collaboration.

Holistic Understanding of Health

We value approaches to human physical and mental health that incorporate a consideration of all aspects of a human being, integrating physical, mental, spiritual, and social dimensions.

Respect for Cultural Diversity

We honour the diversity of beliefs and practices that make up individual value systems. Overall health and positive service is promoted when there is an effort to increase awareness and respect of each client's ethnicity, nationality, spirituality, gender, sexual orientation, level of ability, and socioeconomic status.

Responsibility for Reconciliation with Indigenous Communities

We recognize the privilege that comes with being invited into Indigenous communities to train and work alongside people from these cultural traditions. We understand that with this privilege comes a responsibility to acknowledge cultural biases, as well as to honour the impact of colonialism and intergenerational trauma. Fundamental to all our work with Indigenous peoples is building relationships and listening humbly with an open heart and mind.

Recognition of Diverse Natural Strengths and Paths to Healing

We value that people needing support have natural strengths and ways of healing. Our training strives to incorporate a strengths-based approach that includes both formal and informal strategies for helping.

Acknowledgement of Multiple Roles of Helpers

We recognize that care and service is provided in our communities by both formally trained counsellors and paraprofessionals. Our material strives to be accessible to all care and service providers.

Integration of Best Practices and Promising Practices

We recognize that the development of strategies for helping and service delivery are continually evolving as learning and research advances. We build our training materials by integrating the best research evidence relevant to each field with both established and emerging promising practices. These are identified using the clinical expertise and collective wisdom of experienced practitioners and in consideration of the best fit for the communities we work with.

Working with people is a calling that requires lifelong learning. Those of us in helping roles also need our own helpers to guide us so we don't get isolated or depleted. I hope this book can offer you some camaraderie in your work, solid guidance to navigate the tricky turns, and an enjoyable voyage inspired by human stories of perseverance.

Vicki Enns
Editor and Clinical Director, Crisis & Trauma Resource Institute

CHAPTER ONE

DEVELOPMENTAL TRAUMA

By Vicki Enns

IT IS POSSIBLE THAT EVERY HUMAN BEING HAS BEEN TOUCHED BY trauma in some way, whether through personal experience, the suffering of a loved one, or the effect of shared fears communicated through world news or community events. It has become increasingly apparent that being impacted by a traumatic experience is extremely common throughout the lifespan (Larkin, Shields, & Anda, 2012). Some people go on to develop post-traumatic stress disorder, with lingering symptoms that affect many areas of their lives, while others are able to live with the impacts affecting their lives less often or less severely (Schalinski et al., 2016). Regardless of the direct impact, a person who has experienced trauma becomes more vulnerable to other life stresses and is more likely to develop other health concerns (Lanius, Vermetten, & Pain, 2010).

Trauma can be defined in many ways, and the same experiences will not have the same impact on every person. For an experience to be traumatic, it involves an overwhelming sense of powerlessness or horror, or a sense of threat to one's well-being that causes a person to feel their emotional or physical survival is at stake.

A traumatic experience sets off deep instincts in a human being to survive, which can lay down a pattern of emotions, beliefs, and behaviours that continue long past the originating experience (van der Kolk, 2014). These patterns often contribute to the development of other struggles, such as anxiety, depression, suicidality, and substance use, so the themes of traumatic impact will show up across many chapters in this book. Understanding the mechanics of trauma, and the basics of how to acknowledge and support those who carry trauma in their bodies and memories, will allow helpers to approach these other struggles more effectively.

Trauma can occur in many different situations. It may be the lasting effect of an isolated experience (see the chapter on Situational Trauma in this book), or it may result from many accumulated experiences over time. When the originating experience (or experiences) occurs in the early years of life, the trauma can have unique and profound impacts on the ongoing development of a person. This is called developmental trauma.

Traumatic experiences during childhood and adolescent development can have a distinct shaping influence on the rest of one's life. Not every bump and bruise will have an impact, and many events will be completely forgotten. However, overwhelming or threatening experiences may yield a traumatic impact and weave themselves into the ongoing development of a person's body and mind.

The word *trauma* usually evokes images of threatening or devastating events, such as near-death accidents, assaults, wars, or natural disasters. More common, and sometimes overlooked, are the experiences that involve persistent doses of fear and helplessness within the daily relationships or environments of a person's life.

INEZ

In her 14 years, Inez has moved 10 times. She occasionally sees members of her biological family, but she has lived under the roofs of foster families since her toddler years. Inez keeps a suitcase under her bed packed with her favourite clothes and keepsakes, as she never believes she is staying anywhere long. She is sure that it is a question of when, not if, she'll be made to leave again. Inez longs for a permanent home but has come to believe she is too damaged to really fit in anywhere.

She is well aware of how challenging others find her quick emotional swings, her flaring temper, her sudden patterns of disconnection when she refuses to engage, and her face in a vacant stare.

In my office, Inez sits taut, perched at the edge of the couch like she's ready to flee at any moment. Her fingers jump across her phone's screen as she squeezes in one last text before looking at me. She starts describing a battle of wills over the last three days as she has intentionally disengaged at home. Inez recounts details of how her foster family tried to "trick" her into doing activities with them. Suddenly dropping her phone down beside her, she slumps back looking totally deflated.

"I don't understand why they try so hard. Why do they even care about whether I spend time with them? It's like they pretend to love me, but they don't really know me."

BUD

At the age of 53, Bud is a muscular, looming man with a tall frame. As the oldest and biggest brother of four siblings, he has always lived his life protecting others. Bud was the loud kid who could sometimes get their raging drunk father to back off and give them some peace to sleep. When they were all younger, he made sure he and his siblings got to school every day. At the age of 17, Bud fought his way out of the family home and created a life for himself with a steady job. Now, as an adult, he has devoted the last 10 years to supporting his one daughter, who is a single parent to his only grandson.

Three weeks ago, an accident at the manufacturing plant where Bud works resulted in his co-worker's arm getting caught in the machinery. Bud worked next to the man and rushed over to hit the emergency brake, but he was unable to stop the crushing force that did permanent damage to his friend's arm. Bud has been unable to return to work since the accident, because he is experiencing high anxiety, trouble sleeping, flashbacks, and exhaustion. Bud comments that he used to be the "rock" to his friends, unwavering and strong. Now he's completely confused and demoralized by his inability to stop his tears or to tolerate the noise of his grandson's weekly soccer practice.

Shuffling into my office, Bud notes how his whole body aches. As he slowly lowers himself into the chair, he says, "I don't know why I'm back here … it's a mystery why I'm so different since that stupid accident. You can't change what happened. I'm just broken."

With bags under his eyes, a deep slump in his shoulders, and his voice shaking, he describes another night of little sleep. He sighs and turns to the window. With tears brimming, jaw and fists clenched, he declares quietly, "I should be put down. Can you help me with that?"

Bud and Inez each have a unique blend of life experiences, genetic temperament, and cultural contexts that shape their current struggles. However, they both share a common background of developmental trauma that affects how they cope with life.

Any traumatic experience is a violation of one's sense of safety, evoking survival responses to eliminate or avoid the threat. There are predictable symptoms that show up when something wakes up the memory of these experiences: high anxiety, troubling memories that disrupt sleep, and a quick temper that flares unexpectedly.

Symptoms become more complicated in cases where the genesis of these experiences was during infancy, childhood, or adolescence. There may also be a whole range of events that have contributed to setting up this cascade of fear and defence. People who have experienced childhood trauma may not have clear memories to provide an explanation for their symptoms, but they may have built a life of coping with the persistent feeling that something is wrong.

The experience of developmental trauma leaves a distinct impact on the growing individual that is the result of two interweaving factors:

➤ The direct hit of an experience of helplessness and terror due to a real or perceived threat to one's well-being. This may be a single event or an ongoing accumulation of many experiences.

> The inherent vulnerability of the still-developing physical, intellectual, emotional, and social capacities of a young person. These capacities predict a person's ability to cope and are continually shaped by their environment, so they are partially formed by the trauma.

Living in an unpredictable or frightening environment during these developmental years can result in a baseline of sensitivity and anticipation of recurring threat. Research shows that people with these experiences become highly stressed more quickly, which then informs their mental and emotional understanding of everyday life (Schore, 2003; Siegel & Bryson, 2011; van der Kolk, 2005). Persistent neglect or repeated misattunement from caregivers builds an expectation of not getting one's needs met. As a child grows into adulthood, this background noise can continue to shape how they see themselves, their environment, and every relationship they enter.

INSIGHTS AND GUIDING PRINCIPLES FOR COUNSELLING

The prevalence of developmental trauma means that counsellors will regularly encounter people living with a complex array of symptoms. Common post-traumatic impacts reflect survival stances of flight (anxiety, avoidance, and urges to withdraw), fight (urges to lash out, rage, and control situations), and freeze (numbness, disorientation, and urges to shut down). Developmental trauma may add layers of impact affecting subsequent relationships to self, others, and the world in general. Examples include

> chronic and persistent fears and worries that spill into everyday life;
> an inability to trust others or develop any form of intimacy;
> general passivity and a struggle to form opinions or make decisions;
> confusion, lack of motivation, and a sense of futility;
> struggles with setting or recognizing boundaries;
> physical struggles, body aches, pains, and dis-ease that are not easily linked to a source;

➤ profound negativity toward oneself and persistent feelings of guilt and shame;

➤ chronic dissociation, fogginess, and a sense of disconnection from the rest of the world.

Just as Inez sees every potential caregiver through the lens of her original loss of family, a person may be reliving parts of their trauma history through their present daily life. There may be additional situational trauma that brings fragments of these memories to the surface, as Bud experienced when he suffered the shock of seeing his friend hurt.

There are three main developmental patterns that are particularly shaped by the legacy of developmental trauma: attachment, self-regulation, and self-perspective (Gil, 1996; Siegel, 2012; van der Kolk, 2014).

Attachment patterns affect how a person reaches for and lets in connections with other people. Inez's attachment history makes it difficult for her to trust anyone enough to let them try to care for her. As her counsellor, I want to help her risk feeling cared about and express her needs clearly.

Self-regulation patterns affect how a person manages their physical and emotional responses to stresses in daily life. Both Inez and Bud experience their emotions and physical energy swinging quickly from intense agitation to a collapsing feeling of shutting down. One of the goals in our counselling work is for both of them to be better able to adjust the intensity of whatever emotion they are feeling, so they can stay connected to life without fearing it.

Self-perspective patterns describe the quality of one's relationship to self. Living with persistent feelings of fear, shame, and humiliation has left Bud questioning the worth of his existence and has left Inez with no understanding of why anyone would fight for her unless they had ulterior motives to exploit her. Healing this kind of self-perspective is a slow, yet foundational goal for resolving the impact of developmental trauma.

From working with many people like Bud and Inez, I have come to rely on the following four principles to guide how I support change in these patterns:

1) **Build a secure relationship foundation**
   Develop secure, healthy, and nurturing connections.

2) **Create developmental bridges**
   Recover skills from gaps left in developmental capacities.

3) **Develop a positive connection to the body**
   Cultivate a sense of safety and stability in one's own body.

4) **Order the story across time**
   Create a cohesive life story that separates the past from the present and future.

1) BUILD A SECURE RELATIONSHIP FOUNDATION

Children have an amazing capacity to align themselves to their caregivers and stay connected. The human brain is a social organ, and we need relationships to expand our social engagement capacities for ongoing development of the whole nervous system (Schore, 2003; Siegel, 2012; van der Kolk, 2014). The way caregivers respond to a child and to stressors in the environment will directly shape the child's experience. Ideally, children receive secure enough caregiving responses that allow them to recover from stress and experience the necessary nurture to re-establish a sense of the world as good and reliable.

Without such support, a child may develop patterns of anxious, clingy behaviours that reflect the continual search for reassurance, or they may develop patterns of shutting down their awareness of fear, allowing them to survive by believing they don't need support. Underlying such patterns is usually a deep river of disturbance and disconnection, along with feelings of shame, humiliation, and loss. We see this with Bud's experience of putting so much energy into supporting others, yet feeling intense shame that he is now in a position of needing help for himself.

Developmental trauma compromises a person's ability to "read" themselves or other people accurately, making it harder to enter and maintain supportive relationships. When a person feels persistently under threat, their nervous system shifts to rely on pure survival instincts instead of staying connected to others. This leaves them with reduced opportunities to develop skills for "cooperation, nurturing, and the ability to function as a productive member of the clan" (van der Kolk, 2014, p. 349).

When caregivers are the source of threat, a child is presented with an impossible puzzle of both desperately needing and fearing the same source of connection. As the child grows older, these same expectations and coping patterns will often emerge in other relationships when feelings of stress and uncertainty arise.

Whenever Inez spends time with her biological family, she receives messages that she is too much to handle and gets in the way of their needs. Inez expects this response from every caregiver and believes herself to be unlovable. After a short time in a new foster home, she feels the overwhelming urge to protect herself from her greatest fear of inevitably being sent away. She walls up, shuts off communication, and becomes a sullen, combative teenager who can play the "I don't care" card better than most.

The accumulation of unmet needs leaves the person on guard against others, repeating these patterns. Internally, the person is constantly scanning to determine the following:

➤ "Can I reach them when I need them, or are they absent and hard to make contact with?"

➤ "How do they respond to me – are they predictable and comforting, or are they confusing and dangerous?"

➤ "Do I trust them to be there when I need them in a predictable way?"

A common factor for effective counselling work is the quality of the relationship between counsellor and client. Building a secure, nurturing, helping relationship becomes the initial task and is the foundation upon which all other ongoing counselling work rests. It's not unusual for much of the time spent with a client who experienced developmental trauma to revolve around building, monitoring, and repairing this foundation. The steps can seem simple, yet they can have a profoundly powerful impact on the quality of your working relationship.

COUNSELLING STRATEGIES

Building this foundation requires focusing on the following tenets of secure attachment:

1) Accessibility that is consistent, non-judgmental, and open

   ➤ Be sure that your verbal and nonverbal communication is congruent. Open body language, with eye contact and sensitivity to boundaries for physical space, conveys a message that you are available but not coercive.

   ➤ Be certain to offer opportunities for your client to practice making choices. These may be simple things, such as where they sit or what time you meet. Give them a chance to make the choice to engage.

   ➤ Be clear and honest about your availability. It is important you say only what you can do and not make promises you can't keep. Having firm and clear limits that you can explain is reparative for clients and key for your own well-being.

   ➤ Be clear that there aren't conditions attached to connecting with you, and that they aren't responsible for taking care of you.

2) Responsiveness that is authentic

   ➤ Always be honest and sincere without crossing your own personal and professional boundaries around sharing too much information.

   ➤ Follow through on what you say you will do. Be willing to acknowledge and work to repair any relationship ruptures. For example, having to cancel an appointment because you get sick may trigger a reaction of abandonment from your client. Hold firm by attending to your own needs while reflecting empathically the fear and vulnerability this may stir up for your client.

   ➤ Expect disrupted attachment responses from your client. If you can predict anxious, clingy behaviours or dismissive, angry behaviours as all reasonable through the lens of disrupted developmental attachment, this will allow you to stay open and not take things personally. Gently offer invitations for healthy re-engagement without coercion or negative consequences.

3) Flexibility balanced with consistency within the boundaries of the relationship

➤ Incorporate playfulness and levity into your interactions, encouraging your client to take in small doses of pleasure through laughter, joy, and curiosity. We often need to build up this dosage slowly.

➤ Celebrate with your client as their capacity to have more choice and let others in expands.

CASE APPLICATION

INEZ

In sessions with Inez, she talks easily about her friends or favourite music. When any mention of her family occurs, however, she transforms into a sullen teen with arms folded and one-word answers of "dunno," paired with masterfully contemptuous shoulder shrugs. I intentionally acknowledge the hidden message: "It seems like this is not a comfortable topic right now. I hear that."

Shifting back to a craft project we had started earlier in the session, I invite her to tell me which colour she wants for the next part of her project. As I move gently and slowly to get the supplies, I shift my attention a little further away, then come back closer, increasing my energy to match hers as we chat about paint colours. Inez slowly re-engages with the activity and starts chatting again about her latest best friend.

BUD

In my first sessions with Bud, he would shut down any questions about feelings with a glance and curt response of "It's all fine." With some rapport established, I could risk responding more directly.

[Counsellor] "I believe you can be just fine. Sometimes I notice that people who are the strongest and most capable of taking care of themselves have had to learn they can't afford not to be fine, or else the people they care most about might fall apart and come undone. This is a noble but very lonely way to live."

Bud tilts his head with his chin jutting out, looking at me from under the hood of his bushy eyebrows.

[Counsellor] "I want you to know if you feel something other than fine, I can handle it. I have ways to take care of myself, and I'm really interested in just being able to sit beside you for a moment, so you're not always having to hold that all by yourself."

Pausing, I smile gently at him and carefully hold his gaze.

[Counsellor] "Then you can go back to being just fine and I'll leave you be – I promise."

Taking a big breath, his face softens for a moment.

[Bud] "Well that sounds maybe okay. Not today though."

[Counsellor] "Okay, I'll check in again next time. How did your grandson do at his last soccer practice?"

2) CREATE DEVELOPMENTAL BRIDGES

With accessible and responsive caregiving, children learn to be able to depend on others and accurately read their own needs, so they can reach for and accept support. This baseline of security allows a person to explore, risk, and learn, advancing in cognitive, emotional, and social development. When a person experiences developmental trauma, this nurturing foundation is compromised, and it is common to see many gaps in development (Szalavitz & Perry, 2010).

Two common gaps in the development of healthy self-perception include struggles with the following beliefs:

➤ The belief in one's worth and value without the need to prove it through actions. Without this belief, a person may be confused by others' kindness, praise, or unconditional caring.

➤ The belief that it is healthy and normal to have needs and to want to try to get them met. A person may struggle to even recognize basic physical needs, such as hunger or thirst, and emotional needs, such as longing for connection or needing reassurance. They may feel confusion about what is "normal" or reasonable to expect from themselves or others in any interaction.

These same gaps will often emerge within the counsellor–client relationship. This happens with Bud when he is feeling worried and extra tired. At those times, he can barely tolerate a kind greeting or words of encouragement. The underlying mistrust floods his nervous system with feelings of unworthiness, shame, and confusion over what is happening. It was dangerous for Bud to show vulnerability or need as a child, so he is fearful of showing this now. He has learned to guard himself by being brusque and irritable to cover up his vulnerability.

The indirect protective coping that a client must use can feel manipulative, hostile, or resistant to a counsellor, evoking punitive responses that perpetuate experiences of invalidation and a lack of "good fit."

Alternatively, a person may cope by turning against him or herself, believing their own existence to be the source of the problem. For example, this is reflected in Bud's desire to take himself out of the equation and Inez's solution to detach or run away to solve the problem.

It can be helpful to watch for times when these gaps show up in how a client responds or utters a belief about themselves and to use gentle observation and curious questions to build bridges that allow the client to grow this capacity.

COUNSELLING STRATEGIES

Concrete ways to support development around the value of self-worth and needs include:

1) Sending messages that say your client is worthy, just by virtue of existing

   ➤ Tell them they are worthy in a matter-of-fact way, perhaps many times.

   ➤ Really *see* your client by giving honest, accurate feedback with respect.

   ➤ Listen carefully for childlike beliefs, such as magical thinking and self-blame, or adolescent all-or-nothing patterns in their ways of making sense of daily experiences.

   ➤ Offer observations and information to help give alternate and accurate ways of understanding both everyday events and stressful, overwhelming ones.

   ➤ Stay close to your client's experience by being willing to talk about it and feel with them (Knox, 2013) when shame, humiliation, or self-doubt show up. Avoid cheerleading or trying to pull them along to feel better. Support them in tolerating and shifting these emotions themselves.

2) Supporting your client's attempts to meet their needs

   ➤ Be persistent about providing opportunities for your client to voice their needs and make choices. This may be about simple things like picking a flavour of tea, choosing a time to meet, deciding what activity they would like to do, or taking time to use the washroom.

   ➤ Be patient with indirect or confusing ways of communicating needs, such as irritated language and behaviour when they need a different response from you.

   ➤ Acknowledge risky and self-harming ways of meeting needs. Take a reasoned, clear, and caring approach to developing coping skills.

   ➤ Give lots of permission for a client to have veto power over what you focus on in your work together. Give information and listen carefully for unspoken, non-verbal messages from them, verbalizing them to make them conscious.

➤ Pay careful attention to transition times in your interactions, such as when your meetings are beginning and ending, if your availability is changing, or if your client has successfully completed a program. These are times when old developmental gaps may resurface.

CASE APPLICATION

INEZ

Inez's angry outbursts, followed by extended hideouts in her room, continue. Her foster mom learns how important it is to calmly and consistently repeat the message that she does not want to send Inez away and that she can understand Inez's need to protect herself when she gets so scared. In our session, we debrief one of these interactions.

[Counsellor] "What is that like for you when you hear the message they don't want to send you away?"

Inez ducks her head down.

[Inez] "They're probably lying. Everybody always lies about that."

[Counsellor] "Hmm. You know, I think this is the fourth time you've described a conversation like this to me. So far, they seem to be staying consistent and true to what they say. Do you notice that, too?"

Inez looks at me and furrows her brow, as I can see her working to reconcile this information that contradicts her belief.

BUD

Bud typically looks exhausted when coming to sessions. He automatically refuses my offer of a glass of water before he even registers the invitation. As we begin to talk about his earlier family life, Bud's stories are filled with examples of attending to the needs of his mother and making sure his siblings had meals and got to school until he moved out at 17. During those early years, he was focused purely on surviving and protecting those under his care.

Now that he's struggling to even get out of bed each morning, Bud feels confused and agitated by his daughter's assurances that she is happy to support him with meals and a place to stay in her home while he is off work. Bud is visibly uncomfortable while he talks about this. His belief that he doesn't deserve to live if he can't function as the protector of his family is starting to surface.

[Counsellor] "I wonder if your daughter feels grateful to be able to offer back to you some of the care you have given her so abundantly over the years. It is a common thing in the life cycle of a healthy family that adult children can offer back some caregiving to their parents as needs change. Your current family experience is very different from your childhood family."

Bud visibly hardens, then breathes and softens as he thinks this through. We slowly focus on taking the risk of accepting her offers of care and allowing it to sink in that she loves him just for being her father.

3) DEVELOP A POSITIVE CONNECTION TO THE BODY

Survival of a traumatic experience leaves a person with very sensitive instincts for detecting any further possible threat. The memories related to these experiences become associated with intense emotional and physical responses. A memory is made up of many different parts: the bodily sensations; the sights, sounds, and smells; the thoughts that went through one's head; the behaviours of people involved; and the emotional intensity that they felt at the time. Later experiences that match even one part of these memories may set off the alarm in a person's survival instincts, sending them into a full defensive response, as if the trauma were occurring again.

The defensive responses of fight, flight, or freeze begin in the body with changes in heart rate and breathing, while the large muscles of the legs and shoulders get ready to move, and all the senses become sharply focused to detect any further sign of threat (Levine, 2010; Ogden & Fisher, 2015). Thinking becomes secondary, and it is very difficult to take in new information or change course once these responses have begun.

When I am working with a trauma survivor, I can feel these shifts as they happen for my client in my own gut, chest, and limbs. I know that unless we can turn off the alarm in my client's nervous system, the conversation will not work to make any shifts in how they carry their trauma. The alarm bell will continue to ring and keep their body braced and activated, ready to fight, flee, or shut down.

Once there is a relational connection between counsellor and client, it's possible to use the relationship to bring a sense of support into the experience of threat the client is feeling. I often think that, in these moments, the client and I become one collaborative nervous system. Their body is focused on organizing all the sensations necessary to survive, while I bring my thinking brain and conscious awareness to help us both notice that the threat has passed. Then the alarm can turn off in both nervous systems, allowing our bodies to settle and minds to settle, which gives us the option to make choices rather than just react.

For this shift to happen, we both need to be able to pay attention to what is currently happening physically to register that there is no external threat. I know that when my client is on high alert, I need to approach this carefully and slowly.

With Inez, each time her alarm sounds, I see and feel her shut down like a wounded animal fleeing and hiding behind anything she can find in her mind. I feel her disappear. With Bud, his nervous system prepares him to fight, clenching his jaw and limbs, the fire building in his belly, getting ready to get loud or big to ward off any threat. I feel the air in the room get a little more charged and my own heart rate start to rise.

It can be very helpful to practice noticing these small physical shifts with clients when they are not in a full alarm response. The body can become a scary place for a trauma survivor. Our goal is to rediscover and re-inhabit the body as a safe home base.

COUNSELLING STRATEGIES

Learning to pay attention to the sensations of feeling safer is crucial for experiencing the freedom of knowing the threat is actually over.

1) Learn to tune in to the physical sensations of your own body

   ➤ You will only be able to invite your client to a place you've already been. Practice noticing and regulating your breath, muscle tension, and posture. Pay attention to and soften your chest and belly areas.

   ➤ Practice holding your attention on these areas to track how sensations shift over a short period of time.

2) Help your client practice noticing and tracking their body sensations

   ➤ Invite your client to pause and briefly notice the rhythms of their breathing and shifts in sensations in their body, especially when you notice these shifts.

   ➤ Encourage more than talking about what they feel. Be persistent in encouraging them to tune in to visceral sensations by using touch, smell, taste, hearing, and seeing. It can be helpful to practice this with everyday experiences, such as going for a walk outside or experimenting with holding different objects and exploring them through various senses. Playful games such as the Sensation Charades activity can also encourage your client to express themselves with more than just words. *See page 278 in the Resources section for a description of this activity.*

   ➤ Make a point of inviting your client to recognize sensations when they are more settled, such as the feeling of stability while leaning into a solid surface or noticing the sounds and sights of a soothing song or image. Expanding their sensation vocabulary can be helpful. *See page 280 in the Resources section for a sample sensation vocabulary list.*

➤ Practice gentle and purposeful movement with your client to deepen their ability to connect to their body in a settled, freely moving state. Example movements may be full-range stretching, simple yoga poses, free movement to music, or simply standing, sitting, and walking with their head held straight on top of their spine and their chest open to breathe freely.

3) Use the *reparative moments* of connecting your awareness with your client's experiences of fight, flight, and freeze to help them turn off the alarm

➤ Watch for the moments when your client is moving into a survival state and guide them to attend to their body *now*, while you stay carefully attuned. This is where the magic happens. If they are able to stay connected to you while they become aware of what they are sensing, this allows the traumatized brain to learn something new.

CASE APPLICATION

INEZ

We are talking about a recent visit Inez had with her aunt and uncle. Inez mentions that her cousin was there, and the familiar veil of disconnection comes down as I see her face become expressionless and hard. Her body shrinks back in her chair, and somehow she seems to get smaller. I stay very still and tune in to my own body, feeling my breath catch in my throat and my arms become stiff and braced. Intentionally breathing more slowly, I relax my shoulders and tune in for a moment to the stable support of my chair. I keep my voice slow and steady, making sure I am not speaking from a fearful place.

[Counsellor] "Inez, I notice you have pulled away. I wonder if you can just notice your feet on the floor. Can you see mine and yours both on the floor? Let's both wiggle our toes a little just to feel the carpet."

Here I pause and breathe, tuning in to my own toes slowly moving and sensing my socks and the carpet. As we do this for a few moments, I feel a bit of warmth return to my own face, and I can see Inez's shoulders let down slightly.

[Counsellor] "Yes, that's it."

I carefully acknowledge the shift.

[Counsellor] "Let's make sure we're breathing nice and slow."

After spending several more minutes noticing and tracking both my own and her sensations, eventually Inez moves around in her chair. Her energy comes back up, and we agree to leave that topic for now. Next time, she may be able to tolerate a little more time focusing on how her past experiences have impacted her.

BUD

Bud has a scowl on his face after I ask him to feel his breath in his chest. I have to create some buy-in for Bud to tune in to his body differently.

[Bud] "I'm breathing like I always do. It's fine."

[Counsellor] "You know, Bud, from what I've begun to understand, I think your whole body has probably been braced and ready to fight the world most of your life."

Bud nods at this, and I notice he takes a bigger breath as he briefly connects with this feeling.

[Counsellor] "It's an interesting thing how our breathing will automatically change to support what our body is trying to do. When you are braced all the time, your breathing has to stay fast and up in your chest to pump oxygen quickly to your muscles. Your stomach muscles develop to keep this pattern going – just like when you lift weights at the gym. It's like you're constantly doing the same exercise too much and never allowing those muscles to stretch and recover."

Bud looks quizzical at this, nodding tentatively.

[Counsellor] "Would you be willing to try something with me? I want to see if we can practice stretching those muscles. If we slowly and carefully breathe in more deeply, down to our bellies, it can be like stretching an overworked muscle, allowing it to use its full range of motion."

We spend a few moments taking longer, slower belly breaths. I encourage him to think about gently pushing the air down toward his belly. Bud looks up suddenly.

[Bud] "That felt weird. I don't know why, but it seems like I haven't taken a breath like that since I was a kid!"

Tears come to his eyes, and he looks confused. We spend the next 20 minutes gently talking about how hard Bud has worked to be on guard most of his life. His tone and demeanour become much softer.

[Bud] "I never realized how heavy that armour is that I carry all the time and how angry I always am. Maybe I don't have to fight all the time."

4) ORDER THE STORY ACROSS TIME

Each time a person is faced again with the reality of surviving a past experience, their present experience is disrupted as well. It becomes very challenging to have a clear sense of self with a distinct past, present, and future. Present life becomes a disjointed, partial expression of the past recurring over and over, making it hard to discern what is different now, or whether any change is possible. Memories of past experiences are like puzzles with pieces missing, stored out of order and with mismatched meaning and emotion attached, adding to the confusion and fear.

If there are accessible, nurturing, and responsive caregivers supporting a child or adolescent when they experience an overwhelming event, it is possible to process and resolve the experience at that time. With a supportive caregiver, they can share the emotional intensity – as the counsellor may be able to feel more of the full emotion than the client is able to at the time (Knox, 2013) – make accurate sense of what occurred, and internalize how to shift out of fear and back onto their developmental track.

If they don't have this support available, a young person must compartmentalize these feelings and memories off into dissociated fragments to keep them manageable and to stay connected to their caregivers. Inez found it easier to intentionally shut off her feelings and be numb rather than feeling the hurt and loss of her own mother rejecting her.

Once there is a foundation of connection with a client, I turn my attention toward noticing with them when a piece of their trauma story puzzle comes to the surface. I help shine the flashlight on verbal and nonverbal expressions of their story that seem connected to the past, emotionally significant, or incongruent with the present. I can give them the opportunity to share the emotional intensity now and to make more accurate sense of what occurred.

There are many ways to piece together a story, including speaking, drawing, writing, moving, making music, painting, sculpting, or connecting with the stories of others. Bud began to rework his own childhood story, as he was able to see it in comparison to the current story of his grandson.

We don't have to go through every part of the story, and indeed, the client may not have access to all of their memories, particularly when events happened at very early ages. If we can help find the language or expression of the parts of the memory they are aware of in a way that feels *experience-near* enough for a client, this process allows a fuller and more integrated record to be stored in their memory (White, 2007). Once a person is able to face and work with even one piece of their experience, with support to understand it outside of the panic of survival, they have the tools to allow the other pieces to fall into place.

COUNSELLING STRATEGIES

1) Hold the flashlight but let them choose when to move forward

   ➤ Create opportunities for clients to express parts of their experience
   with your support. This may be through curious questions or invitations to draw, play, or move in some way that gives expression to part
   of their experience. Key to this is that their internal alarm stays off.
   Therefore, this may need to happen in very small steps, interrupted
   by opportunities to come back to a sense of safety and stability.

   ➤ Stay carefully attuned to your client, so you can help them notice
   if the alarm starts to ring and if they need to stop or say no to
   something. Help them honour their own boundaries.

2) Experiment with different ways of expressing parts of their life story

   ➤ Using different senses or ways of articulating thoughts and emotions allows a client to access different parts of their experiences
   and find freedom to choose what feels best. Often the symbolic
   language of play or the use of metaphor can help to provide some
   distance, yet allow them to explore meaning deeply.

   ➤ Help the client stay connected to their body sensations while
   doing this. Learning to read and trust their own gut about the
   accuracy of their expression can bring relief and reduce the inner
   tension of self-doubt.

3) Unwind the past from the present

   ➤ Don't start with the hardest parts. Like untangling a tight knot in
   a string, we can pull on various places to slowly loosen its grip. It
   works best to start at the outside, where the knot is already a little
   looser. Invite clients to practice with experiences that are more
   recent, that feel less confusing, or that happened when they had
   some support.

   ➤ Stay actively involved and attuned. You are inviting a person to allow you to come with them into an experience that has been isolating, shameful, and terrifying. Consciously ground yourself and gently keep them aware that you are there with them.

➤ Pay close attention to the transition from focusing on the past back to focusing on the present. This is often pushed through too quickly. Take the time to really help the person notice, verbalize, and engage with the present environment, what they will be doing next in their day, and how they are thinking and feeling now about what they need.

CASE APPLICATION

INEZ

I haven't seen Inez for a couple of months. She has been doing better and focusing on beginning Grade 9 in another new school. Her social worker set an appointment after a string of skipped classes and the beginning of old patterns resurfacing at home. I reflect on possible parallels between what is happening now and what I know about other chapters of Inez's life.

The beginning of the school year is often hard for Inez. This difficulty is likely connected to her experience in the fall of Grade 4, when she was abruptly moved to yet another new foster home. It was discovered that her older cousin had assaulted her on a weekend visit close to her former home, and, as a result, she was moved to a different part of the city. Inez didn't often bring up this experience, and any invitation to do so was usually very short lived. I wondered if this might be an opportunity for her to process these memories a little more.

I have a variety of craft options out on the table, as doing something together with our hands has often helped Inez settle in the past. She decides to continue working on a collage about her future dreams that she had begun last time we met. She is flipping through magazines and stops, looking intently at an ad for winter jackets that shows a young girl laughing, holding hands with an adult, both of them decked out in puffy, shiny parkas.

[Inez] "I bet this girl has secrets that she can't tell anyone, because no one will really believe her ... and it's really, really uncomfortable to talk about them ... it makes her feel really sick inside to talk about them."

Inez glances up and makes eye contact with me for a brief second as she says this.

[Counsellor] "It looks like she's figured out how to get through so she can be happy sometimes and not have to feel sick inside all the time. She's creative ... I wonder what she'd like to be able to do with those secrets when they pop up in her mind."

I watch Inez's body language carefully to see what direction this is taking her.

[Inez] "I think she just wants this woman to keep smiling with her and just to know ... just to know it happened. She doesn't want to talk about it."

[Counsellor] "That sounds reasonable and like she knows what she needs right now."

Sitting taller and flipping the page to an image of a sports car, Inez enthusiastically rips it out.

[Inez] "That's going in my future!"

And we continue the collage.

BUD

Bud is talking about his struggle to go to his grandson's soccer practices. He finds them overwhelming now and is expressing his sadness over the loss of a previously joyful activity. The weight of sadness feels particularly heavy today.

[Counsellor] "This really affects you deeply. I sense that sadness goes back a long time."

[Bud] "I know what it is like when the adults in your life never show up. It's like they can't be bothered, and you just don't matter!"

A sob catches in his throat. I gently encourage Bud to allow some of that emotion to come through and surface rather than swallowing it back as he usually does. After a few minutes, we continue.

[Counsellor] "You know what it is like to be so alone … I wonder if you can also notice how your grandson's life is different? Maybe you aren't attending all of his practices, but what happens when he gets home?"

[Bud] "He comes to my room, and we go through the plays he learned. We practice with a small ball that we sneak in, so his mother doesn't get worried we'll break anything."

[Counsellor] "You make sure he knows you still care about and know him. You engage the best you can. What effect do you see in him?"

[Bud] "Yeah, he knows I care, I think. We have fun. He says he misses me at the practice … and I want to get back there."

[Counsellor] "As a little boy, you desperately needed someone like you – someone to really see you and care about you."

More settled now, Bud looks sad but not panicked.

[Bud] "Yes, I did need that. My parents couldn't do that for me."

Bud is looking alert and thoughtful.

[Bud] "I can really see he is not me. His life is much better. I can make sure his life is better. He's healing me too, you know!"

FINISHING THOUGHTS

The legacy of developmental trauma can leave a long-lasting shadow over a person's life, sounding the alarm of past threats in daily life, leaving them confused, overwhelmed, and helpless.

As a counsellor, I have found it important to understand the unique ways in which trauma during developmental years can affect how people move through their everyday lives, including the way they interact with other people, the volatility of emotion that can arise suddenly like a gale-force wind inside their own bodies, and the complicated negative perception they typically have of their own self.

The healing journey from developmental trauma is often long and winding. A person can slowly untangle the impacts of their trauma to fill in the developmental gaps that were left along the way as they struggled to just survive. As a companion on one small part of this journey, I have learned to trust the process of following the guiding principles described in this chapter. Often, the steps are small and subtle. However, as the pieces of long-held memories can be placed in their past, clients can start to engage with their present up to their full potential. Rather than just surviving in spite of fear and helplessness, they can live their way into a future with more choice and joy.

ABOUT THE AUTHOR

Vicki Enns, MMFT, RMFT

Vicki is the Clinical Director of the Crisis & Trauma Resource Institute, an Approved Supervisor with the American Association for Marriage and Family Therapy, and an instructor in the graduate program for Marriage and Family Therapy at the University of Winnipeg. In her private practice, she specializes in the area of trauma recovery for individuals of all ages and helps individuals, couples, and families build positive mental health and relational skills across all stages of development.

REFERENCES

Gil, E. (1996). *Treating abused adolescents.* New York, NY: Guilford Press.

Knox, J. (2013). 'Feeling for' and 'feeling with': Developmental and neuroscientific perspectives on intersubjectivity and empathy. *Journal of Analytical Psychology, 58*(4), 491-509.

Lanius, R., Vermetten, E., & Pain, C. (2010). *The impact of early life trauma on health and disease: The hidden epidemic.* New York, NY: Cambridge University Press.

Larkin, H., Shields, J., & Anda, R. (2012). The health and social consequences of adverse childhood experiences (ACE) across the lifespan: An introduction to prevention and intervention in the community. *Journal of Prevention & Intervention in the Community, 40*(4), 263-270.

Levine, P. (2010). *In an unspoken voice: How the body releases trauma and restores goodness.* Berkeley, CA: North Atlantic Books.

Ogden, P., & Fisher, J. (2015). *Sensorimotor psychotherapy: Interventions for trauma and attachment.* New York, NY: W. W. Norton & Company.

Schalinski, I., Teicher, M., Nischk, D., Hinderer, E., Müller, O., & Rockstroh, B. (2016). Type and timing of adverse childhood experiences differentially affect severity of PTSD, dissociative and depressive symptoms in adult inpatients. *BMC Psychiatry, 16*(295). https://doi.org/10.1186/s12888-016-1004-5

Schore, A. (2003). *Affect regulation and the repair of the self.* New York, NY: W.W. Norton & Company.

Siegel, D. J. (2012). *The developing mind: How relationships and the brain interact to shape who we are* (2nd ed.). New York, NY: Guilford Press.

Siegel, D. J., & Bryson, T. P. (2011). *The whole-brain child: 12 revolutionary strategies to nurture your child's mind, survive everyday parenting struggles, and help your family thrive.* New York, NY: Delacorte Press.

Szalavitz, M., & Perry, B. (2010). *Born for love: Why empathy is essential – and endangered.* New York, NY: Harper Collins.

van der Kolk, B. A. (2005). Developmental trauma disorder: Toward a rational diagnosis for children with complex trauma histories. *Psychiatric Annals, 35*(5), 401-408.

van der Kolk, B. A. (2014). *The body keeps the score: Brain, mind, and body in the healing of trauma.* New York, NY: Penguin Random House.

White, M. (2007). *Maps of narrative practice.* New York, NY: W. W. Norton & Company.

CHAPTER TWO

SITUATIONAL TRAUMA

By Michelle Gibson

TRAUMA CAN RESULT FROM MANY DIFFERENT TYPES OF EXPERIENCES and at any stage of life. The impact of trauma on one's life cannot be determined by the number or objective severity of traumatic experiences. However, it can be helpful to distinguish between general types of trauma in order to begin to understand common patterns of impact.

Situational trauma refers to isolated incidents and traumatic events that are relatively short lived (also referred to as Type I trauma). This is set against more complex and repetitive traumatic experiences (also referred to as Type II trauma), which often involve interpersonal elements like physical abuse, sexual abuse, or cumulative relationship losses (Courtois, 2008; van der Kolk, 2009; van der Kolk & Courtois, 2005).

Traumatic experiences that occur during the early years of life can be either situational (if a single incident) or complex (if repetitive). Because of the ongoing development of the person at the time, these earlier experiences tend to leave that individual more vulnerable to later trauma. Therefore, it is more often the case that childhood developmental trauma contributes to a pattern of complex, repetitive trauma.

To distinguish between situational and complex trauma, we can consider whether there is a memory or memories related to the same situation (Type I or situational trauma), or whether there is a complex history of trauma that often begins in childhood or continues over a period of a person's life and requires attention to repeated traumatic experiences (Type II and developmental trauma).

When we engage in any trauma work, we are working with clients who have been exposed to violence, serious injury, or a threat to their well-being. It is important to note that the determination of what is perceived and experienced as a threat is very personal and may vary from person to person. For example, two people may experience the same event, such as a car accident. While one person may experience the accident as highly overwhelming and incur traumatic impact (situational trauma), the other may be shaken for a short period of time and then continue without any further impact or trauma.

Similarly, with complex (Type II) trauma, the experience of threat is shaped by an individual's unique history, personality, and sources of support. When there are already patterns of traumatic impact in a person's nervous system from past experiences, situations that may seem benign, such as a dental checkup or a routine medical procedure, may set off these implicit patterns and be experienced as threatening.

Traumatic experience throughout the lifetime is very prevalent, and the majority of these experiences are related to single-incident or situational traumas. Single incidents of accidental injury requiring hospital admission are one of the most common trauma occurrences in childhood (National Center for Injury Prevention and Control, 2006; Nixon, Sterk, & Pearce, 2012). For adults, the most common types of situational trauma are motor vehicle accidents, workplace incidents, and physical assaults. Because of the varying experiences of trauma, we cannot assume that one type of trauma has an inherently greater impact on individuals than another. In my practice, working with people who have experienced both situational and complex, developmental trauma, I have seen that the impact varies much more by the individual than by the type of traumatic experience. This chapter focuses on principles for addressing the impact of situational trauma on a person's life.

BRANDON

Brandon, who is 19 years old, entered counselling to address trauma associated with a motor vehicle accident several years prior. Brandon had sought support following the accident, but continued to struggle with intrusive thoughts, nightmares, and emotional flooding related to memories of what happened. These symptoms appeared most frequently at night but were also triggered by the act of driving and the squeal of car brakes.

His experience – a car accident – is one of the most common forms of situational trauma. His experience has led to severe symptoms of traumatic stress that leave him feeling overwhelmed. In my office, Brandon was quiet and had difficulty talking about his accident. His body was quite rigid, his muscles were tensed, and his hands fidgeted along the arm of the chair. This was his first experience with formal counselling, and he had a lot of questions about what was expected of him.

CAROLYN

Carolyn came to counselling at the recommendation of her family physician. She is a 37-year-old woman who survived a break-and-enter in her home, during which she was assaulted. She has not experienced trauma in her past, and has only had one short-term experience with counselling, which was when she attended for relationship concerns.

Carolyn has a demanding job and found that her work was being impacted by persistent traumatic stress symptoms. She took a leave of absence from her employment, because she found it difficult to concentrate on her work.

Now, she generally feels unsafe in the world and has difficulty trusting others. She fears another assault will happen and has begun triple-checking all locks in her home before being able to go to bed. When Carolyn feels unsafe, her body enters into a state of mobilization, with muscles tensing and preparing to move into a flight response. In my office, Carolyn expresses feeling her heart rate increase, and often I notice her eyes moving rapidly around the room.

INSIGHTS AND GUIDING PRINCIPLES FOR COUNSELLING

This chapter will explore the impact of situational trauma on the brains, bodies, and minds of our clients. It will begin by exploring the impact of trauma on individuals and will then discuss a phased approach to Type I trauma care.

In my work with clients who have experienced situational trauma, such as Brandon and Carolyn, I have learned that a holistic approach to trauma is best. There is no static model to trauma work that is effective for all clients, which means that we, as counsellors, have to come to the work with mindfulness towards client safety and with knowledge and skills that we can adapt to suit a client's needs.

Because the experience of trauma is often overwhelming and can impact all aspects of a person, trauma work must be done with careful attention to developing tools to assist in stabilization and self-regulation before the processing of traumatic memories. I hold the following principles as especially helpful when helping those who have experienced situational trauma:

1) **Establish the brain, body, and mind connection**
   Use a holistic view to understand the impact of trauma and the potential for healing.

2) **Follow a phased approach to ensure that the work is not overwhelming**

   Phase one: History and stabilization
   Slowly and carefully build a solid foundation for the rest of the work.

   Phase two: Process trauma memories
   Stabilize and work through traumatic memories.

   Phase three: Meaning-making and resilience
   Re-insert the trauma into a full life story that has a past, present, and future.

1) BRAIN, BODY, AND MIND CONNECTION

The brain, body, and mind are connected, and so a change in one area has ripple effects through the whole system. Consider the act of bumping your elbow on a hard table edge: your brain sends a message to alert your elbow of the pain and potential injury, your body feels the pain of the incident, and your mind may be flooded with an emotion – such as frustration – and a thought about the event. This process occurs through the brain-body-mind connection for all experiences of emotional and physical pain. Practicing from a stance that recognizes the interconnected nature of the brain-body-mind is important in all areas of counselling, but especially in trauma work. To begin, let's explore the foundation of an approach that incorporates the brain, body, and mind to consider how it can fit within your practice.

Brain

Theorists have distinguished between *top-down* or *bottom-up* approaches to how the brain functions. The brain is built, like most things, bottom-up, meaning that it develops level by level. The lower (bottom) part is the reptilian brain, which is responsible for all the needs and sensations beginning in infancy (responses to hunger, temperature, fatigue, etc.). In the reptilian brain, the hypothalamus and brain stem control energy levels in the body, coordinating functioning of organ systems in the body. Signals from this area also initiate instincts for self-protection, such as thrusting one's arms out to break a fall.

The middle part of the brain, the limbic system, can be thought of as the emotional brain. For people who have experienced trauma, the limbic system senses danger – like an alarm being set off – and sends a release of hormones into the body as a response to move a person into action.

The upper part of the brain is the neocortex or the rational-cognitive brain. Bessel van der Kolk (2014) calls this the "watchtower." When danger is observed by the limbic system, the neocortex attempts to determine if the threat is real by observing our surrounding environment. It also attempts to make sense of new information and allows for the use of language. It is the hot spot for higher order thinking, reflection, and decision-making.

When trauma occurs, the limbic system sends a message to the reptilian system, stimulating the autonomic nervous system (ANS) to trigger a whole-body response. The ANS sets off survival responses, colloquially known as fight, flight, or freeze. By the time the upper brain (neocortex) recognizes what is occurring, the body may be in a state of mobilization (fight and/or flight) or immobilization (freeze). Once the threat has passed, the parasympathetic branch of the ANS works to return the whole nervous system and body to homeostasis, or a sense of calm (Porges, 2009).

Understanding the brain's processes can help counsellors and clients as they recognize the natural survival system that is alerted by perceived threats. After trauma, the brain has difficulty discerning between the real threat of the trauma and perceived threats in everyday life. When we share this information with clients, we provide them with language to explain their experience and an explanation for their post-traumatic experiences.

For example, Brandon expressed confusion and embarrassment over his high anxiety when riding as a passenger in a car. After explaining how his nervous system was responding to protect him, his sense of shame was reduced, because his experience was normalized. Psycho-education about the brain's response to trauma can help to alleviate clients' feelings of isolation and to establish a foundation of trust and information sharing between client and counsellor. In adopting a client-centred approach, remember to consider your client's ability to understand information about the brain. This information can easily become overwhelming to a client who is experiencing symptoms of trauma. Consider using a diagram and changing the terms to language that is more appropriate for your client. For example, talking about the "alarm system" in the nervous system may be more accessible than using technical neurobiology terms.

Body

The impact of the brain's survival response on the body cannot be overstated. The ANS sends messages throughout the body to alert it to danger. In considering how much the body is impacted by trauma, Daniel Siegel's theory of the window of tolerance is helpful. Siegel (2012) states that we all have a window of tolerance within which we can experience a range of stress, yet we can still stay emotionally regulated by using learned coping strategies. If a threat to one's survival or way of life occurs that is too great for the window to maintain, the ANS is triggered, and the person can be pushed out of the window of tolerance either into hyper- or hypoarousal.

In *hyper*arousal, we fly up out of our window of tolerance into the mobilization defence of fight or flight. Common body changes include tensed muscles, increased heart rate, shortness of breath, reddening of the face, increased rate of speech, and irregular eye movement. The body is being told it is in danger and must respond, which makes it very difficult to regain a sense of calm and safety.

Alternatively, a person may fall out of the window of tolerance down into *hypo*arousal and into the immobilization defence of freeze. Common body changes may include numbness, slowed speech, difficulty answering questions, irregular eye contact, and rigidity. It can appear as if the client's conscious awareness has left the present moment. A helpful way of distinguishing between the two states is whether the body that has experienced trauma is feeling too much (hyperarousal) or feeling too little (hypoarousal).

For example, Carolyn's reaction to triggers is to experience tense muscles and increased heart rate, which are symptoms of a body feeling too much. The sensations from these physical changes cause her to panic and feel like she can't control her bodily experiences.

In contrast, at times, Brandon's reaction to triggers is to become disconnected from his body. When his symptoms of stress are elevated, he becomes stuck in his mind and unable to discern any sensation in his body. He will say his body feels calm, even when expressing significant emotional responses. His body feels too little. By following an embodied approach to practice, we can help clients connect to their bodies in a safe way.

Following the experience of trauma, many body sensations may feel unsafe, and, in turn, many people disconnect from their bodies to avoid discomfort. As our clients understand how and why the body reacts to trauma, they can begin to re-establish trust in their bodies. A simple technique for this is to ask clients to connect with the ground, notice what surrounds them, and breathe as their bodies connect to the present moment as a safer environment. This practice can help to begin the process of reconnecting to the body and the present moment.

Mind

In counselling, the mind is the focus of most interventions. The activities of the mind should include the connection between our bodies, emotions, and thoughts. However, much of our day-to-day activities are determined by the mind's cognitive processing. The mind is where we organize information, make to-do lists, and decide how we are going to execute tasks. It is also where feelings are put into words. With trauma, the emotional and cognitive processes do not always match or work well together. In a trauma state, emotions can no longer be trusted as guides for thoughts because emotions are felt as both intense and urgent, which can lead to cognitive processes that are impulsive and irrational.

One of the primary goals of trauma counselling is to slow down and notice the difference between emotions, bodily sensations, and thoughts. When heart rate increases (physique) out of fear (emotion), then the thought "I am not safe" (cognition) emerges. This leads to a brain-body-mind connection that is overwhelming and that can push a person outside of their window of tolerance.

In the trauma healing process, we must help our clients to slow down and notice these distinctions. This has the dual purpose of normalizing the experience of responding to trauma and of teaching our clients how to calm themselves down and to settle their bodies and minds.

For example, when Carolyn hears a loud noise in her home, she jumps, her heart races, and she immediately thinks someone is breaking in. As we carefully notice each part of this experience, she is able to work on slowing down her body's response, which helps her be able to think more clearly. She can then use her thinking brain to help her more calmly choose what to do next, such as investigating the source of the noise and recognizing that she is not in danger.

The brain-body-mind connection is presented here as a framework from which to root the rest of your practice. Trauma presents as an overwhelmingly complex set of symptoms and responses and can be experienced this way by both the client and the counsellor. Separating the experience of trauma into the brain-body-mind connection can help to simplify and normalize the trauma response and also provides a framework for effective practice.

COUNSELLING STRATEGIES

1) Strategies focused on the *brain* are grounding techniques that facilitate a sense of safety to calm the ANS response. When the brain's alarm system is triggered and the client feels unsafe in the present moment, you can apply the following strategies

   ➤ Use grounding techniques, which help clients centre themselves in the present moment. For example, ask the client to feel their feet on the ground, to use their senses to notice their surroundings, and to generally pay attention to what is actually happening in the present moment.

   ➤ Observe with your client the act and effect of these activities while you do them. By clearly and transparently inviting your client to do a grounding activity while noticing the sensation of their feet on the ground, for example, you can help build a calming connection in their brain between the prefrontal cortex and the ANS. This helps the brain to notice fully that it is safe in this moment and that the trauma is in the past.

2) Strategies focused on the *body* bring the mind's awareness to the body. These approaches teach the client how to move back into a sense of safety and calm, even when the client is experiencing physical discomfort. A slight increase in tension, change in rate of breathing, or butterflies in the stomach are signs of something coming up in the body. Invite your client to notice these shifts so they can expand their ability to discern where the trauma is being held with these techniques

➤ Use more active exploration through movement exercises. Ask clients to stand and root themselves into the ground by feeling their feet connecting with the floor. If you practice yoga or other body-based approaches, such as reiki, this is an excellent point in which to introduce techniques to your clients.

➤ Teach progressive muscle relaxation. In this approach, you can direct the client to work from the top down or from the bottom up by moving from head to toes, holding the muscles in a tensed position and then releasing the muscles to a relaxed position, and working along the whole body. I use this approach with clients who have difficulty connecting to their bodies. The practice of tensing then releasing the muscles reconnects the person with their body from head to toe (or toe to head), in a way that is controlled.

➤ Facilitate a body scan. The process involves inviting a client to scan from the top of their head to their toes and to notice any tenseness, tightness, or pain, and to just notice the sensation without changing anything. I encourage clients to breathe through the body scan and imagine they are shining a light of awareness along their body as they do the scan. This practice helps to re-establish a brain-body-mind connection and to find comfort and calm amid the discomfort and stress of the body.

➤ Teach the client to approach discomfort with techniques like pendulation. Pendulation activities ask the client to move their attention from the area of discomfort to any area of the body that feels calm or relaxed, and then back and forth repeatedly. This is paired with deep and regulated breathing, as well as encouraging the client to just notice the sensations in their body. If your client reports that the discomfort is still present, continue with the pendulation (moving back and forth repeatedly). If your client reports the discomfort has lessened or disappeared, invite your client to lead themselves through practicing the pendulation to enjoy the calming feeling of their body. *See page 282 in the Resources section for a description of this activity.*

3) Strategies focused on the *mind* engage both feelings and thoughts. By using the client's name, making eye contact, and modelling calmness, you embody safety. Additionally, offering psycho-education about feelings and thoughts while engaging clients in conversations about how they feel and what they think when they experience symptoms builds collaborative safety. Often symptoms of trauma feel so overwhelming that thoughts and emotions cannot be separated

➤ Using an emotion wheel or list (a diagram with the primary emotions labelled along with related feeling words), ask your client to identify the presenting emotion. It's not uncommon for clients who have experienced trauma to lose track of their emotional experiences. This can present as a loss of emotional vocabulary. If you work with an individual who has suppressed their experience of trauma for a prolonged period of time, they have likely distanced themselves from emotions that feel unsafe. *See page 283 in the Resources section for an emotion vocabulary list.*

➤ Help your client recognize and identify negative thoughts such as "I am not safe, I am worthless, I should have done something, and it is not safe to feel my emotions as they are shared in session." Negative thoughts can become so ingrained for clients that they perceive them as normal. These negative thoughts become the baseline for viewing the self and the world. Use a ready-made negative and positive thoughts list to help your client identify their thoughts, or make a list with your client of their negative and positive thoughts. With this awareness, the client can begin to identify these thoughts as a result of trauma, rather than as the truth.

CASE APPLICATION

CAROLYN

Carolyn benefitted from approaches that grounded her in the present moment and directed her awareness into her body. Below is an excerpt where she talks about her experience of nightmares.

[Counsellor] "As you're telling me about the nightmare, what are you noticing in your body?"

[Carolyn] "I don't know. I am scared."

[Counsellor] "You're feeling scared as you think of the nightmare. I want you to know you are safe now. Can you take a breath, inhaling through your nose, and slowly releasing it through your mouth? Feel your feet on the ground, connecting to the present moment. [pause] If you were to do a scan from the top of your head to your toes, where do you notice the scared feeling?"

[Carolyn] "In my stomach."

[Counsellor] "Just notice it there, that scared feeling. As you do the body scan, is there anywhere that you feel is calm or relaxed in your body?"

[Carolyn] "My feet now."

[Counsellor] "Okay, slowly bring awareness to the scared feeling in your stomach, and then swing your awareness to the calm feeling in your feet. Like a pendulum, just swing your awareness. Now move your awareness back and forth, back and forth, between your stomach and your feet. Breathe as you do this. Back and forth. As you bring your awareness to your stomach now, what do you notice?"

[Carolyn] "It feels lighter now."

[Counsellor] "Remember, you can remind yourself that you are here now and use your body to ground you."

2) FOLLOW A PHASED APPROACH

Working through trauma follows three distinct phases: (1) history and stabilization; (2) processing traumatic memories; and (3) meaning making and resilience from trauma. Weaving the first principle of attending to brain-body-mind interconnection into each stage allows us to offer more effective support in this difficult work.

Phase One: History and Stabilization

Phase One is the most important phase, as it lays the foundation for all future progress and builds resilience. It is also the phase that counsellors tend to move through too quickly. At the urging of clients who want to feel better immediately, speedy progress through the phases is sometimes prioritized over best care of our clients. I draw upon the phrase "go slow to go fast" often in trauma work. A slow approach to Phase One can make for better progress in Phases Two and Three.

COUNSELLING STRATEGIES

1) Build therapeutic rapport

Phase One starts with the development of therapeutic rapport, which is built by establishing trust. Counsellors are working with their clients' deepest fears, so they need to be able to trust us to be non-judgmental, caring, and empathetic when they bare their most difficult experiences. We create new meaning through interacting with others, and the therapeutic relationship provides the client with a safe person they can share and collaborate with.

To be rapport focused, the counsellor should take a collaborative approach to exploring the client's experiences and should remain attuned to the client's need for a slower pace. Ideally, therapeutic rapport can develop to a point where the counsellor becomes a safe person within a calming space for the client. The client can use the counsellor as an example of a secure and calm base from which to model their own emotional regulation. This doesn't develop in one session and wholly depends on the counsellor's ability to create and model calmness and self-regulation for the client, from which point therapeutic counselling can be undertaken.

2) Do a historical review

During the first sessions of trauma work, it is helpful to conduct a thorough historical review of the client's life. The history sessions may progress at a slow pace as your client begins to feel safe sharing their story. We do not want the history session to be overwhelming or triggering. Some standard questions to ask are:

➤ If you were to play your life like a movie, where would it begin?

➤ What are your first memories of your family?

➤ Can you tell me about each member of your family?

➤ What or who were your main sources of support and comfort growing up?

➤ What was your first experience of loss?

➤ What are your greatest successes in your life?

➤ Can you tell me if you have ever experienced abuse, assault, bullying, death/loss, accident (work- and automobile-related), illness, and injury?

Before asking these questions, gauge your client's level of comfort. I open and close these sessions with some breathing and stabilization strategies, which are outlined below. Some of my clients prefer to prepare a list of events they feel are important to share or bring a written narrative of their life. In helping clients to prepare this, I ask, "What is important for me to know about who you are and what you have experienced in your life?" We can then use the client-prepared narratives as a road map for exploring history.

CASE APPLICATION

BRANDON

When Brandon came to counselling, we began by spending a session talking about his experience of trauma and his goals for treatment. In the second session, we planned to discuss history. I quickly noticed that there was something more to Brandon's experience of trauma than the traumatic memory itself.

[Counsellor] "We were talking about your life up to the accident, and I wondered if you could tell me about your first experience of driving?"

[Brandon] "Um, I think I was with my mom. She was sitting beside me, and I had just received a pass on the (driving) test. She was nervous."

[Counsellor] "Your mom was nervous?"

[Brandon] "Oh yeah, she gets nervous in cars. She says, 'It's easy to die in accidents' to all of the kids, and she told me that it was a dangerous thing."

[Counsellor] "Your mom told you that it was easy to die in car accidents and that driving was a dangerous thing. Do you think that impacted your driving experiences at all?"

[Brandon] "Oh, um, well I didn't really feel worried driving, but I always had that voice saying it's dangerous."

[Counsellor] "What does that voice say now, after the accident?"

[Brandon] "That Mom was right."

These questions address the developmental aspect of history. While we are not working with developmental trauma, these questions have several purposes:

➤ The information received helps to determine if there is developmental trauma present. If the client reports past experiences of abuse, attachment issues, major losses in childhood, or general, persistent, and cumulative traumas, then a developmental model for trauma work is needed.

➤ The information received can assist in determining if there are related factors that may be connected to the incident at hand. These factors can have a cumulative impact on the client's current functioning. This means that there are additional memories to address.

➤ The information received can help us find hidden strengths and past coping abilities. In the case example, Brandon's mother's worries about driving were not traumatizing on their own, but they did worsen his fears about driving as an unsafe activity following the accident. This helped inform later work in Phase Two, when we incorporated a focus on addressing "Mom's voice." Historical reviews provide much more than standard information, and also give us important guidance for future work.

3) Provide psycho-education

Throughout the history-taking and stabilization process, incorporate a psycho-education component. Psycho-education is simply providing clients with information about how the brain operates during trauma, as well as the functions and names for emotions and thought processes. Often, clients report feeling "crazy" or "alone" and as though no one else understands what they experience. While we want to value the individual experience of trauma, we also want to normalize the common impacts of trauma on one's mind and one's body. Handouts and online resources are useful for psycho-education, but it is also important to discuss ideas with our clients to ensure their understanding.

4) Teach stabilization and regulation skills

Stabilization is more than providing some strategies for clients to practice at home. It's the basis of teaching clients how to self-soothe toward a state of calm. Using a brain-body-mind approach to stabilization ensures that the processing of Phase Two is safe for the client. Consider how you engage the mind, the body, and the brain in the strategies used. All stabilization strategies impact one or all of the areas for trauma processes, but it is helpful to touch upon each aspect. The strategies listed in the previous brain-body-mind section are examples.

When using stabilization strategies, the counsellor should recommend approaches that are a good fit with the client's lifestyle. Spend a session discussing the client's openness to physical-based activities versus visualization activities. Explore their interest in and commitment to spending time practicing these strategies and develop a tailored coping plan. These discussions will inform you about what is most likely to appeal to their lifestyle.

When are clients ready to move from Phase One to Phase Two? What are the signs of progress that tell counsellors that it's safe to move forward? There are no easy answers to these questions. Each of our clients is unique, and we need to be responsive to their readiness to move to the next phase. The goal of Phase One is to increase the client's adaptive functioning by learning to experience emotions and arousal safely while staying in their window of tolerance. It can be helpful to ask yourself the following questions:

1) Does the client show an active engagement in counselling? Do they attend appointments as scheduled and arrive on time?

2) Does the client show an attunement with you? Have they comfortably shared their experiences, or are they nervous in attending counselling?

3) Have you conducted a thorough history to gain a full understanding of the client's past and of their presenting concerns?

4) Has the client been provided information about trauma, stabilization, and the counselling approach being used? Has the client been able to engage in stabilization strategies in your presence? Have they developed a coping plan or self-care plan? Are they able to engage in stabilization independent of your presence?

5) Are they able to self-soothe? Are their symptoms reducing in severity?

6) Does the client have access to healthy, positive, supportive relationships and the ability to reach out for support when they need it?

If you answer yes to these questions, it's likely that your client is ready to move into Phase Two of treatment. If we move too quickly into Phase Two, we can inadvertently trigger the client to a state of crisis, and we run the risk of harm to our clients. Instead of stabilizing our clients, we destabilize them. If contact is short term, it is in the client's best interest to spend this time in Phase One, unless the client has already developed Phase One tools. Careful, slow work in the beginning sets the stage for progressing through the later phases in a safe and timely manner.

Phase Two: Processing Trauma Memories

In Phase Two, the focus is on working directly with traumatic memory to resolve trauma-related symptoms. Traumatic memories often emerge as fragmented pieces of the whole experience. It is common for a client's memory to be disjointed, to be missing spans of time, to seem out of order, or to contain inconsistent details of events. While successful trauma processing depends on the recollection and reflection of traumatic experiences, we are often working with only fragments of the whole story. With a traumatic memory, a person may have conscious access to only some of these pieces, or they may not be clearly connected. The parts of the memory available may be non-verbal, rather than full, detailed stories. A person may only remember images, smells, sounds, emotions, physical sensations, or thoughts (Figure 2.1).

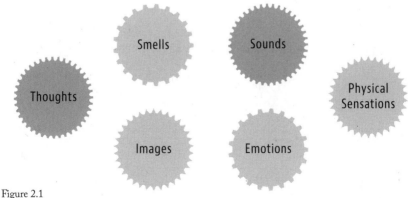

Figure 2.1
Parts of a memory

The work of Phase Two aims to stabilize the traumatic memory, so that it does not come up for the client unexpectedly and cause traumatic stress symptoms. The following principles are used to work effectively with the traumatic memory.

COUNSELLING STRATEGIES

1) Strengthen stabilization tools

Through Phase One work, the client has successfully learned and integrated stabilization strategies into their lives, creating a safe base from which to begin to work with traumatic memory. These stabilization tools need to be continually strengthened throughout Phase Two. A simple check-in is effective, such as asking clients about their ongoing self-regulation practices or asking clients to keep a journal or log of their practices. As a counsellor, your client's continued practice of stabilization is reassurance of their engagement in counselling and readiness for processing.

2) Connect mindful presence to a memory

Memories naturally change with new experiences, which allow us to continually use and learn from past experiences. Non-traumatic memories naturally undergo the change process, which occurs when memories can be recalled and reflected upon without triggering a traumatic stress response. When traumatic memories are recalled, they cause the brain to feel under threat, and this causes the ANS to come online. During Phase Two, our primary goal is to help clients process their traumatic memories to a point where clients can remain within their window of tolerance (and feel calm) when reflecting on the memory.

CASE APPLICATION

BRANDON

Brandon's memory was quite fragmented. He remembered few details about the accident itself, but he ruminated on his mother's words, the image of the steering wheel, and the squeal of brakes. To encourage a mindful approach to processing, we worked on noticing the feelings that emerged when he brought up the memory, while he remained aware of a sense of calm.

[Counsellor] "When you think of the accident [his word for the memory], what comes up for you now?"

[Brandon] "It feels like a story, like someone else's story."

[Counsellor] "Where does the story start?"

[Brandon] "Well, getting in the car to go to work, then I don't know, I just hear the squeal, and I see blood and the steering wheel, and then I am in a hospital room. There are missing parts, like I don't remember how I got there."

[Counsellor] "What else comes up for you as you think about this?"

[Brandon] "My mom, my mom saying it's dangerous, I am going to die, you know, that I am not safe."

[Counsellor] "Just be aware of these parts of the accident memory, then take your awareness to your body. Is there anywhere that feels tense?"

[Brandon] "My chest."

[Counsellor] "Just notice that. Don't try to change it. Just notice it. Is there anywhere that feels calm?"

[Brandon] "Um, my feet."

[Counsellor] "Just bring your awareness there. Notice the calmness. Move your awareness back and forth between these two areas, back and forth."

3) Choose a theory map to guide processing the memories
Processing memories and their impact is the core of most psychother-

apeutic approaches to trauma, and the steps of processing vary depending on which approach is used. Having a clear map to guide this stage of work is important to help both the client and counsellor remain clear about what steps are safe to take and when to take them.

Across approaches, or modalities, counsellors ask clients to stay with the treatment, to stay connected to the trauma memory, to become less reactive, and to develop an ability to reflect upon the memory without moving into a traumatic stress response.

We don't have space in this chapter to explore all trauma modalities in great detail, but here is a brief summary of some trauma approaches that are currently popular:

> A cognitive behavioural approach to trauma processing assumes that dysfunctional thinking patterns are the cause of psychological distress and thus focus largely on cognitions in processing.

> A psychodynamic approach would focus less on cognitions and more on concepts of denial, repressed emotions, and the notion of therapeutic catharsis or releasing emotions.

> Eye movement desensitization and reprocessing (EMDR) therapy uses bilateral stimulation of the brain and exposure to the traumatic memory to complete Phase Two of treatment (Shapiro, 2001).

> Somatic experiencing therapy uses pendulation between somatic sensations and traumatic memories to assist the client's processing of traumatic memories (Levine, 2015).

Most approaches to trauma use some form of exposure to the trauma in their Phase Two work. I use imaginal exposure in my work, where I invite the client to envision themselves in the moment of the trauma or to replay the memory in their mind. Some approaches use in vivo exposure, which means the client is exposed to real stimuli of the trauma. For example, in vivo might include taking Brandon to the scene of the accident or into his car. Exposure teaches the client to self-regulate while experiencing the impact of the traumatic memory and has the effect of changing the experience of the memory itself. Any exposure should be approached within a phased model, ensuring the client stays within their window of tolerance through the process.

I use an eclectic approach that integrates somatic approaches and EMDR for Phase Two processing of traumatic memories and is tailored to the individual client's needs and preferences. For example, if I have a client who is quite disconnected from their body, I might begin Phase Two with a somatic approach. Additionally, when I have a client who experienced a recent trauma, I prefer to move into EMDR first to help to process the new, fragmented memory. When consulting with new counsellors, I recommend they research the various treatment approaches and select a modality that is the best fit for their practice philosophy.

Having a modality to rely on in Phase Two helps to ensure that you are practicing responsibly and effectively. There is no one best approach, and each method has its merits. However, when the counsellor believes in the benefits of the modality they use, their passion will shine through to their client.

A counsellor needs to be well trained in their chosen modality, so they can be sure they stay within the bounds of their competence. It is imperative that a helper can ask for further supervision or support, or refer a client to additional resources as needed. For counsellors who don't have specialized training in these modalities, working collaboratively with a consultant or supervisor who does can help them continue to support their client effectively.

Regardless of which map is chosen, it's wise to include a brain-body-mind approach. Consider how the modality chosen integrates body sensations and brain processes, as well as emotions and cognitions, into its techniques. If there are gaps, consider integrating another modality or a stabilization strategy that integrates the missing component.

Determining the end of Phase Two is also tailored to the individual in counselling. Phase Two for situational trauma is often shorter than Phase Two for developmental trauma. We're working with one memory and its associations, rather than a lifetime of occurrences. We're ready to move to Phase Three when the client can bring up the memory and feel relatively calm.

I use a scaling question by asking the client, "When you think of the memory now, using a scale of zero to 10, with zero being calm and 10 being the worst possible feeling, where is the memory sitting for you in this moment?" Some memories will never be a zero, but we want to help our clients process their memories to as close to zero as possible before moving forward.

CASE APPLICATION

CAROLYN

Carolyn's processing was done using EMDR therapy. She began this session imagining she was in the moment of the attack and noticing her thoughts, emotions, and bodily sensations as she did this. She had the recurring thought, "I am not safe," and a strong feeling of fear that was showing up in her stomach as a sharp pain. To showcase the end of processing, consider this excerpt:

[Counsellor] "What is coming up for you now, in this moment?"

[Carolyn] "Well, it happened. I mean when I think about them in my house, then, I don't feel scared. I feel mad but calm. I don't know how to explain, like it happened, it shouldn't have, but it happened."

[Counsellor] "The mad feeling, can you tell me more about that?"

[Carolyn] "It shouldn't have happened, but it did. It's less of a 'mad' and more of an injustice."

[Counsellor] "The injustice feeling, how does it feel on a scale of zero to 10, zero being calm and 10 being the worst feeling you can imagine – where would you put the injustice feeling?"

[Carolyn] "Like a zero. It happened, it shouldn't have, but I am okay."

[Counsellor] "Would you like to just sit with those statements: It happened, it shouldn't have, and you are okay."

[Carolyn] "Yeah."

[Counsellor] "Just sit with this and notice the feeling that comes from hearing these statements. Take a breath and notice how it feels in your body. [After few moments] What do you notice?"

[Carolyn] "I feel like something cleared or something. Like it's okay now. It's okay today."

Phase Three: Meaning Making and Resilience

Phase Three is the reintegration phase, when the counsellor helps the client to integrate traumatic experience into their present and future storylines. When people enter into counselling, they are often focused on the problem of the traumatic memory. The traumatic memory and symptoms are overtaking their life and their sense of self.

In Phases One and Two, we aim to increase our clients' strengths and resilience in the face of trauma and then decrease the impact of the traumatic experience. In Phase Three, we aim to help our clients construct a plan for their future. Prior to Phase Three, the focus is on difficult memories of the past, and on how awful life is now, which does not allow the client to hope for a future without trauma. At this phase, our clients are ready to begin to move towards a future that does not include the impacts of trauma that brought them into your office in the first place.

COUNSELLING STRATEGIES

1) Construct a new narrative

In Phase Three, we are tasked with co-constructing a new narrative – a life story that includes the traumatic experience as part of a person's past, separate from the present, in order to plan for a future without traumatic stress. This new storyline moves away from the trauma memory and fosters hope for what the future may hold.

Narrative therapy is an excellent psychotherapy approach to draw upon in Phase Three. Narrative approaches focus on the concept of re-authoring

(White & Epston, 1990), which is a beautiful way of saying rewriting past knowledge. With trauma-informed support, individuals have the opportunity to re-author their traumatic experience into something meaningful.

This is not putting a positive spin on a negative experience, but rather it is coming away from a troubling experience with meaning that is transformative and adaptive. It is the difference between "This is the worst thing that ever happened to me, I will never be the same," and "It is what it is, it happened, and it's over now." Sometimes this meaning making can be thick and complex in its description, such as "I am now stronger for having survived that," and other times, this meaning making is simply "It's over now," or "It is what it is."

Sessions in this stage involve discussions of the client's life moving forward and reflections of the past, all while standing in the present moment. Questions to facilitate this can include:

➤ What does it mean to grow from this experience?

➤ What did it take for you to overcome this?

➤ What does your growth (use client's word or your own) say about you? What does it say about what you believe in about yourself and others?

➤ If you were able to keep this knowledge about your life close to you, to draw support from this, what's your guess about what this would make possible for you?

➤ While thinking about what this would make possible for you to do, what steps could you take that would fit this?

2) Celebrate pivotal moments

We want to work with clients to co-construct a story about their traumatic experience, from the beginning to the unknown (but hoped for) future. We want to explore the moments of change and realization, also known as pivotal moments, in one's healing.

Duvall and Beres (2011) describe pivotal moments as those in which people experience realizations, release, and movement as they are pulled toward their hopes and new ways of being in the world. These moments occur in a present-centred, new meaning-making context. A counsellor may hear shifts in client language, and these are the first signs that the client is engaging in change. A movement away from catastrophic language that paints the future as negative and the use of present-centred language that acknowledges the past while endorsing hopes for the future can be observed in sessions.

Until Phase Three work, Carolyn was stuck in the notion that she would always feel unsafe and that she could not trust others. After processing her memory of the attack, she was suddenly speaking in hopeful terms, and saying "I checked the locks twice last night, but I thought then that I was doing it more out of habit than need. I realized I'm okay just locking it and saying it's okay."

Here, Carolyn presented a sudden and new realization that she does not need her past habits of safety to feel safe. As a counsellor, this is an exciting shift, because we're now able to have conversations around new meaning and experiences post-trauma. These realizations are based on reactions from the outside world. Carolyn felt a deeper sense of safety and progress each time she locked her doors without checking multiple times. Take this phase slow and spend time getting to know – and celebrating – the healing process your client has taken.

3) Collaborative letter writing

Past clients have truly appreciated letters either provided by me or co-constructed together. Pennebaker (2004) wrote that release is one benefit of letter writing and the opportunity to know oneself more deeply. Putting pen to paper and directing the mind to release thoughts and feelings is a therapeutic experience in itself. One approach to letter writing involves asking the client to write a letter to their future self, focusing on their hopes for the future, or writing a letter to their past self, focusing on their growth, with the message of recovery and healing. Another approach is to instruct clients to write letters to another person, someone who hurt them or someone who supported them, outlining the story of their experience and healing. These letters to others are often never sent, but they allow for creative expression and emotional release. These letters are not meant to be controlled by the counsellor or to be a perfect narrative of the experience. Rather, letters are much like conversation. They shift and flow in a fluid way.

CASE APPLICATION

BRANDON

Brandon and I invited his mother into the room through the use of his imagination during Phase Three work. She was such an important voice in the counselling room during Phases One and Two, that both Brandon and I felt that she was a part of the process.

[Counsellor] "As you look back to the accident memory now, what does your mom's voice say?"

[Brandon] "She still says it's dangerous. She definitely still worries."

[Counsellor] "What do you think about this voice now?"

[Brandon] "That she worries so much that she makes everyone else worried."

[Counsellor] "What do you want her to know about her worrying?"

[Brandon] "That it takes her away, and that it was hard for me to be okay because of it."

[Counsellor] "Can you imagine bringing your mom into the room here with us? What would she say about all that you've worked through?"

[Brandon] "She'd say she was happy for me and proud of me."

[Counsellor] "What would you say about her worrying? Talk to her as if she was here."

[Brandon] "Um, Mom, it's hard when you worry, because I can't be okay. I need you to be okay so I can feel safe to drive and do the stuff I want to do."

[Counsellor] "What might your mom say?"

[Brandon] "I don't think she would even know that it impacts me. She just thinks she's protecting me or something."

[Counsellor] "What might it be like for her to know that?"

[Brandon] "She might think about how big her worries are."

[Counsellor] "Do you think you'd like to share this with her?"

[Brandon] "Yeah."

[Counsellor] "Sometimes, the people I work with like to use letters to share their experiences with others, as well as information that is tailored to a specific reader. Would you be interested in writing a letter to your mom about how big her worries are and how you feel about them?"

[Brandon] "I think so. She would definitely read it, and I think I might get more out that way."

My closing activity with clients also involves letter writing. I provide my client with a letter summarizing their growth and movement through counselling, using words and expressions the client has shared during sessions, and ending with their stated hopes for moving forward. These letters don't need to be long, and they can be written by hand or emailed, but the message to my clients is that their stories are important, meaningful, and worth remembering. The letters that I prepare for clients honour their healing process and our time together.

We know that our clients are ready to end counselling when they are no longer experiencing trauma symptoms, when they are practicing effective stabilization, and when they feel ready to move forward without our support. Planning an ending session is useful. The session can summarize your work together and discuss your client's hopes for the future.

FINISHING THOUGHTS

Trauma work can feel heavy. It takes a toll on our own well-being to be emotionally attuned to the traumatic experiences of others. Despite the potential to be exhausting, it is also rewarding to offer assistance. Traumatic experiences are not doomed to be long lasting in their impact. There is always potential for growth and recovery.

My continued passion for this work comes from the notion of post-traumatic growth. Drawing on the writing of Tedeschi and Calhoun (1995), post-traumatic growth is a benefit of surviving trauma. Recovery from trauma offers the opportunities to strengthen one's sense of self, to have a greater openness to possibilities in life, to develop stronger relationships with friends and family, to have a greater appreciation for life, and to maintain a stronger sense of spirituality.

Overall, the growth offered through the recovery from trauma offers an opportunity to experience oneself and one's personal relationships in new ways. Doing efficacious and compassionate trauma counselling provides the opportunity to see recovery from situational trauma and to find meaning in the helping role.

ABOUT THE AUTHOR

Michelle Gibson, MSW, RSW

Michelle is a Registered Social Worker who holds a master's degree in clinical social work. She is a trainer with the Crisis & Trauma Resource Institute and is also an instructor at Western University, where she teaches counselling and trauma courses to family studies and social work students. Michelle has a private practice specializing in the area of trauma recovery for youth and adults. She is an empathetic practitioner who believes in the importance of therapeutic attunement and collaboration with clients as the basis for recovery.

REFERENCES

Courtois, C. A. (2008). Complex trauma, complex reactions: Assessment and treatment. *Psychological Trauma: Theory, Research, Practice, and Policy, S*(1), 86-100.

Duvall, J., & Beres, L. (2011). *Innovations in narrative therapy: Connecting practice, training, and research.* New York, NY: W. W. Norton & Company.

Levine, P. (2015). *Trauma and memory: Brain and body in a search for the living past: A practical guide for understanding and working with traumatic memory.* Berkeley, CA: North Atlantic Books.

National Center for Injury Prevention and Control. (2006). *CDC injury fact book.* Atlanta, GA: Centers for Disease Control and Prevention.

Nixon, R., Sterk, J., & Pearce, A. (2012). A randomized trial of cognitive behaviour therapy and cognitive therapy for children with posttraumatic stress disorder following single-incident trauma. *Journal of Abnormal Child Psychology, 40*(3), 327-337.

Pennebaker, J. (2004). *Writing to heal: A guided journal for recovering from trauma and emotional upheaval.* Oakland, CA: New Harbinger Publications, Inc.

Porges, S. (2009). The polyvagal theory: New insights into adaptive reactions of the autonomic nervous system. *Cleveland Clinic Journal of Medicine, 76*(2), 86-90.

Shapiro, F. (2001). *Eye movement desensitization and reprocessing (EMDR): Basic principles, protocols, and procedures* (2nd ed.). New York, NY: Guilford Press.

Siegel, D. J. (2012). *The developing mind: How relationships and the brain interact to shape who we are* (2nd ed.). New York, NY: Guilford Press.

Tedeschi, R. G., & Calhoun, L. G. (1995). *Trauma and transformation: Growing in the aftermath of suffering.* Thousand Oaks, CA: Sage Publications, Inc.

van der Kolk, B. A. (2009). Developmental trauma disorder: Towards a rational diagnosis for chronically traumatized children. *Praxis Der Kinderpsychologie Und Kinderpsychiatrie, 58*(8), 572-586.

van der Kolk, B. A. (2014). *The body keeps the score: Brain, mind and body in the healing of trauma.* New York, NY: Penguin Books.

van der Kolk, B. A., & Courtois, C. A. (2005). Editorial comments: Complex developmental trauma. *Journal of Traumatic Stress, 18*(5), 385-388.

White, M., & Epston, D. (1990). *Narrative means to therapeutic ends.* New York, NY: W. W. Norton & Company.

CHAPTER THREE

ANXIETY

By AnnMarie Churchill

ANXIETY IS A NORMAL PART OF HUMAN LIFE, AS WELL AS A COMMON mental health issue. Every person is unique in the amount of anxiety they feel in response to everyday stressors. This is largely due to the individual baseline that is considered a fairly stable part of each person's personality (LeDoux, 2015). Regardless of one's general level of anxiety, most people can recall a time in life when extreme worry or fear gripped them. Human beings tend to be on the lookout for danger and will instinctively take steps to avoid threat. This risk avoidance is rooted in an ancient fear response that reacts to *immediate* danger by triggering the survival instinct to fight, flight, or freeze. When someone experiences anxiety, that same fear response is engaged, but it's in relation to a potential *future* threat. This can be useful when it helps us prepare for or avoid something dangerous or unpleasant. But when that fear response is triggered unnecessarily, people can experience maladaptive and disordered patterns of anxiety that are excessive in their frequency (Hofmann, Ellard, & Siegle, 2012). These false alarms create significant distress and cause people to avoid everyday situations.

MARK

As the end of senior year in high school approaches, Mark is increasingly stressed about his grades and college applications. He is having difficulty concentrating, and he lies awake for hours worrying about school and his future life. In the last month, Mark has been absent from school more often than he has attended because of various physical ailments and related medical appointments. No underlying physical illness has been detected, yet Mark continues to feel unwell, and his absenteeism is making matters worse.

Mark's mother scheduled a counselling appointment for him on the recommendation of his guidance counsellor. In my office for his first appointment, Mark sat on the edge of his chair with his hands folded tightly and right leg shaking. He spoke about his many concerns and described himself as "a worrywart, but with good reason." When asked about his goals for counselling, Mark replied, "I have to maintain my average and get into college. I need to concentrate, but I can't stop worrying. Can you help?"

IRENE

At 72 years old, Irene has been widowed for two years. She has two adult children and four grandchildren, but she often feels lonely. Since her husband George died, Irene hasn't been going out much and has been keeping to herself, even forgoing family events. Irene is aware that getting out of the house and socializing is good for her and usually plans to attend events. However, when the time to go out arrives, she feels nervous and develops a queasy stomach, which causes her to cancel. Lately, Irene has been asking her children to pick up groceries and other necessities for her, because she doesn't want to leave the house.

Irene's daughter convinced her to attend a seniors' mental health walk-in program. At the beginning of the first session, Irene seemed uncomfortable. She avoided eye contact and apologized for taking up my time, saying, "People have worse things to deal with than no social life."

As the session continued, Irene relaxed and discussed feeling lonely and embarrassed.

"I was never very outgoing, but it was easier to go out when my husband was with me. Sometimes I feel better if I stay home, but then I feel bad cancelling on people, especially my friends and family. It seems I don't know my own mind."

AMIR

Amir, who is 40 years old and has a solid family life and a recent career promotion, felt his hard work had finally paid off until he had his first "episode" a month ago. Amir arrived at his desk on a Monday morning, and he had just opened his calendar when he felt the room spin. His heart began to pound, and he felt short of breath. Amir gripped his desk in fear that something horrible would happen until the sensations subsided. The episode lasted about two minutes, but as Amir explained, it felt like an eternity. Later in the week, it happened again, and this time he called his wife, who insisted they go to the hospital. Amir felt calmer as he sat in the waiting room with his wife, even though he expected to be told he had a dire illness. Instead, he was informed that he likely suffered a panic attack. He went home relieved but found himself dreading going back to the office.

The following day, Amir experienced another "episode" at his desk, and he cancelled work for the week. On the advice of a friend, he contacted the Employee Assistance Program and made his way to my office. At his first appointment, Amir looked tense and worried as he wondered aloud about what he should do. "Should I be at work? What if I faint or do something crazy? How can I make it stop?"

Although Mark, Irene, and Amir are in different circumstances, and their reactions vary, all three clients are experiencing disordered anxiety, which is persistent, distressing, and causing interference in their daily lives.

Challenging situations such as a job interview or driving test can commonly evoke an ordinary anxious response. Most people experience butterflies in the stomach, worrying, sweating, feeling jittery, and other nervous sensations before and during a stressful situation. These sensations usually subside as the situation ends. This normal level of anxiety is routinely managed and does not significantly impact performance or behaviour.

However, anxiety is considered disordered when the level of distress is more extreme, and the nervousness and worry is prolonged or reoccurs. With disordered anxiety, there is an overestimation of threat and underestimation of one's ability to manage or cope, causing intense and irrational fear and avoidance of normal life situations. Common components of disordered anxiety include

➤ activation of the fear response, including physical and psychological distress, in the absence of immediate danger;

➤ a sense of uncertainty, loss of control, and/or impending doom;

➤ future-oriented worry with repeated "What if?" rumination;

➤ attention and over-focusing on potential internal and/or external threats;

➤ uncomfortable physical sensations;

➤ an instinct to avoid everyday situations;

➤ initial avoidance of one situation becomes habitual and spreads to other situations.

Physiological sensitivity, cautious or reactive temperament, and adverse life events contribute to the development of disordered anxiety. Mark's "worrywart" temperament makes him prone to ruminating on impending life changes after Grade 12. His current challenges have likely overwhelmed his sensitive internal warning system, causing dysregulation and disordered anxiety. For Irene, as a naturally shy and cautious person, the loss of her husband (who was also her main social support) put her at risk for disordered anxiety. Amir, in contrast, is a self-described "Type A" personality, not prone to worry or internalizing. However, the demands of his new position and his tendency to push through without respite likely caused nervous system overload. This buildup of tension and stress triggered his first panic attack. Fear of a recurrence of panic added additional threat, creating disordered anxiety.

Anxiety disorders are among the most prevalent mental disorders (Langlois, Samokhvalov, Rehm, Spence, & Connor Gorber, 2011). In addition, anxiety is often an important component of physical illnesses and other mental disorders, such as depression, eating disorders, and post-traumatic stress disorder. Because of this prevalence, it's important for counsellors to have a comprehensive understanding of anxiety and practical strategies to assist clients.

INSIGHTS AND GUIDING PRINCIPLES FOR COUNSELLING

Clients experiencing disordered anxiety are in a heightened state of vulnerability. Their internal and external worlds seem out of control and uncertain. At the initial session, Mark, Irene, and Amir all reported feeling nervous and unsure of themselves. A calm environment can make room for clients to feel hopeful about resolving their anxiety problem.

Normalizing anxiety is an important starting point for intervention. Many clients feel embarrassment or shame, believing that they are flawed or weak because of their problem with anxiety. It's helpful to inform them of the prevalence of anxiety and to provide examples of common and disordered anxiety.

Explaining how anxiety works, including its adaptive nature, can be empowering and helpful in reducing and managing anxiety. Clients are often worried about their anxiety symptoms. Mark is worried that he is flawed in some way, and Irene and Amir are concerned that there is something seriously wrong with them. Connecting these anxiety-related symptoms with the underlying fight/flight/freeze response helps clients understand their experience of anxiety and the rationale for treatment.

The pattern of disordered anxiety involves a feedback loop of threat-based thoughts, associated feelings (emotional and physiological), and reactive behaviours. For example, being stuck in traffic on the way to a concert or presentation can create an anxious response. Thoughts such as "This is horrible … I hate being late … everyone will be looking at me" can trigger feelings of nervousness and tension, leading to behaviours like clenching the wheel, horn honking, and possibly turning around and going home. These behaviours will increase tension and anxiety and reinforce worry and negative thoughts, leading to repeated anxiety and avoidance. Clients can learn to interrupt this loop by noticing and changing anxiety-related thoughts, feelings, and/or behaviours.

I find the following principles key for guiding my work with clients experiencing disordered anxiety:

1) **Use the counselling relationship to activate calm**
   A consistent and stable environment allows a client to come out of their "alarm" state.

2) **Explain anxiety**
   Accurate information normalizes a person's experience and provides rationale for treatment.

3) **Build physiological awareness**
   Understanding and expecting to feel the physical side of anxiety allows clients to regulate their fear response.

4) **Expand cognitive flexibility**
   The ability to broaden one's perspective and shift one's attention to notice positive events, as well as the frightening ones, allows clients to reduce threat perception.

5) **Practice exposure**
   Gradual practice of turning toward situations and events that produce anxiety allows clients to reduce anxiety in these contexts and increase their abilities to approach more of life.

1) USE THE COUNSELLING RELATIONSHIP TO ACTIVATE CALM

A calm, therapeutic approach helps soothe the client's nervous system, reducing the sense of threat, and allowing for new insight and awareness. In a state of high arousal, the sympathetic nervous system is activated, which generates a flood of stress hormones through the body. In this state, survival instincts take precedence over higher order thinking and planning. Clients often report they can't think straight, feel keyed up, and have the urge to escape. For counselling to be effective, this alarm must be deactivated. Counsellors can use themselves, the counselling environment, and the counselling process to promote connection and calm. This soothing approach activates the parasympathetic nervous system, which regulates the body back into rest and recovery.

COUNSELLING STRATEGIES

1) Maintain a calm presence

   ➤ Create a *before-session* ritual to tune in to your own internal state to induce calm and focus. I leave my office for a short walk down the hall and use this time to tune in to my breathing and physical movement.

   ➤ Initiate *in-session* self-regulating strategies, such as taking an intentional deep breath or having a beverage on hand, to slow yourself down and ensure your system isn't activated by the client's anxiety.

2) Provide a calm environment during the session

   ➤ At the introduction stage, ask clients about their preferences (including seating arrangement and lighting). This provides a sense of control and comfort for clients and helps to ease the threat response.

   ➤ Offer physical or sensory objects to help create calm and focus. I find clients respond well to beach rocks, silly putty, a miniature Zen rock garden, soft music, landscape pictures, and natural scents.

3) Use the counselling process to create connection and motivation

   ➤ Pace session progress and content according to the client's state. For some people, it's important to slow down the process and focus initial work on rapport building and emotional regulation. Other clients show up eager to learn about anxiety and ready to make changes. These people may require a more businesslike approach that is informative and efficient.

➤ Tailor your approach to match the client's unique experience. Although anxiety problems are common, the stories presented in this chapter show that client experiences are quite different. Demonstrate attunement through language, metaphors, and strategies that are salient for the client.

CASE APPLICATION

MARK

Mark is agitated at his first session, appearing tense and jittery. As I introduce myself and ask questions to get to know him, Mark sits on the edge of his seat and seems ready to bolt. It is obvious that he is nervous and uncomfortable. It is important for me to help Mark settle down so he can make it through the session, is able to engage, and will return for further work on his anxiety. I work on grounding by talking about things that interest him. I draw his attention to a hiking poster on the wall and talk about the seating arrangement in the room. I offer him silly putty as a tool to contain his nervous energy and to help focus him to both his external environment and to the present moment. Mark responds well to the putty and the casual nature of the conversation. Halfway through the session, he sits back in his chair and begins to share his concerns.

IRENE

Irene attends the first appointment on the urging of her family. She has never been to counselling before and is concerned that she is wasting my time. Irene seems rushed, embarrassed, and unsure of why she is here. It is important for me to pay attention to her discomfort and use strategies to create connection and calm. Approaching her in a relaxed manner, while assuring her she isn't taking up my time and that her presence is important, helps build connection. I create a calm environment by providing opportunities for empowerment and engagement. I prompt her to choose her seat, offer her a choice of water or tea, and normalize her discomfort with this novel experience of counselling. It is also helpful for me to model calm by intentionally slowing down my speech and behaviour and making space for quiet reflection. As Irene listens and sips her tea, there is a noticeable change in her demeanour. She settles into her chair, her breathing slows, and she becomes less skittish and more open.

Irene explains that things changed after George died. She is less active and often feels lonely and nervous. Irene expresses embarrassment and frustration with this change in herself but is unsure of what to do about it. It will be important for Irene to understand her anxiety in terms of her temperament and the significant loss of her husband, who was also her primary social support.

AMIR

Amir appears tense and "all business" at his first session. He is eager to learn about anxiety and expresses an interest in trying something – anything – to stop the panic. In the presence of Amir's tension, I notice myself stiffen and sense the urge to speed up. It is important for me to intentionally regulate my breath and speech to help him calm down and engage in the process. Matching Amir's style, my approach in the session is efficient and focused on explaining panic, as well as discussing the rationale for well-established anxiety management strategies. Through this information sharing, Amir becomes noticeably less tense and begins to open up about his embarrassment and intense fear related to the panic attacks. Matching the pace and content of the session to Amir's needs and temperament helps him feel comfortable in the session and confident in the counselling process.

2) EXPLAIN ANXIETY

It is important for clients to develop an understanding of their anxiety as a malfunctioning protective instinct that they can learn to regulate. Understanding the biology of anxiety and the fear response is often the first step in reducing distress and avoidant behaviour. It helps to explain that the fear response, triggered by an imagined or future threat, is the same reaction that is triggered by an immediate danger. Stress hormones are released that work to focus attention on the threat and ready physiological processes for fight, flight, or freeze. It can be said that with anxiety, the alarm system is working extremely well, but it's in the wrong place at the wrong time, like a smoke detector over a toaster, creating a false alarm.

Helping clients understand this process and relating it to their experience of anxiety is extremely effective in reducing distress and addressing behaviours that maintain and reinforce disordered anxiety.

COUNSELLING STRATEGIES

1) Explain the fear response, making the connection to anxiety

   ➤ Normalize the experience of anxiety, noting the evolutionary nature and prevalence of phobias and specific anxieties that cause people to avoid everyday situations.

2) Provide books, handouts, or other reference material

   ➤ Offer details of informational and interactional websites on anxiety that can extend the client's learning and understanding of their anxiety beyond session time.

3) Help clients map out their personal experience of anxiety

   ➤ Cultivate a curious, adaptive, and, if appropriate, humorous approach to the client's experience of anxiety.

   ➤ Include the client's perceived threats, potential triggers, and physiological and behavioural reactions associated with their fear response.

CASE APPLICATION

MARK

Mark can identify his many worries, but the act of listing them at an appointment leaves him feeling nervous and scared. It is helpful to practice grounding techniques (slow breathing and body awareness) and to normalize anxiety, including the fear response. Mark is particularly interested in this ancient survival instinct, so I pursue that area to emphasize the adaptive nature of anxiety.

[Counsellor] "The fear response is amazing and interesting. The human species survived because of that instinct. We wouldn't be here today if we couldn't sense threat and avoid danger. Some people, like you, have a sensitive warning system – sort of like a canary in a coal mine. As the air in the mine becomes toxic, the canary stops singing, providing an early warning signal that alerts the miners to danger. Your warning system overreacts and is often triggered when there is no danger, creating false alarms. The good news is that you can learn to detect a false alarm and turn it off or down, reducing your worry and fear. What do you think?"

[Mark] "I never thought of it like that – like a false alarm I can turn off. How can I do that?"

The shift from fear to curiosity about his anxiety is significant for Mark, and the change is noticeable in his thinking. Instead of focusing on the fear of a doomed future and other negative possibilities, Mark becomes interested in what he *can* do. He seems energized and hopeful about getting back to school and his "normal life" with reduced worry and anxiety.

IRENE

Irene benefits from the explanation that her brain is interpreting social situations as dangerous, triggering an alarm that makes her feel unwell and unsafe. We discuss her natural tendency toward shyness and how George provided a sense of safety and comfort in social situations. It isn't surprising that worry and fear have escalated in George's absence.

Irene recognizes that being by herself and going out on her own feels frightening, and that she will need to find ways to make it more comfortable. It is important to normalize Irene's situation by letting her know that many people experience this kind of social anxiety that causes them to stay away from social events, leaving them isolated and lonely. Irene can then see that her way of trying to make herself feel better is making her feel worse. This discussion creates important insights for Irene, leading to the beginning of a plan to manage her nervousness and become more social. Irene seems relieved to have an explanation that makes sense to her and gives her confidence that she can live a satisfying life on her terms.

AMIR

Amir is particularly worried about what his panic experiences mean for him. The personalization of his "episodes" creates additional stress and makes him feel weak and vulnerable. It is helpful to reassure him from the start that he isn't "crazy," and that panic attacks are common and not fatal.

Amir needs more than reassurance and empathy. He is deeply concerned that something is wrong and that he isn't behaving like a "guy in control." Explaining the biology of anxiety, including the power of the amygdala and the survival instinct, in relation to Amir's experience of panic provides a rational explanation for an otherwise terrifying experience. This understanding creates a sense of control, which is vital for Amir and works to ease his fear.

It is also helpful to normalize Amir's experience by making the connection between his anxiety experience and common fears related to flying, elevators, and public speaking. Amir's posture and mood change as he engages in this discussion. He relaxes in his chair, is animated, and laughs as he shares a story about his wife "freaking out" at the sight of a spider. Through this session, Amir's worry and embarrassment decrease, allowing him to become curious about methods to manage (rather than avoid) the panic.

3) BUILD PHYSIOLOGICAL AWARENESS

The physical symptoms of anxiety usually create discomfort and distress. As a result, clients commonly set a goal of never feeling anxious again. Understandably, anxiety is viewed as a problem to be solved. It is important for clients to understand that it's normal to feel anxious, just as it's normal to feel hungry – it's not always comfortable, but it isn't dangerous. Anxiety sensations, like hunger pangs, are built-in signalling mechanisms, drawing attention and focus to internal functioning and important external events.

Many clients are surprised to learn that anxiety can be helpful in achieving goals. Mounting tension and the quickening of one's heart rate help to trigger alertness and attention. In small doses, this physical arousal or agitation can serve to help people wake up or to draw attention to something important, which improves focus and performance. For Mark, moderate levels of anxiety can provide energy and alertness that help him study for exams. That amount of anxiety can also provide enough agitation or concern to motivate him to get enough sleep for exam day.

As anxiety increases beyond a moderate level, it becomes less helpful. At high levels of anxiety, the alarm centre of the brain takes precedence over the thinking and planning centre of the brain, sacrificing performance for survival. Symptoms of high anxiety, such as a pounding heart, shaking limbs, and racing thoughts, undermine motivation and performance. For example, Irene experiences butterflies in her stomach when her anxiety is low. When her anxiety gets higher, her whole body feels shaky and she experiences nausea, preventing her from feeling able to do her other activities. Learning to recognize when anxiety is low, moderate, or high increases self-awareness and the ability to self-regulate.

COUNSELLING STRATEGIES

1) Increase regulation skills

> ➤ Help clients identify physical cues for various emotions. Use pictures from magazines or emotion cards to identify nonverbal cues for each emotion. Practice by using activities such as charades or a

"feelings walk." *See page 284 in the Resources section for a description of the feelings walk activity.*

➤ Explore the nature and intensity of symptoms associated with anxiety in more depth.

- Invite clients to identify specific areas of their bodies affected by anxiety. Use a blank template with a body outline and invite clients to draw in symptoms or body clues. Participate with your own outline and body clues to normalize anxiety and the fear response. *See page 287 in the Resources section for instructions.*

- Introduce clients to techniques that activate the relaxation response. Practice with a variety of strategies, such as relaxation breathing and progressive muscle relaxation. *See pages 285 and 286 in the Resources section for sample activities.*

2) Teach mindful awareness by helping clients focus their attention on the present moment without judgment (Kabat-Zinn, 2016)

➤ Invite clients to simply notice their breath and body sensations as they inhale and exhale.

➤ Help clients become aware of their physical state by doing an internal scan of their bodies from one end to the other, or by focusing in on one specific area, and noticing the presence or absence of tension.

➤ Encourage clients to practice being mindful in their daily life by noticing physical sensations associated with everyday activities, such as walking, eating, showering, and doing chores.

3) Encourage clients to develop a wellness plan with specific activities

➤ Recommend they include physical activity, time in nature, and social time.

➤ Encourage clients to choose from their personalized wellness menu for strategies to manage distress and face challenges.

➤ Provide clients a prompt list if they have difficulty identifying soothing activities or strategies.

➤ Encourage clients to set realistic goals for building rest and recovery behaviours into daily life and help monitor their use to encourage motivation and effort.

CASE APPLICATION

MARK

To develop physiological awareness and help Mark *turn off his alarm*, I explain in general terms how emotions are expressed in the body and specifically explore the physical sensations associated with fear and anxiety. I normalize this process by sharing my own physical sensations related to low and high anxiety. To emphasize the usefulness of these sensations, I refer to them as body "clues" for emotions. I ask Mark to identify the body clues he gets when he feels nervous or worried.

[Mark] "I have so many. My jaw hurts, my neck and back feel tight and sore, my legs get stiff, and my head hurts. If I'm at school and the teacher asks a question, my heart pounds, and my mouth gets dry. It's like I can't talk and feel like an idiot."

I explain that these body clues are signs that his alarm is activated much of the time, either responding to important matters or false alarms. It is important for Mark to recognize the helpful early signs of anxiety, so he can respond more effectively and prevent unnecessary high anxiety.

Mark has difficulty identifying early signs, which is common for people who experience chronic anxiety. Clients may describe feeling tense and keyed up as their normal state. To help Mark become aware of his body, we do a short body scan activity in the session. I invite him to tune in to his body and notice where he feels tension. Mark is unsure of how to tune in, so I take him through a body scan practice by inquiring about tension in different parts of his body and giving him time with each to make an assessment. I start by asking him if his shoulders are tight or relaxed. After a pause, I ask him to notice his hands, whether they are clenched or relaxed, then his stomach, his feet in his shoes, and finally, to notice his breathing – is it fast or slow, comfortable or uncomfortable?

Through this scan, Mark can detect tension in his shoulders but cannot assess his breathing. I explain that tuning into body sensations can be difficult and takes practice, but that this is the first step to being able to turn off his alarm. I introduce progressive muscle relaxation as a strategy to help with awareness and developing a sense of calm. I encourage Mark to practice tuning in to bodily sensations and intentionally tensing and releasing areas of his body throughout the day at home and at school.

IRENE

The physiological sensations associated with anxiety are a major factor in Irene's experience. She mentions several times in the session that she can't go out because she is "sick." Irene misinterprets her stomach upset as illness, which prevents her from carrying on with regular activities. It is helpful to explain that, along with worry and fear, stress hormones can upset the stomach and cause her to feel unsettled. The stomach problems are real, but they are not caused by a physical illness. The underlying cause is worry and fear. This helps Irene understand why she began to feel better physically when she made the decision to stay home, and why the physical symptoms returned before the next outing.

The understanding that her queasiness before an outing is likely from anxiety, or "bad nerves," provides a different perspective on her situation that opens up possibilities for Irene to cope differently. Rather than cancel an outing and retreat to bed, Irene decides to expect to feel nervous and "sick" and to try different strategies, such as relaxation breathing, music, and walking, to soothe her nerves and stomach.

AMIR

Amir can understand his panic as a false survival alarm and can connect it to his physical symptoms, but it is difficult for him to identify early signs of tension and anxiety. He reports that, for him, "the attack comes out of nowhere. I'm just sitting there, and boom, I'm in a full-blown panic."

It is important to help Amir become more aware of his body, to notice when he is tense, and to practice calming his nervous system. Tuning in to the body is an unfamiliar process for Amir and, like Mark, he requires guided instruction. Amir notices that his hands and feet are clenched, and his breathing is shallow and short. He is surprised that by simply paying attention to his hands and feet, he can release the tension. Eventually, Amir reports that he can recognize when his hands are clenched, and he uses this signal to intentionally release his hands and slow down his breathing.

I outline the connection between chronic tension, stress, and panic, and this motivates Amir to regularly practice body awareness to avoid extreme anxiety. I also introduce mindfulness practice to facilitate this awareness and to reduce unhelpful reactive behaviours. Amir begins to practice allowing uncomfortable body clues like dizziness and tingling to come and go without tensing up or fighting them. To reinforce this practice, I suggest that Amir try mindful awareness beyond anxiety management and use mindfulness strategies at home and work.

4) EXPAND COGNITIVE FLEXIBILITY

The tendency to over-focus on threat is a key factor in the development and maintenance of anxiety. Human beings tend to pay greater attention to negative events and possibilities than positive events, creating a negative cognitive bias (Hanson, 2013). For example, it's natural for negative comments from a supervisor to have more staying power than the supervisor's complimentary remarks. When giving a presentation, it's normal for our attention to be drawn to one scowl, rather than 10 smiling faces.

Although this attention to threat is a natural human instinct, when anxiety patterns take hold, a person's attention gets stuck on the negative, and we'll miss positive things that happen. Cognitive flexibility refers to the ability to see things from different perspectives and notice positive experiences alongside the challenges. The counselling process encourages this flexibility as clients like Mark, Irene, and Amir begin to recognize the personal growth they achieve through their struggles with disordered anxiety.

It is important for clients to understand that how they think about a situation affects how they feel and respond. Developing awareness and understanding of unhelpful self-talk and thought patterns that trigger and reinforce the fear response is important cognitive work for reducing anxiety. There are some common patterns of thought traps, such as those listed in Figure 3.1, which can be useful to explore with clients. Mark begins to recognize that he tends to think about negative events or challenges in a way that increases anxiety and avoidance, falling into a catastrophizing thought trap. Worrying about being sick at school, receiving bad grades, or being late for class expands to thoughts of personal and academic failure that zap his confidence and motivation, leading him to take refuge at home on the computer.

THOUGHT TRAPS	EXAMPLE THOUGHTS
Catastrophizing	If I don't get into college, my life will be ruined. If I don't find a job, I'll end up living on the street.
All-or-nothing thinking	Being late on a project means I can't do my job. The party was a waste of time. I didn't meet anyone new.
Mind reading	I can tell she doesn't like me, because she didn't say hello. If I vomit at school, they will think I'm disgusting.
Over-generalizing	I failed my math test. I'm a terrible student. I can't find my keys. My life is a mess.

Figure 3.1 *Common negative thinking patterns or traps that reinforce anxiety*

It is also important for clients to understand that helpful thinking doesn't change a difficult situation. Rather, it changes their approach to the situation. Thinking in a helpful way won't turn Irene into an extrovert and the life of a party, but shifting thoughts from "I'm sick, so I can't go" to "I'm worried about going" will create a mindset that helps get her to the party.

Focusing on positives and thinking in a helpful way can help people feel better and cope better.

CASE APPLICATION

AMIR

Although Amir learns to identify automatic catastrophic thoughts and shift to more helpful self-talk, his panic symptoms reduce but are not eliminated. Instead of "I'm losing my mind" and "Something horrible is wrong with me," Amir practices telling himself "This will pass" and "I'm just wound up" in response to panic sensations. Amir reports that thinking in a more helpful way eases the urge to flee from work to the safety of his home. Amir explains that he doesn't worry as much about his anxiety as he did before. Changing his thinking changes what he does.

At a later session, Amir reports, "I don't feel so out of control. I know what's going on, so I just calm myself down and get on with my day."

For some clients, especially those prone to rumination, challenging repetitive anxious thoughts may cause them to over-focus on the negative thought, which can intensify and prolong anxiety. It can be helpful for clients to understand that thoughts are not facts, but rather mental events that can be helpful or unhelpful, acted upon or ignored.

IRENE

Ever since George died, Irene is bothered by threatening thoughts that wake her up at night. She worries about what will happen if someone burglarizes her home and imagines confronting an intruder. The more she tries to convince herself that a burglary is unlikely, the more she imagines how it can happen, which increases her anxiety and causes insomnia. Irene learns that some scary thoughts, especially at night, are best left alone. She learns that she does not have to understand or entertain every thought that enters her mind. Irene practices simply noticing the thoughts and then intentionally moving on to pleasant thoughts, a strategy Irene refers to as "changing the channel."

COUNSELLING STRATEGIES

1) Introduce positive attention-training activities to reduce negative cognitive bias

   ➤ Encourage clients to notice everyday positive events, such as the brilliance and warmth of sunshine, a blooming flower, a hug from a loved one, or an enjoyable cup of coffee.

   ➤ Suggest clients make a daily practice of listing things that are going well or things for which they're grateful, shifting attention to the positive.

   ➤ Use humour, if appropriate, to challenge irrational thoughts.

   ➤ Help clients identify something they learned or personal growth they experienced through difficult life events.

2) Identify anxious thoughts and beliefs

   ➤ Help clients become aware of unhelpful self-talk and connect their thoughts to feelings and behaviours.

   ➤ Use in-session roleplays and thought journals to create awareness.

3) Practice categorizing negative self-talk and irrational beliefs according to thinking traps or cognitive distortions as illustrated in Figure 3.1, and introduce strategies to reduce and manage anxious thoughts

   ➤ Encourage clients to "test" the helpfulness of their thoughts by noticing the associated emotion or mood.

   ➤ Suggest clients practice accepting or postponing worrisome thoughts.

   ➤ Introduce the idea that people are not their thoughts. Have clients practice mentally observing negative or threatening thoughts moving through their mind without reacting or trying to change the thought.

   ➤ Invite clients to think of personalized coping thoughts. A specific thought that is meaningful can be written on a cue card or posted in their phone as a reminder.

CASE APPLICATION

MARK

Imagining a typical morning helps Mark identify physical sensations and unhelpful thoughts that cause him to stay home. A nervous stomach triggers the thought that he could vomit in the classroom, in front of his classmates, which terrifies him. Mark is convinced that this would be "the worst thing ever." I explain to Mark that it is possible that he could vomit in the classroom, but it's debatable whether that would be the "worst thing ever."

By holding such a catastrophic belief about vomiting at school, Mark reinforces the fear response and avoidance of school. I use reality testing and humour to develop flexibility in his thinking about being sick at school. Compared to the possibility of the office roof caving in on us or a natural disaster, vomiting at school is probably not the worst thing that could happen. To empathize, while also challenging the notion, I suggest it is possible to be sick at school, for it to be embarrassing and uncomfortable, *and* for it not to be the worst thing ever.

This challenging exercise helps loosen up Mark's rigidly held belief that being sick at school would be disastrous, and it serves to highlight the effect of irrational beliefs in maintaining anxiety. Repeatedly telling himself that vomiting at school would be the "worst thing ever" or that he "would die if that happened" escalates the anxiety and strengthens the connection between school and the fear response, which reinforces the instinct to avoid school.

To counteract this pattern of negative thinking, Mark is encouraged to write out a more rational thought in relation to the possibility of vomiting at school. I explain to him that many people, myself included, need reminders of helpful thoughts when feeling worried or anxious. Mark responds, "I'm going to write 'It won't kill me!' because sometimes it feels like that."

AMIR

Amir can eventually recognize that experiencing a panic attack is not all bad, which enables him to be more accepting of himself and his vulnerability. Before his experience with panic, Amir believed that he could and should be in control of himself and in control of all aspects of his life. This worldview held little tolerance for mistakes or short-comings. Amir learns that panic, although frightening, is also helpful. At the end of the counselling process, Amir can see that it takes the intensity of panic to slow him down enough to examine his beliefs and develop a healthier work–life balance.

5) PRACTICE EXPOSURE

Avoidance is the behavioural hallmark of anxiety. It's normal for people to move away or avoid something that is threatening or scary. However, avoiding anxiety-provoking thoughts or situations can result in higher sensitivity. A person's internal alarm may go off more quickly in anticipation, making them more rigid in their reactions to try to protect themselves.

In Irene's case, she began by avoiding leaving the house for social events and reached a point where she avoided leaving the house altogether. Mark began staying at home whenever he felt unwell. It was only at home, and eventually in his room, that he felt safe and comfortable. Amir's first panic attack occurred at the office. After the second attack in the same place, he began avoiding the office, choosing to work from home. All three clients are doing what comes naturally by moving away from a perceived threat. However, the perceived threats are important life events and challenges that require management, not avoidance.

Some people believe facing fears directly is the best approach. However, being thrown in the deep end of a pool doesn't guarantee you'll learn to swim. It's just as likely you'll sink, which could create a fear response.

This direct approach might lead to a lifelong avoidance of swimming or anything associated with pools or water. In contrast, learning to swim by starting out in the shallow end, receiving lessons, and using supports like water wings is a more gradual and effective approach. The perception of threat is lessened by an approach that helps a person face the fear and approach the challenge gradually with strategies and support. When working with anxiety, this approach is referred to as gradual exposure and is considered a key ingredient in anxiety treatment (Foa, 2011; Kendall et al., 2005).

Clients can be encouraged to develop a systematic plan for gradually approaching challenging thoughts or situations. Rather than facing difficult situations in a way that triggers intense anxiety, clients identify small manageable steps they can take to approach the fear. Building in aids such as social support, self-regulating strategies, and helpful self-talk can make it more manageable for clients to approach a source of fear. In some cases, for unrealistic or exaggerated fears, exposure can be done through imagination. In other situations, real-life exposure is ideal.

COUNSELLING STRATEGIES

1) Invite clients to identify anxious thoughts or situations they fear and/ or are avoiding

   ➤ If there is more than one concern, invite the client to rate these from low to high, creating a hierarchy of fears.

   ➤ Encourage clients to start addressing fears on the low end of the hierarchy to minimize anxiety and create a sense of competence.

2) Help clients develop a step-by-step plan for approaching each feared situation

   ➤ Remind clients to use support, calming techniques, and helpful self-talk as they approach challenging situations. For example, if a client fears making a phone call, their exposure plan could include writing out a script for the call, practicing with a support person, using relaxation breathing to calm down, and creating a helpful coping thought.

3) Introduce a rating scale that goes from zero, for no anxiety, to 10, for highest anxiety, to help you and your clients track their arousal or distress as they face fears (I introduce the rating as SUDS, an acronym for subjective units of distress scale)

➤ Remind clients to be aware of their arousal so they can maintain a low to moderate level of distress when engaging in exposure. Practice using SUDS with clients and help develop a plan to initiate rest and recovery techniques to de-escalate their anxiety.

➤ Encourage clients to prepare for escalating anxiety by identifying a sensory object or grounding technique that works for them ahead of time. Slow breathing, cold water, relaxing pictures, a sprig of lavender, or a beach rock are examples of common things people use to feel calm.

➤ Emphasize effort rather than outcome and celebrate partial success. Remind clients that any effort or movement toward situations they fear is success and should be reinforced through positive self-talk. Clients with disordered anxiety tend to be all-or-nothing thinkers. If the exposure plan does not work out perfectly, it's considered a "failure," and this labelling can reinforce anxiety and undermine willingness to engage in future exposure tasks.

➤ Prepare clients for setbacks. Exposure doesn't always happen smoothly or go as planned. It's possible to make progress quickly in facing a feared situation and then experience extreme anxiety and retreat back to avoidance. This back-and-forth movement toward behaviour change should be explained and normalized.

CASE APPLICATION

MARK

I encourage Mark to try exposure through using imagination (also called imaginal exposure) to face his fear of vomiting at school. This scenario is one of the last fears for Mark to tackle. I remind Mark that we will approach this scenario in a gradual way, maintaining a mild to moderate level of anxiety. If his anxiety escalates above a six on the SUDS scale, he will pause and use calming strategies. At the beginning of the exposure, Mark reports a SUDS rating of eight. To bring down his arousal, he uses slow breathing and tactile support with putty. After a few minutes, he reports that his SUDS is at four and begins his gradual exposure again.

As Mark imagines step by step what it would be like to be sick at school, I ask him about his SUDS. The high point of his anxiety is when he imagines vomiting and the other students' reactions to this. Because his SUDS level is eight, Mark stops and goes back to breathing and playing with the putty. After several minutes, he reports a rating of four and returns to the story, picking up where he left off. Mark goes on to imagine the drama of the classroom and the cleanup process, and his SUDS level remains below five.

I encourage Mark to imagine the immediate aftermath and the longer-term effects (over one year, five years, and 10 years) if this incident occurred in real life. This future perspective helps him think more rationally about the fleeting importance or significance of this fear. At the end of the exposure, Mark reports his fear of vomiting at school as five out of 10.

Avoiding or suppressing fears increases their power and intensity. When Mark approaches the fear in a controlled way, he gains perspective and learns that it is not as bad as he thinks it is. When I asked how he would feel if he had to imagine the whole incident again, and repeatedly, he thought he would be bored, instead of feeling anxious or worried. Facing his fear removes the sense of threat that supports his anxiety.

IRENE

Irene's exposure work focuses mostly on her attending social events. She decides to start with attending her grandson's piano recital, as she feels that will be the least difficult. Irene decides that once she makes the arrangements, she will notice her stomach upset but will not react to it. Her plan includes engaging in calming activities, such as positive self-talk and knitting, for the hour before she has to leave the house. Irene also decides to enlist her daughter's support by telling her about the anxiety and sharing her plan. To help her feel better when she is out of the house, Irene plans to bring along a CD for the car, to use her relaxation breathing, and to try to focus on her grandson.

Irene chooses to write out her plan and is eager to practice for this step. Knowing there is a realistic way she can become more involved in events and activities helps Irene feel more hopeful and motivated to change.

AMIR

Amir approaches going back to work gradually. He starts with meeting a colleague in the coffee shop at his office building. The following week he goes into his office for scheduled meetings. By the end of the month, Amir's attendance is more regular as he manages half days at the office. Eventually he works up to full days, with occasional lunch breaks at home.

While practicing this gradual exposure, Amir experiences another panic attack. He stays home for a couple of days and says that he feels discouraged. We discuss how this recurrence of panic demonstrates that it wasn't harmful to have an "episode." Amir is able to realize that bracing against the possibility of panic and constant monitoring of his panic is stressful and anxiety provoking. Through this recurrence, Amir learns that accepting anxiety and using strategies as needed reduces his fear and creates a sense of confidence. The presence of anxiety also provides motivation for Amir to practice a variety of calming strategies and to maintain a healthy lifestyle. Amir eventually tweaks his original plan to incorporate fresh air breaks throughout the day, a consistent lunch break at mid-day, and regular exercise.

FINISHING THOUGHTS

While disordered anxiety is distressing and limiting, it also reveals important information about clients' natural defences and abilities. Anxiety work, as outlined in this chapter, helps clients make sense of their worries and cultivates their natural coping. When people learn to manage anxiety problems, they often report that they feel stronger and freer than before the difficulties began. In a life dominated by anxiety, a lot of time and energy is spent on being preoccupied with threatening possibilities. With proper support and coping strategies, people experiencing anxiety can better accept uncertainty and develop confidence in their abilities to face the challenges of life.

ABOUT THE AUTHOR

AnnMarie Churchill, PhD, RSW

AnnMarie is a trainer with the Crisis & Trauma Resource Institute. She is a Registered Social Worker who holds a PhD in experimental psychology and a master's degree in clinical social work. In addition to advanced study and training in the areas of anxiety, trauma, and resilience, AnnMarie has 30 years of direct clinical experience. She has worked as a psychotherapist and consultant in various workplaces, including EAP programs, schools, community settings, and hospital settings. Much of her work over the years has involved working with Indigenous communities, including 20 years as a member of the mental health team on the Akwesasne Mohawk Territory.

REFERENCES

Foa, E. B. (2011). Prolonged exposure therapy: Past, present, and future. *Depression and Anxiety, 28*(12), 1043-1047.

Hanson, R. (2013). *Hardwiring happiness: The new brain science of contentment, calm, and confidence.* New York, NY: Harmony Books.

Hofmann, S. G., Ellard, K.K., & Siegle, G. J. (2012). Neurobiological correlates of cognitions in fear and anxiety: A cognitive-neurobiological information-processing model. *Cognition & Emotion, 26*(2), 282-299.

Kabat-Zinn, J. (2016). *Mindfulness for beginners: Reclaiming the present moment – and your life.* Boulder, CO: Sounds True Publishing.

Kendall, P. C., Robin, J. A., Hedtke, K. A., Suveg, C., Flannery-Schroeder, E., & Gosch, E. (2005). Considering CBT with anxious youth? Think exposures. *Cognitive and Behavioral Practice, 12*(1), 136-148.

Langlois, K. A., Samokhvalov, A.V., Rehm, J., Spence, S. T., Connor Gorber, S. K. (2011). Health state descriptions for Canadians: Mental illnesses. *Statistics Canada, catalogue no. 82-619-MIE2005002.* Ottawa, ON: Statistics Canada.

LeDoux, J. (2015). *Anxious: Using the brain to understand and treat fear and anxiety.* New York, NY: Penguin Random House.

CHAPTER FOUR

DEPRESSION

By Sheri Coburn

THE WORD DEPRESSION GETS THROWN AROUND A LOT. SOCIALLY, THE word has become an overused synonym for sad, annoyed, frustrated, or simply disappointed. People often make offhanded comments like "I am so depressed that sweater hasn't gone on sale," which shows little thought or regard for those who bear the true weight of the word. The flippancy of its use can distract from the intensity of the lived reality of depression and can undermine those who have an intimate connection to it.

The reality of depression is that it is often all-consuming. It can steal the joy out of things once loved by the sufferer, alter perception of self and others, and, at its worst, manipulate a person into planning for the relief anticipated from death. Depression is calculating, vindictive, and strategic. It thrives when left unattended and unmanaged (Strosahl & Robinson, 2008).

Depression symptoms can arise around adverse circumstances or overwhelming periods in one's life. These result in what is known as situational depression, which can either be short-lived or continue over a long period of time, especially if additional stressors arise during the recovery period.

In contrast, a person may have persistent emotional, cognitive, and behavioural clinical depression patterns linked to chemical changes in the brain, known as clinical or major depression. These changes are influenced by neurobiology, as well as by external stressors and other contextual factors.

For both situational and clinical depression, recurrent episodes of symptoms increase a person's vulnerability to subsequent and more ingrained patterns if left untreated. People who have more persistent and major episodes of depression throughout their lives may need multiple layers of treatment that address biochemical, cognitive, social, and emotional symptoms. Depression is more likely to show up when a person has had experiences of early life adversity or experiences of trauma (Schalinski et al., 2016).

From the clinician's perspective, working with depression can be exhausting and overwhelming, but also rewarding. It is exhausting when clients struggle to make progress and suffer setbacks along the way, making the pace feel slow or stuck in place. The work is often overwhelming due to the effort it takes to stay positive and motivated in the face of the influence that depression can bring. However, this work can be very rewarding when signs emerge to show that the cloud is potentially lifting and progress may be more sustainable. Working with depression requires as much commitment from the clinician as is needed from the client.

Although depression is an acknowledged and recognized formal diagnosis in the mental health field, the purpose of this chapter is to be broadly applicable for helpers working with people in both formal and informal settings – whether one meets the diagnostic criteria within the Diagnostic and Statistical Manual of Mental Disorders (5th ed.; DSM-5; American Psychiatric Association, 2013) for Major Depressive Disorder (MDD), whether one is experiencing an isolated and situational depressive episode, or, in the absence of a formal diagnosis, whether the symptoms can overwhelm and paralyze the strongest of individuals.

Despite the existence of common symptom patterns, depression is often a unique and individualized experience. This chapter works to validate, empathize, and provide applicable strategies in acknowledging the diversity of depression.

DAN

Dan is 49 years old, occupationally successful, financially stable, and multitalented. He has been the emotional leader within his family and has always been a good problem solver. He's gained much of his happiness throughout his life by using his dependability and skill set to make sure others are well taken care of. He has many examples in his life when his needs and wants were placed secondary (consciously in adulthood and more subconsciously in his childhood) to those around him. He is adamant that this approach to life, in which he puts others' needs ahead of his own, feels right to him, and he has no desire to become "selfish."

Dan greets me with an obligatory nod as I invite him into our session. He does a controlled collapse into the hardest chair in my office. He chooses this seating arrangement despite the availability of a more conveniently placed and far more comfortable couch. Sitting to the awkward left of me, he looks a combination of angry and annoyed. I have known him long enough to know that his presentation and the energy he brings with him are connected to nothing that I have said or done.

Recently, Dan's wife decided to end their 15-year marriage, noting that she "just isn't happy." Despite lengthy inquiries as to the cause of her unhappiness and a belief that things could be fixed, Dan is being forced into the reality that he cannot make his wife happy. He cannot fix this, and she is not changing her mind.

Dan continues to live with his soon-to-be ex-wife as they organize the logistics of separation, divorce, relocation, and co-parenting two active children. It has been almost six months since his wife's declaration and final decision.

He is irritable, confused, not sleeping, losing weight, and questioning his purpose. Dan is often defensive when we discuss his behavioural pattern of struggling to set boundaries with others and is very concerned that I am going to coach him into being selfish as part of our work together. Much of his self-esteem, self-worth, and identity as a man are dependent on being able to make others happy.

Dan has stated on more than one occasion during our time together that, "if you are going to tell me that there is something wrong with making others happy, we're not going to get very far. What's the point if you can't make others happy?"

LILING

Liling is quiet, creative, sensitive, and, in many ways, wise beyond her 14 years. She describes always feeling things very intensely, always knowing the world can be a scary place, and always being acutely aware of life's unfairness. At the age of nine, Liling learned of the sponsorship programs that exist for children in developing countries. She remembers feeling an overwhelming sense of shame for her own privilege, panic that children could be left to starve, and a paralyzing helplessness of not knowing how to help. She remembers dreading every day of school after that. She feared any new knowledge as potential roadways to the intense sadness that never quite lifted once she confirmed what she suspected were the immense cruelties of the world. She began to see life as simply "putting time in." Liling describes life as an experience whereby her plan is to struggle through until she can decide for certain if she wants stay in this life or leave it. Basically, she views life as an indeterminant game of "Can I handle it or not, and if I can, do I even want to?"

Liling has come to the conclusion she won't kill herself until she is 18. I silently breathe a sigh of relief, for two reasons. One, I believe her, which means we have more time. Two, this is progress.

This "not now" safety plan has been re-affirmed between us after much dialogue, a genuine willingness on my part to explore her life-long battle with depression, and an authentic acknowledgement of the intensity and reality of her pain. In addition, and probably most importantly, this required a purposeful and very hard conscious shift on my part. The shift happened when I committed to working with Liling in a way that was aimed at making her feel better, not just at making me or the other adults in her life feel better.

I had to be willing to hear her, to know that we might still get her to 18 and she still may determine that she doesn't want to do "this life" anymore. I don't like the idea of Liling ending her life at all. In fact, I hate it. However, Liling can tell the difference between the times when I am saying and exploring things with her because they quell my own discomfort with the idea of her death, and the times when I am truly connecting to her and working to quiet her pain and discomfort with life. When my discomfort is quieted, progress stalls, and when her discomfort is quieted, progress happens. I remind myself frequently during our time together that I am the adult, I am the helper, and I must manage my own discomfort on my own time.

Although Dan's and Liling's current life stages, their past and present lived experiences, and their overall interpretations of their worlds are so different, they are sharing the experience of depression. Depression can be influenced by a variety of factors with no clearly identifiable or scientifically proven absolute cause. Factors may include, but are not limited to, genetic predisposition, early life experience, major or chronic illness, significant loss, unmanaged intrapersonal or interpersonal conflict and substance abuse, and external or internal messaging systems that leave an increased vulnerability. Depression symptoms (regardless of cause) often include

- ➤ depressed mood or irritability nearly every day;
- ➤ loss of interest in activities most every day;
- ➤ change in sleep, such as insomnia or hyposomnia;
- ➤ change in activity or fatigue;
- ➤ guilt and worthlessness;
- ➤ reduced concentration and indecisiveness;
- ➤ changes in appetite, such as overeating or undereating;
- ➤ body aches and pains with no identified physiological cause;
- ➤ increased desire to isolate socially;
- ➤ suicidality.

Depression has a way of altering both one's perception of self and one's perception of others. Unlike other primarily physical struggles in which people tend to be highly motivated to seek treatment, depression can result in the opposite. As motivation decreases and self-deprecation increases, people often experience a depleted sense of desire and deservingness around seeking and receiving treatment. This then acts as a barrier that prevents people from reaching out, furthering the isolation that is an accompaniment and aggravator to depression. Depression signs and symptoms then have a greater opportunity to settle in, becoming more ingrained and more difficult to shift.

INSIGHTS AND GUIDING PRINCIPLES FOR COUNSELLING

To explore everything about depression far exceeds the scope of this chapter. Instead, I want to offer some nuggets of knowledge that I have gathered in my work with people both struggling with and living successfully with depression. There are three key thinking and behavioural patterns in the experience of depression that often require special attention and some reworking: *core beliefs*, *motivation*, and *social connection*. These areas, dependent on how they are explored and solidified, have the potential to be the most influential or the most paralyzing patterns in the depression and healing journey.

Core beliefs refer to our primary guiding thoughts about how we see and feel about ourselves, others, our world, and the future. Both Dan and Liling have navigated their lives with some very strong core beliefs. Some of these core beliefs have both increased their vulnerability to depression and also now serve as aggravators to their relationships with depression. Many people hold core beliefs that increase susceptibility and give foundation to depression. These can be referenced as depression-friendly belief systems. It can be helpful to identify or work with clients to highlight what core beliefs they hold that serve to reinforce, aggravate, or prevent them from moving ahead of their depression patterns.

Examples of belief themes that can reinforce depression include but are not limited to

- I am weak;

- my worthiness is dependent on my ability to make others happy;

- I am unworthy of comfort in a world in which others are suffering;

- I am helpless in changing my circumstances;

- I should be thankful, because others have it way worse than me;

- my depression is confirmation that I don't deserve happiness;

- the world is unsafe, unforgiving, and exhausting;

- I should suffer like others suffer, it's only fair;

- if I were smarter, stronger, more deserving, this wouldn't be happening to me.

Motivation is the desire to do things. Depression is the antithesis of motivation. The cognitive distortions, the emotional and physical exhaustion, and the sense of disconnection from others and the world all work against motivation. The drive to think, feel, and behave in opposition to depression is compromised, and yet these elements are critical to the healing process. Setting people up for success and challenging the motivation myth becomes essential for building on the small wins that ultimately move people in a healthier direction.

The motivation myth is the false belief that one must first *feel* like doing something before doing it (Burns, 1981; Smith, 2013). Herein lies the critical challenge: who feels like doing anything when they are depressed? Let's be honest, who feels like doing most of the logistical and mundane things needed to navigate life even when they are not living with depression? The catch with depression is that it can block motivation for not only the logistically necessary things, but also for the pleasure-filled things in life.

The truth about motivation is that it follows a behaviour but is not needed and often does not exist before it. Not being able to follow through on something, such as a healthy eating and exercise plan, is not necessarily because of being depressed. It could be that a person doesn't feel like embracing a healthier lifestyle, because they haven't done it yet!

Doing what we don't feel like doing is the beginning of teasing out and cultivating motivation. Waiting until we feel like eating properly, creating a sleep routine, introducing exercise, getting out with some friends, or finishing a chapter in a book may result in never feeling like doing it. Motivation builds as we do things, even including those things that we never felt like doing in the first place. Planning a structured way of moving into action becomes imperative for moving out from under depression.

Social connection is a need. It is one of the quickest ways we can regulate when we are dysregulated. As we tap into and embrace the energy and comfort from those around us, we feel more supported, more capable, and more confident in our ability to negotiate the joys and hardships life brings. Without this, a sense of isolation and fear can grow. Intuitively, we are drawn to people who make us feel good or who meet a need that we have. Most of us can identify the friend we want to laugh with, cry with, grab a beer with, or watch a movie with in comfortable silence. In much the same way, we intuitively or consciously try and avoid those who don't.

Depression serves as an interrupter or inhibitor to this need. Sometimes, it tells the sufferer that their presence is an annoyance to others and they have nothing to contribute. Other times, depression makes the physical energy of others or the expectations of being social feel overwhelming and unmanageable. Reconnecting to the social world and capitalizing on the energy of others is essential. Whether it is working with people to eliminate depression-friendly distortions that encourage social isolation or developing the skills needed to function more comfortably in the social world, ensuring that one can and will build on positive social connections is imperative in the fight against depression.

A clearly outlined path of intervention can offer hope for the client, accountability for the helper, and momentum to the therapeutic process. From working with many people like Dan and Liling, I have come to rely on the following five principles to guide how I assist individuals with accepting, navigating, and shifting their current – and for some, potentially lifelong – relationships with depression:

1) **Make the mind-body connection**

Address persistent cognitive distortions and self-deprecating thinking patterns that aggravate and reinforce depression symptoms and behaviours. This also includes tending to and using the body through movement to work against depression.

2) **Distinguish depression from the depressed**

Recognize when depression is overruling an individual's ability to intake, generate, process, and/or apply information and strategies. This may include having the "is it time to have a conversation with your doctor about medication" conversation.

3) **Ignite hope in the face of hopelessness**

Empathize, normalize, and capitalize on the counsellor's effect to generate the necessary engagement needed to implement thinking and behaviour-change strategies.

4) **Motivate the unmotivated**

Develop strategies for increasing behavioural change in the face of what can be chronic emotional and physical pain.

5) **Build positive social connections by building connection capacity**

Explore social isolation as both a cause and symptom of depression. Identify the influence of negative social experiences and the necessity of positive relationships for healing.

1) MAKE THE MIND-BODY CONNECTION

One thing I have noticed throughout my counselling career is that people gravely underestimate the mind-body connection. The mind and the body can neither survive nor live separately. Cognitive distortions can dysregulate physiology (a top-down effect of brain to body), and dysregulated physiology can influence cognitive distortions (a bottom-up effect of body to brain), or both can occur simultaneously. An effective intervention plan gives the unbreakable and reciprocal relationship between the mind and the body the appropriate credit and attention.

COUNSELLING STRATEGIES

1) Address cognitive distortions or problematic core beliefs

   ➤ Listen for past and present patterns in thinking and belief systems that reinforce the current state.

   ➤ Explore your client's thoughts about identified beliefs and their origins.

   ➤ Once therapeutic trust is established, gently challenge their distortions when they prevent insight from occurring.

   ➤ Explore times when they have behaved in alignment with their core beliefs and examples of when they have acted in opposition to them.

   ➤ Assess for motivation in altering core beliefs.

2) Highlight the mind-body connection and the importance of engaging both in healing

   ➤ Explore physiology by reviewing nutrition, hydration, hygiene, and sleep patterns and identifying areas for improvement. *See page 288 in the Resources section for a sample chart.*

   ➤ Explore socialization and activity levels and ask what they are doing for social connection, how often, and with whom.

   ➤ Encourage your client to explore ways of getting more connected to or improving physical health, including identifying vitamin or hormone deficiencies that could be causing or aggravating depression symptoms.

   ➤ Make referrals to other health care providers (dieticians, physiotherapists, occupational therapists, massage therapists, homeopaths, naturopaths, and so on).

   ➤ Use movement and posture awareness to explore the capacity to shift current emotional states by shifting physical states.

➤ Look to introduce or build on regulation activities, such as walking, dancing, running, drumming, or playing an instrument.

CASE APPLICATION

DAN

Dan looks a little less defeated but a little more exhausted today as he enters the room. He sits in the same chair and waits for me to initiate today's discussion. I purposely wait and create an awkward pause. Dan notices and chuckles under his breath, both of us acknowledging that we are playing a game of conversational chicken.

[Dan] "Well, I'll start then … I was somewhat proud of myself today."

Dan tells me that he went looking for a new house with his ex-wife for her to purchase. He tells me that he absolutely did not want to go, but she asked, and he knew it would make her happy. He describes how she smiled and laughed as she talked about redecorating, and that he did his best to play along.

[Dan] "When I got home, I was so exhausted, I slept for four hours. I don't know too many ex-husbands who would do that for their ex. Aren't you proud of me?"

[Counsellor] "You mentioned that you really did not want to go house hunting but went anyway – because you knew it would make Linda happy?"

[Dan] "I like making people happy – what can I say?"

[Counsellor] "Yes, I can see that!" [We both chuckle.] "It also sounds as though it was very exhausting and emotionally painful for you to go. That speaks to how strong your belief is that making others happy is more important than your own happiness, doesn't it?"

I purposely interject doses of humour into our sessions. I do this for a variety of reasons and not because I think depression or Dan's situation is funny. Humour reminds the mind and the body of their capacity for laughter. Humour in the face of depression highlights the ability for dual awareness: the human capacity to hold two sometimes-conflicting thoughts and/or feelings at the same time. It also reminds us that we deserve and need the social connection that shared humour brings.

I also am purposely using very direct questions to generate dissonance. The lightened mood allows me to highlight patterns in Dan's thinking that may be constraining him.

[Counsellor] "What do you think you might have done instead, if Linda had not asked you to go with her?"

[Dan] "I don't know. I didn't really think about it."

[Counsellor] "Let's just think about it for a moment. What would be something you would love to do if you had all time in the world and no obligations to anyone?"

[Dan] "Oh, probably go fishing or for a hike with the dog on a beautiful day like today."

[Counsellor] "Well that sounds a lot more fun than house hunting with your ex-wife!" [We both laugh.] "It sounds as though your beliefs about making others happy can sometimes prevent you from taking care of yourself and feeding your own happiness. I wonder if you are open to talking about how we might modify that belief so you could still find purpose in making others happy but not trade *all* your happiness in return?"

[Dan] "Well, based on how I feel, it may be time for a 'modification'" [as he makes air quotes in jest at my use of the word modify]. "I think I may already be out of happiness to trade."

LILING

Liling is wearing one of her many awesome graphic tees celebrating an alternative music band that I (of course) have never heard of. I am trying inconspicuously to read the name of the band as I am banking on this nugget of information for my lead-in to today's session. Liling's arms are crossed straight in front of her at the elbows with both hands protectively tucked between her knees and chin towards her chest. This is one of many ways Liling uses her body to hide herself from the world and reinforce to herself that she is not worth the space she takes up. The smaller and more cocooned, the better.

After a brief pause, I blurt out:

[Counsellor] "I give up."

Liling looks up at me.

[Counsellor] "I can't read the name of the band on your shirt, so I can't pretend I know them."

Liling makes a modest smile, letting me know she catches my humour.

The way Liling is shielding her body sets the stage for a great opportunity to invite her into an experiment. I talk with Liling about how, often, the way people sit, stand, or walk tells a story and tell her what I notice as an observer to her story.

[Counsellor] "I notice that the story you tell with your body often matches what you have told me in our sessions, things like the world feels unsafe to you, unfair to others, like you don't deserve what you have."

I ask Liling to notice how she is sitting right now.

[Counsellor] "What kinds of feelings or story do you think might be happening for someone … or you … when sitting that way?"

[Liling] "I don't know." She pauses for a while. "Maybe nervous, embarrassed, insecure."

[Counsellor] "Nervous … insecure … embarrassed. Those are all ways you have described feeling to me at some point. Your body matches your story, so to speak. Let's try changing the way we are sitting and see what happens."

I shift myself in my chair and invite Liling to copy me. I sit taller, chin up, hands placed comfortably clasped on my legs in front of me. I make comfortable eye contact with her. She does the same.

[Counsellor] "What story do you think I am telling you right now?"

[Liling] "Like you feel good about yourself, like you want to be here, like you know what you're doing."

[Counsellor] "You are sitting exactly like me right now! How do you feel?"

Liling looks a little surprised before she answers my question and then smiles.

[Liling] "A little weird ... like not bad weird, just weird different."

[Counsellor] "Do you think I am feeling nervous, insecure, or embarrassed right now?"

[Liling] "Not at all."

[Counsellor] "Are you feeling nervous, insecure, or embarrassed *right now*?"

[Liling] "Not at all."

2) DISTINGUISH DEPRESSION FROM THE DEPRESSED

Sometimes when we work with people who are struggling with depression, they come to a point when they simply are unable to participate. They are totally disengaged in the counselling process. They are paralyzed. Early on in my relationship with Liling, she was almost catatonic. She was unable to maintain eye contact, and not just in that typical adolescent defiance sort of way. It looked painful for her to lift her head and make eye contact.

Liling was not experiencing an episode of situational depression, but she was experiencing another cycle of her recurring, ingrained depression that she had experienced since her childhood years. These recurring bouts caused her physical, emotional, mental, and spiritual pain. She was a wealth of two-word responses, even to my strategically placed and well-formed (if I do so say myself) open-ended questions. She looked drained. She was attending school intermittently, spending more time drowning herself in social media, and spending less and less time anywhere near people. We were at a crossroads.

Even my well-intentioned efforts at relationship building were impossible for Liling to respond to. I knew I was not talking to Liling at all. I was talking to, and only to, her depression. For Liling, appropriate medication following a medical and psychiatric consult was a necessary part of her talk therapy (Greenberger & Padesky, 2016). I needed to be able to spend some time working with and talking to the other parts of Liling. Her depression was so chronic that it was not allowing any other part of her to participate.

COUNSELLING STRATEGIES

1) Assess your client's baseline

   ➤ Gather information about your client's usual demeanour, behaviour, level of activity, hygiene, diet, and sleep patterns. Include family members whenever possible to get a more accurate and full picture of the person. *See page 290 in the Resources section for a sample chart.*

   ➤ Explore your client's overall attributional style. Is their general perspective more glass half-empty or glass half-full?

   ➤ Express concern to your client or concerned others (if appropriate) regarding their level of disconnect from the regular baseline. Explore their perspective and level of concern.

2) Model an open mind and healthy curiosity for any conversation about potential pharmaceutical interventions

   ➤ If needed, encourage your client to connect with a primary care provider as part of the larger intervention and wellness planning.

➤ Reinforce that a healthy mindset is open to exploring all options, including medication, before accepting them or ruling them out. Help your client research or get more information on medications if their primary care provider suggests them.

➤ Assist your client in exploring critical questions about the potential benefits and risks of introducing medication into their plan.

3) Build your team

➤ Don't let your pride as a helper get in the way of building a team around the client. No matter how good you are at what you do, depression has many faces. Reaching out to other professionals to ensure the client gets holistic and inclusive care is essential. Having an interdisciplinary team ensures both the helper and the client have access to all appropriate intervention and support systems.

➤ Be confident in what you know about the client and your assessment of the situation. This could mean sharing your knowledge with other professionals or challenging roadblocks to appropriate intervention strategies. In cases where immediate risk to the client or others is not present, secure consent from the client to discuss their situation for the purpose of formulating an effective intervention plan.

➤ Introduce to the client the idea of connecting them with other helping professionals.

➤ When patterns of depression are particularly ingrained, arrange for a psychiatric consult to explore pharmaceutical and/or complementary interventions in addition to talk counselling.

4) Determine if suicide risk requires a more formulated or immediate action plan

➤ Perform regular suicide assessments (see the chapter on Suicidality in this book).

➤ Know the protocols in your workplace around suicidality.

➤ Collaboratively develop safety and wellness plans that include positive coping strategies and sources of support the client can realistically turn to if they feel they are in crisis (Stanley & Brown, 2012). *See page 297 in the Resources section for a sample wellness plan.*

CASE APPLICATION

LILING

Liling enters the room sheepishly. She looks up and greets me with an awkward hello and a genuine – albeit very shy – smile.

Approximately five weeks earlier, Liling had undergone an in-depth psychiatric assessment that included consultation with her family, teachers, counsellors, and family doctor and was prescribed appropriate medications.

[Counsellor] "Hey Liling, how are you feeling today?"

[Liling] "A little better."

[Counsellor] "What's 'a little better' feel like?"

[Liling] "I don't feel so tired."

This brief description is followed by silence. I struggle to leave the space for silence, as I want to relieve my curiosity about what is going on for her. My struggle pays off as Liling starts talking again.

[Liling] "I've been going to school, and I went grocery shopping with my mom before I came here."

[Counsellor] "It seems like it's been a while since you had the energy to do those things. That must have been hard to be so tired all the time."

[Liling] "Yeah, it totally makes you feel lazy and stupid."

[Counsellor] "What was it about not having any energy that made you feel stupid?"

[Liling] "Well, I would have thoughts in my head when people were talking but couldn't get them out fast enough, because I felt so exhausted. I would just end up sitting there and looking stupid. Now at least I know I could say stuff if I wanted to … not that I want to … but at least I know I could."

3) IGNITE HOPE IN THE FACE OF HOPELESSNESS

Depression often partners with hopelessness. The ability to look positively toward or conceptualize a future in which you don't feel overwhelmed, exhausted, and troublesome to others is impossible. Instead, it is replaced with the feeling that this is as good as it will ever get. A counsellor's ability to stay connected, regulated, optimistic, and motivational is of the utmost importance. In many cases, the counsellor is the only one in the room who can see the colour-filled pathway out of this black-and-white life. Having a plan, being able to articulate that plan to the client, and maintaining hope is the foundation of the therapeutic alliance and the springboard to better times.

When Dan first started coming to see me, it was because his business partner had told him that he was worried about him and that he thought he "should talk to someone." When Dan told me this at our first session, he was angry. He was angry at the suggestion that he needed a "shrink" and angry that he felt like his business was also on the line. He was very clear in telling me that he was only sitting in my office so he could say that he came. He was reluctant, unmotivated, and highly suspicious of the process. I had a lot of igniting to do.

During our first few sessions, I focused entirely on relationship building. I used every minute I had to make myself likeable, make the office inviting, demystify the process, and create a therapeutic alliance to build the foundation of hope. After our third session, Dan turned to me as he was walking out the door. "Oh yeah, we forgot to book my follow-up." Dan's use of the word "we" is not lost on me. That, for me, is the spark of hope igniting – a sign that we have a partnership forming and a sign that he is taking some initiative in his own therapeutic experience.

COUNSELLING STRATEGIES

1) Have a plan and know why you are choosing it

   ➤ Decide where it makes the most sense to start for this particular
   client, based on their comfort level, interest, and where you think
   you'll have the most leverage to see change begin. In general
   terms, you can start with thinking patterns (top-down) or body
   work (bottom-up).

   ➤ Top-down strategies: explore core beliefs; introduce mindfulness
   activities; document thought records; explore thought and mood
   connections; identify, document, and practice recognizing and
   undoing cognitive distortions; keep a mood calendar to assess
   patterns or activities that influence thoughts and moods.

   ➤ Bottom-up strategies: build a pain-management plan; introduce
   body-focused therapies (like massage therapy); explore using
   movement to alter mood; create activity goals and logs; assess
   physiology, nutrition, hydration, sleep, and personal-care hygiene
   routines.

   ➤ Articulate to your client the mind/body connection and why you
   are doing what you're doing. Experiment to find ways of connecting to their body that they find comfortable.

2) Choose frameworks to serve as a map for the journey

   ➤ Identify your guiding frameworks and articulate why you have
   chosen them. For example, note why you chose Cognitive
   Behaviour Therapy (CBT), Acceptance and Commitment Therapy
   (ACT), Narrative Therapy, and so on.

   ➤ Be flexible in your approach and relay confidence in moving from
   one strategy to the next. It is important your framework matches
   who and where your client is.

3) Project hope into the session

> Acknowledge the powerful pull of the depression energy on you, the helper, and prepare for it by regulating and grounding yourself before each session.

> Find ways to incorporate humour when appropriate.

> Provide homework to your client and review it with them. Alter it as needed.

CASE APPLICATION

LILING

Liling sits down, takes a deep breath, and tells me very reluctantly that she has decided she "should go vegan." She tells me that it is a small gesture towards showing her support for mistreated animals and modifying her own indulgence in a culture that promotes gluttony while others starve.

I compliment Liling on the level of thoughtfulness that has gone into this decision and acknowledge the limitations of my own knowledge regarding a vegan diet. I ask her some questions about it to show my desire to connect and validate how much it means to her.

[Liling] "I need to do more research, but basically you only eat foods that come from plant sources. No meat and no animal byproducts."

[Counsellor] "Hey, maybe we could plan for you to connect with a nutritionist to make sure you have what you need so we don't aggravate any of your depression symptoms?"

[Liling] "You're not going to just try and talk me out of it? My mom thinks I'm crazy. She says it will make me sick. I think she means sick in the head."

[Counsellor] "If there is a way to respect your feelings and your health at the same time, I am definitely willing to explore it with you.

Not now, but at some point, I would also like to spend some time talking about how your empathy for others might influence your health and feelings about *your* place in the world."

I end our appointment by confirming that I will arrange an appointment with a nutritionist for her. I am busily looking through my list of nutritional contacts when Liling squirms in her chair and coughs a little. I look up at her.

[Liling] "Hey Sheri? Thanks for not thinking I'm crazy." [She says quietly while avoiding eye contact.]

[Counsellor] "Liling, I am really good at diagnosing 'crazy' and you're *not* crazy."

It's the first time I hear her laugh. It sounds hopeful.

4) MOTIVATE THE UNMOTIVATED

Establishing motivation is an intricate process and balancing act between client and clinician. The client has none, we're full of it, they finally begin to generate some just as we're starting to lose it. It's like an unchoreographed dance number, where one is waiting for the other to pick up the count so the other can follow. In the dance routine titled "Motivating Depression," the counsellor must take the lead.

It's time to reinforce to the client that their feelings are not facts. When it comes to depression, feelings can't be trusted anyway. Motivation is generated through direct action, not through thoughts and not through feelings. When it comes to changing, introducing, or modifying a problematic behaviour, the golden rule of motivation is "just do it." Don't *feel* like getting up in the morning? Do it anyway. Don't *feel* like maintaining a hygiene routine? Do it anyway. Don't *feel* like going to a friend's birthday celebration? Do it anyway. Then and only then do feelings get considered. Do it now, feel it later, and definitely don't wait until you feel like doing it as one may never do "it," whatever that is.

When Liling first came to see me she both *felt* and *was unable* to explore or implement anything. However, even after her medication levelled some of her mood and physical symptoms, her depression-patterned behaviour was still very much in play. She was spending hours isolating herself on social media, her attendance at school was still sporadic at best, and she was turning down invitations to spend time even with those she considered friends. It was time for a motivation intervention.

Because Liling and I had built a good therapeutic connection, I put forth a challenge. We collaborated to develop some reasonable behavioural goals, and if she accomplished them, I would memorize the lyrics to a song of her choice and recite them to her at our next session. Make no bones about it, it was a motivation collaboration. If I was solely in charge of setting goals, they would probably have looked something like this: get off social media forever (highly unlikely), attend school even when contagious (yes, a little dramatic), and plan a surprise party for a friend and host it at her house (I am being a little facetious here). What makes goals meaningful and achievable is when they are done with the spirit and the intention of collaboration.

Liling and I built a list of *collaborated* goals. These goals included: social media for no more than 90 minutes a day (she was currently banking at least four hours); accept one invitation from a friend for an out-of-the-house activity; and attend school at least four days the following week. In consultation with her mom and the school, we all agreed that she could choose one day to refuel at home if needed.

The moral of the story is: don't challenge an adolescent to anything, especially when it includes the potential shaming of an adult in their life. Liling literally laughed out loud when I recited the lyric, "Without you I'll be miserable at best." She then told me that it was a song by Mayday Parade, whose shirt she was wearing on the day that I was trying to read the band name. Touché.

I am not suggesting it is always as easy or linear as this – to put forth a challenge, the client meets the challenge, and then forever overcomes the motivation hurdle. It's not a linear process. There were weeks that followed when Liling could meet our collaborated goals and others when she was not as successful. But that first win and any other win after that became a strengthened platform of behavioural change, as well as a recognition that *doing it* resulted in *feeling it* and not the other way around.

COUNSELLING STRATEGIES

1) Homework and accountability without judgment

   ➤ Create clear and manageable behaviour-driven homework.

   ➤ Build on and then use the therapeutic alliance to generate accountability. Clients need to feel connected to the process and, most importantly, to the therapeutic leader. What are you doing to solidify the connection between helper and client? I became a lyrical poet for Liling!

   ➤ People do things for people they like. Your primary job as a helper is simple: be likeable.

   ➤ Project a non-judgmental approach to homework. Be flexible and understanding when it comes to modifying homework goals. Offer support and encouragement, both when clients are successful and when they are struggling.

   ➤ Balance non-judgmental strategies with reasonable expectations and accountability.

2) Just do it

   ➤ Don't allow clients to beat themselves up over not feeling like making necessary behavioural changes. Challenge their perceived idea of laziness and explain the principles behind generating motivation.

   ➤ Use activity scheduling logs and clear action item steps when introducing behavioural goals.

   ➤ Make action steps small and manageable. Generating some wins will help foster motivation.

3) Rework the unworkable

> Be willing to see when the activity is not working, when it is too much or not enough to foster momentum.

> Challenge but don't overwhelm. Inquire with the client: "What do you think is one thing you could do that would push you out of your comfort zone?" Healthy risk-taking is part of the healing process.

> Sometimes our clients' depression paralysis can make us nervous about pushing too hard. It's important to have reasonable expectations of your client, not to let go of expectations altogether. Set up healthy challenges when motivation is at a standstill.

CASE APPLICATION

DAN

Today Dan is coming in, and I know that his wife recently moved out of their shared home. We had spent much of our last session collaborating on a plan to help him balance his need to make others happy while also strengthening his capacity to respect his own need for boundaries. Dan would spend two hours helping Linda move – not all day, as she originally asked for – followed by an activity that would help him recuperate from what would be a very emotionally and physically exhausting experience.

[Counsellor] "What was it like for you helping Linda move out of the home you shared?"

[Dan] "Awful. I felt like crying and begging her not to go and yelling at her at the same time. I didn't do any of that, because I wanted the kids to see me helping their mom and see us getting along. Two hours was plenty though!"

[Counsellor] "I imagine it was! What was it like to give yourself permission to leave after two hours and not spend the whole day like she had asked?"

[Dan] "I felt terrible in that moment. I knew she had so much more to move, but I was also relieved that I didn't have to spend the whole day there. I didn't think I was going to be able to leave … I probably wouldn't have, but I knew Josh was waiting for me. You'd think I would have run out of there. I love hiking, but I really had to force myself to leave. Isn't that weird?"

[Counsellor] "I don't know Dan, is it? Is it weird that you had to force yourself to balance the needs of others while also considering your own?"

Dan quickly picks up on me capitalizing on this far too easy opportunity to toot my own assessment horn, and we both laugh.

With limited prompting on my part, Dan goes on to tell me how much he enjoyed his time hiking with Josh and his new puppy, and that he and Josh made a standing weekly date to run and train the dog. I sit silently engaged as Dan talks more about his love of dogs, hiking, and nature. He stops mid-sentence, almost as though he just noticed me, with a small smile on his face.

[Dan] "Okay, I get it, you can be kind to others *and* still find time for your own joy."

5) BUILD CAPACITY FOR SOCIAL CONNECTION

From the moment of birth, social connection is necessary for survival. Learning how to communicate our needs through the giving and receiving of social signals becomes the basis for all things human. We need others to regulate our nervous systems, and we need others to regulate our emotions. Regulation refers to the ability to move successfully from more hyper-aroused states, such as stress and fear, to our more balanced states of rest and relaxation. It also includes the ability to move successfully from more exhausting emotional states, such as anger, frustration, and sadness, to more energizing emotional states. Regulation is not the absence of stress, fear, anger, or sadness, but rather the ability to handle, move through them, and adapt. We do this most quickly and successfully with the help and influence of others.

When we are dysregulated by depression, being with people is part of the antidote. Social isolation can be both a symptom and a contributor to depression. Depression can take a typically social individual and steal their capacity and their confidence to be social. Social isolation can exaggerate an individual's risk for depression. Whether it is a circular or linear relationship, it is certain that reconnecting socially or building capacity for connection is a critical piece to solving the depression puzzle (Thomson & Broadway-Horner, 2012).

COUNSELLING STRATEGIES

1) Recognize social isolation as a contributor to depression

   ➤ When the therapeutic relationship is safe, identify social deficits or behavioural habits that may be inhibiting social connection.

   ➤ Roleplay with the client to build confidence in initiating and managing social exchanges.

   ➤ Set up safe opportunities to practice with people outside of the counselling relationship.

   ➤ Introduce rejection as social risk and plan for ways to manage the feelings and choices around rejection if it happens.

2) Recognize social isolation as a symptom of depression

   ➤ Work with the client to identify already-existing supportive relationships and to use those in their attempts to reconnect socially. Supporters that understand the struggles and limitations of living with depression are ideal.

   ➤ Set homework goals directly linked to reconnecting socially.

   ➤ Use your counselling relationship to emulate the positives of social connection. This can include injecting small doses of humour, demonstrating empathetic understanding, assistance with reframing, and building motivation.

➤ Encourage volunteering or assisting with something that requires the client to be in a giving role.

3) Stress, reinforce, and then continue to reinforce the importance of positive social connection

➤ Explore existing relationships and help your client assess the health of those relationships.

➤ Identify the risks in social connections that are unhealthy, unsafe, or exploitative in nature.

➤ Work with your client to minimize time spent on relationships that aggravate depression symptoms (such as those that are highly critical, emotionally abusive, or unsupportive) and build on or create more positive relationships.

CASE APPLICATION

LILING

Liling starts our session today with a willingness to be vulnerable with me.

[Liling] "I'm pretty sure Jane and Mosi are only my friends because of Hannah. They like Hannah, so I think they just pretend to like me when Hannah is around."

The reality is Liling struggles socially. I could tell her that she is imagining that students at her school think she is weird, and that others are just pretending to be her friend because they don't want to be "too mean," but I would be lying. Liling is hard to get to know. She has always been more introverted by nature. Her social skills have been compromised, and her battle with depression has not allowed for much in the way of practice.

[Counsellor] "What gives you that impression?"

I show my willingness to not dismiss this worry with an unhelpful and way too common adult reassurance, and Liling is able to support her worry with an example.

[Liling] "When Hannah isn't around, they don't invite me to sit with them at lunch."

I ask a more clarifying question, both to gather more information but also to highlight a skill to Liling that allows for less all-or-nothing thinking and the ability to identify differing perspectives.

[Counsellor] "Have you ever been comfortable enough to approach them at lunch when Hannah isn't with you?"

Liling has obviously been thinking about this, as she doesn't hesitate.

[Liling] "Yes, and they still don't ask me to sit down."

Knowing some of Liling's social limitations, I explore further.

[Counsellor] "What do you say or do when you approach them to sit with them?"

Liling looks a little confused by my inquiry and paints a clearer picture of the potentially awkward interaction.

[Liling] "Nothing, usually. I just wait at the door of the cafeteria with my lunch. They act like they don't even see me standing there. Then I leave."

This confirms what I suspected – that Liling often waits for others to engage her and does so in ways that can be easily missed or miscommunicated to others. Having said that, it is possible that Jane and Mosi do have ill intentions when it comes to Liling, so I explore a little further.

[Counsellor] "How are they different with you when Hannah is around?"

[Liling] "Really good. We all talk and laugh and stuff, you know, normal."

[Counsellor] "Have they ever said or done anything that has made you feel uncomfortable other than not inviting you to sit with them?"

[Liling] "No, not at all."

I propose to Liling that maybe they are misreading her, that maybe they are not sure of her intentions. I wonder aloud to Liling if maybe standing at the door is not a clear signal or message about her desires or intentions around wanting to sit with them. I use this dialogue between us as an introduction to a key concept, the need to build our skill set for communicating our needs and wants for social connection.

[Counsellor] "Liling, maybe we could explore some different ways that you could approach Mosi and Jane before or during lunch to let them know that you would like to sit with them, even when Hannah isn't with you? Are you open to trying a few things with me?"

[Liling] "If you think it will make a difference ..."

DAN

Dan is continuing to make emotional and behavioural progress. In today's session, he commented on what he will do differently in his *next relationship*, highlighting a newly identified ability to envision a more hopeful future. He talks less about his ex-wife and more about the challenges of co-parenting. He has been consistent with scheduling activities that bring him joy and continues to recognize when his difficulty setting boundaries aggravates his depression symptoms. Today, we are exploring his ongoing struggle with self-identity when he is not in a helping role.

[Dan] "More and more, I realize I have always surrounded myself with people who need me. Lopsided relationships. Relationships where I can be the hero." [Partly joking, he adds] "I think I am attracted to needy people."

Dan looks to me for confirmation of his assessment. I am not willing to confirm or deny, but, instead, I choose to further explore with him.

[Counsellor] "If that is true, what do you think this all means?"

Dan has been doing some real thinking and is beginning to apply our discussions and our homework to his knowledge about himself and his relationship with depression. Our dialogues are getting more exploratory in nature. Dan is often the leader of the dialogue, and he is making connections between thoughts, feelings, and behaviours and the power of their influences. Dan proposes a theory to me.

[Dan] "Maybe I think if you need me, I am indispensable, and if you don't need me, I am disposable. Maybe it's too risky *not* to be needed?"

[Counsellor] "What do you mean by risky?"

[Dan] "Risky in the way that if I don't serve a purpose, you will decide you don't need me, you don't want me in your life. Just get rid of me. Like Linda did. Oh my, I am messed up!" [He says with a laugh.]

I love his desire to want to fit the pieces together, but I also don't want him becoming discouraged with a false belief that he is defective in some way, so I am quick to respond.

[Counsellor] "Dan, I don't think you are '*messed up*.'" [I use air quotes, as this is a bit of our thing now.] "I think what you might be referring to is a fear of rejection. Rejection is a very powerful emotion and one most of us like to avoid. Unfortunately, all relationships come with this risk. Are you interested in trying to figure out what role rejection and your fear of it plays in your relationship patterns?"

Dan replies with a mix of exhaustion and interest.

[Dan] "We've come this far."

FINISHING THOUGHTS

For some, depression can be a lifelong journey. For others, it is a very painful hiccup in a larger story. Regardless of its intensity or longevity, it infiltrates one's relationship with both self and others. It alters one's perception of self by highlighting or creating non-existent deficiencies. Depression lies about worth within relationships and inhibits the ability to love and be loved. It prevents the envisioning of a peaceful and functioning future. Combatting depression requires acceptance and commitment. First, it requires acceptance that something is not working and is impacting the ability to experience joy and embrace hope. Commitment is then needed to move through the physical, psychological, emotional, and social toll. Battling depression requires that a person undertake a committed search for a more manageable and hopeful reality on the other side.

Helping people reset their perspectives and regain a sense of control includes approaching depression from a holistic framework. It includes an integration of the mind and body with efforts geared at honouring both. This work also requires a commitment to behavioural change in recognition that motivation will follow and the use of social connection as a critical and non-optional caveat of change. An effective and purpose-driven action plan cannot overlook or underestimate the power of collectively building on these variables.

ABOUT THE AUTHOR

Sheri Coburn, MSW, RSW

Sheri is a Registered Social Worker who holds a master's degree in social work and a bachelor's degree in criminology. She has a diverse professional background with experiences as a correctional officer, addictions counsellor, and developer and coordinator of a domestic violence outreach program. Sheri is a trainer with the Crisis & Trauma Resource Institute and is also a counsellor in a private practice setting. She currently provides individual and family counselling in the areas of mental health, addiction, recovering after relationship breakdown, and trauma.

REFERENCES

American Psychiatric Association. (2013). *Diagnostic and statistical manual of mental disorders* (5th ed.). Arlington, VA: Author.

Burns, D. D. (1981). *Feeling good: The new mood therapy.* New York, NY: Signet.

Greenberger, D., & Padesky, C. A. (2016). *Mind over mood: Change how you feel by changing the way you think* (2nd ed.). New York, NY: Guilford Press.

Schalinski, I., Teicher, M. H., Nischk, D., Hinderer, E., Müller, O., & Rockstroh, B. (2016). Type and timing of adverse childhood experiences differentially affect severity of PTSD, dissociative and depressive symptoms in adult inpatients. *BMC Psychiatry, 16*(295). https://doi.org/10.1186/s12888-016-1004-5

Smith, B. (2013). Depression and motivation. *Phenomenology and the Cognitive Sciences, 12*(4), 615-635.

Stanley, B., & Brown, G. K. (2012). Safety planning intervention: A brief intervention to mitigate suicide risk. *Cognitive and Behavioral Practice, 19*(2), 256-264.

Strosahl, K. D., & Robinson, P. J. (2008). *The mindfulness and acceptance workbook for depression: Using acceptance and commitment therapy to move through depression and create a life worth living.* Oakland, CA: New Harbinger Publications, Inc.

Thomson, B., & Broadway-Horner, M. (2012). *Managing depression with CBT for dummies.* Chichester, UK: John Wiley & Sons Ltd.

CHAPTER FIVE

SELF-INJURY

By Trish Harper

SELF-INJURY BEHAVIOUR IS COMPLEX AND OFTEN MISUNDERSTOOD. When a person is cutting or burning their own flesh, picking and interfering with the healing of wounds, or hitting themselves, it can be confusing and scary for their loved ones, and even for the professionals who try to help. In the last several years, helping professionals have begun to understand that these behaviours are not done with suicidal intent, but rather, they have many other functions (Klonsky, 2007). "Non-suicidal self-injury" is the clinical term to describe the act of intentionally damaging one's own body tissue without conscious suicidal ideation. In this chapter, we will refer to it as self-injury behaviour.

When assessing clients who self-injure, clinicians should consider that individuals who self-injure are more likely to have suicidal ideation, and appropriate screening should always take place (Klonsky & Muehlenkamp, 2007). Intention is key. With suicide, the plan is often to escape pain or overwhelming circumstances, and ending life is seen as the solution. In contrast, the aim of self-injury is usually to ease pain, feel emotionally better, and be able to make it through another day.

In this chapter, we will explore the variety of functions self-injury can fulfil and how self-injury can be viewed as a compulsive, self-regulatory behaviour. For individuals who use self-injury behaviour to manage their emotions (self-regulate), the goals for change are often complicated and need to be explored sensitively and carefully in a way that respects the possible positive functions of the behaviours. This chapter will outline principles for navigating this complex territory.

There are several characteristics associated with self-injury behaviour, including the presence of intense negative emotions, deficits in emotional literacy, higher levels of self-criticism, and the presence of psychiatric conditions, such as depressive and anxiety disorders, eating disorders, and substance use disorders. Self-injury appears to be most common in the early to middle teen years, but can be present in adults as well (Peterson, Freedenthal, Sheldon, & Andersen, 2008).

KATELYN

At the age of 13, Katelyn has been exposed to many dark experiences. She lives with her mother in a small rental house with three brothers and dreams of becoming an artist, as she loves to engage in any creative activity. However, school is a challenge she struggles with on a daily basis. When she was two years old, her father left the family, and several men came in and out of their lives until her mother remarried when Katelyn was five years old. Unfortunately, the one man she considered to be her stepfather sexually abused Katelyn for over four years. When Kaitlyn was 10, her mother ended the relationship with this man, and her stepfather left the home and was never again a part of her life. However, one of her brothers began to come into her room at night and continued the cycle of abuse.

Katelyn came to see me for counselling after her mother, Rhonda, discovered the abuse. Katelyn feared she might be pregnant and went to see their family doctor with her mother. During the appointment, her mother was shocked and scared to discover many thin red scars across Katelyn's arms and inner thighs. Some of her wounds were fresh, and Rhonda immediately assumed Katelyn was suicidal and drove her straight to the emergency room. She did not have any suicidal ideation and was not admitted. She left the hospital several hours later with a recommendation to attend counselling.

In my office, at her first visit, Katelyn looks up at me, her eyes heavily lined with dark makeup, which make her appear much older than her 13 years. She has her phone in her hand, busily checking messages. She then proceeds to look straight at me and declares in a defiant voice, "I don't think this counselling thing will help. I've been before, and it never changed anything." She searches my eyes to see how I will respond.

MARIA

Maria is 16 years old and lives "worlds away" from Katelyn's neighbourhood. Her parents are successful professionals, and she is a dancer who aspires to be a doctor, just like her mother, Carmen. She is plagued by concerns about her body image and perfectionistic expectations of herself in dance class. Despite her best efforts, fitting in at school is not easy. When she was in Grade 6, she changed schools due to the unrelenting bullying by a group of girls in Grade 7 who called her "fat" and used social media to demean her on a regular basis.

Her new school has been a more welcoming place, but feelings of depression still linger. She has considered suicide to escape the constant feeling of unworthiness. She found relief from the suicidal thoughts when she started cutting her arms. Her ballet teacher discovered the marks during a private lesson. Maria was very scared to tell her parents, because she believed they would blame her boyfriend, Carlo. He also engages in self-injury and was hospitalized six months prior when he cut his arm too deeply and needed stitches.

In my office, Maria sits timidly on the end of my comfy chair, polite but reserved. She tells me, "My mother just doesn't understand me. No one in my family does. They are all perfect, and I just can't be that anymore. I tried, but it didn't work. The only person who understands me is Carlo."

TOMAS

Tomas, age 34, is an attorney, married, and has a six-year-old daughter and a three-year-old son. His wife, Lori, also a lawyer, has put her own practice on hold to stay home with their children. Tomas makes a big revelation during our first interview, with tears welling in his eyes.

[Tomas] "I am so scared that increasingly when I look in the mirror, I see my dad. I never want to be that kind of father to my children. He was abusive, and I could never please him. He always told me I was going to amount to nothing and become a lonely old man, just like him."

Tomas mentions, almost as an afterthought, that he recently began burning his chest with a lighter. He says that he used to do it when he was a teenager. He does notice he's had increasing feelings of aggression, and it is starting to concern him.

Tomas is grieving the loss of his mother, who died of lung cancer a couple of months ago. He has been a frequent user of marijuana, and his use has become heavier in recent weeks. His marijuana habit is starting to be a source of conflict with his wife, who reluctantly accepted his recreational use but is now very concerned, as it has become almost daily. Tomas believes he should try to quit "cold turkey," as his father always told him it was a disgusting, dirty habit.

Tomas' parents were divorced after his mother tired of ongoing psychological and physical abuse. After the age of 13, Tomas had very little contact with his father. Once his own children were born, he began to talk to his father more.

Katelyn, Maria, and Tomas all have difficulty with emotional regulation. Emotional regulation involves the awareness of our internal state, the ability to tolerate a range of emotions, and the ability to respond to and adjust the changes in our internal state that may arise as a result of those emotions. The compulsion to self-injure serves as a temporary solution to intense emotions, which have become too big to manage. These big emotions result in either feeling overwhelmed or numbness/lack of feeling. This is followed by behaviour that has been hijacked by impulsive urges and feelings, resulting in intense distress.

Self-injury evolves as an antidote to that intense distress. It provides a feeling of relief, a sense of control, and sometimes even a release of feel-good endorphins, which produce a temporary feeling of calm or happiness. Self-injury can offer an escape from a seemingly intolerable emotional or psychological situation.

A cycle of self-injury (see Figure 5.1) can be triggered by incidents that cause unresolved wounds to surface. For example, experiencing conflict, criticism, or rejection may trigger old beliefs or fears. This leads to escalating emotional tension and is usually combined with distorted and/or negative thinking. This escalation then gives rise to an overwhelming feeling of panic or urgency that results in a strong compulsion to engage in a self-injurious behaviour. The self-harm behaviour then provides a rapid (but temporary) de-escalation of the internal crisis (Sutton, 2007). Often, the initial sense of calm and relief turns into feelings of anger, shame, or guilt, which begin the cycle again.

This cycle of self-injury is often compared to an addiction, however, some researchers distinguish the concepts, because urges for self-injuring behaviour typically arise in very specific situations for individuals involving overwhelming negative emotion, rather than an urge that may start to organize many other parts of a person's life as well (Victor, Glenn, & Klonsky, 2012). The compulsive nature of the cycle, however, can have similar addictive qualities, such as the difficulty to give up the behaviour and the fact that the compulsion and urges can become stronger over time.

1. Trigger
(Trauma, Negative
Beliefs About Self,
Negative Emotions)

5. Aftermath
Reaction of Anger,
Shame, or Guilt

2. Increased
Emotional Tension
and Distorted
Thinking

4. Self-Injury
Action and
De-Escalation: Calm

3. Overwhelm
Leading to:
a) Panic or
b) Shutdown

Figure 5.1
Cycle of self-injury

INSIGHTS AND GUIDING PRINCIPLES FOR COUNSELLING

Self-injury almost always begins in adolescence, as it did in various ways for Katelyn, Maria, and Tomas. This is in part due to the increased sensitivity to stress during this developmental period. The brain system that regulates emotions and stress reactions is essentially being rewired at this time, and responding to both social and environmental stressors is particularly challenging.

Neuroscientists have recently discovered that the adolescent brain works differently than the adult brain when making decisions and solving problems (Shanker, 2016). Behaviours and actions are guided more by the emotional reactivity of the amygdala (within the limbic system of the brain) and less by the thoughtful logic of the prefrontal cortex. This is especially true during times of stress and adversity. When young people are in a state of emotional turmoil and dysregulation, they tend to make more impulsive, and potentially harmful, decisions. People who use cutting, burning, or hitting behaviours may disregard the negative consequences, because they receive social or emotional rewards, such as care and concern, from the people around them. A frequent misperception is that young people injure themselves *simply* to gain attention. This is most common, for example, when fresh wounds are displayed in a highly visible way, or when the person expresses intense emotions in a manner that is perceived as dramatic.

It seems confusing that people try to gain attention with negative behaviour. From a behavioural viewpoint, unwanted actions or impulses are typically met with one of two responses: to ignore the behaviour, or to punish the behaviour.

For youth who self-injure, either of these two responses is unlikely to diminish the behaviour because the *attention* they *need*, and therefore seek, is almost always indicative of unmet needs and is therefore a healthy longing. The *need* for validation, expression, or belonging may be the result of lack of psychological, emotional, or physical safety in a youth's environment. This may be due to violence, bullying, relational difficulties, or complicated bereavement and multiple losses. As counsellors, it is our role to heed the call for attention in a healthy way, helping families and support systems to respond productively.

Identity is a central focus of exploration in adolescence. Peers and the outside world become increasingly influential for teens. Exposure to self-injuring behaviour, especially through social media networks, among peers at school, and from others in extracurricular settings, is an important consideration. There is enormous pressure both to *fit in* and to *find yourself* as an adolescent.

In today's digital world, there is much more access and exposure to media than at any other time in human development. There are thousands of choices for entertainment, role models, communication, and learning opportunities through social media.

Social contagion is a valid concern regarding self-injury, with both positive and negative reinforcement capabilities (Jarvi, Jackson, Swenson, & Crawford, 2013). Maria identifies her boyfriend, Carlo, as her biggest support and acknowledges that his use of cutting as a means of stress management and calming his emotions has been an influence on her. One of

Maria's best friends at school describes cutting as "better than Prozac." Her friend also struggles with attempts to treat her underlying depression with medication because of the side effects. Maria tells me she also prefers to use non-pharmacological means of dealing with her feelings of self-hatred, sadness, and disengagement from others.

Sometimes reinforcement of self-injury behaviour occurs through a shared desire to avoid or escape an unpleasant demand in the environment. In the case of Katelyn, she has a laundry list of activities, people, and places that she prefers to avoid. When she is unable to escape from certain situations, she will sneak away to either engage in cutting or pick away at a scab to distract from her current stressor. Youth who view others using self-injury as a means of managing intense emotions will often strongly identify with self-injury as a successful strategy for reducing their own suffering. If a client's friend has used cutting or burning and found that it relieves distress, it is far more likely that a client will try it as well.

As clinicians, we must also pay attention to past experiences of trauma and the dynamics of the family. Developmental trauma occurs early in life, and examples of it may be attachment disruptions through foster care, death or separation from a primary caregiver, a chaotic family environment involving substance use or violence, or experiences of physical, emotional, or sexual abuse or neglect. Experiences of insecure attachment may indeed lead a person to engage in behaviour to gain attention, often because they have unmet relational needs. Unsurprisingly, early adverse events and circumstances provide fertile ground for difficulties with emotional regulation to take seed.

Tomas was not only a victim of psychological and physical abuse at the hands of his father, he was also witness to his mother being harmed. The lasting impact of experiencing and witnessing violence has led to him only feeling *normal* when he uses substances like marijuana. Substance use is associated with a higher risk of self-injury and, in Tomas' case, it causes even more psychological pain, due to the messages he received from his father about his drug use.

There are four guiding principles that I have found to be very useful when working with someone who self-injures:

1) **Understand the function of the behaviour**

   This knowledge informs what next steps are necessary and provides the most useful insight for setting out on the best treatment path.

2) **Work from a harm-reduction perspective**

   Providing education about harm reduction for key support people in the person's life and paying attention to pacing and unmet needs allows the optimum conditions for positive changes to be undertaken successfully.

3) **Increase safety in the support system**

   Creating an environment that provides emotional validation sets the conditions for improved communication and successful treatment over the long term.

4) **Focus on positive coping strategies**

   New strategies to express and manage negative emotions can be implemented, along with increased capacity for self-regulation.

1) UNDERSTAND THE FUNCTION OF THE BEHAVIOUR

It is critical that helpers understand the function that self-injury behaviour has in a person's life. Many of the responses that people describe as unhelpful involve shock, anger, judgment, and what they perceive as overreaction on the part of others. In some cases, the reaction of those involved can be described as overly complacent or even dismissive. It is also not helpful when helpers or those close to the person who is self-injuring automatically assume that suicidal intention is present. The person inadvertently feels less understood if the clinical interventions (such as hospitalization) that are undertaken do not match with their intention. This assumption can further drive the behaviour underground, as self-injury often already involves shame and secrecy.

Self-injury behaviour primarily serves to regulate emotion, along with several other potential functions, such as relieving feelings of numbness or dissociation, reducing suicidal thoughts, punishing oneself for perceived wrong-doing, or seeking sensation through endorphin release. Emotional regulation is the most typical function of self-injury in both adolescents and adults (Klonsky, 2007). Katelyn describes the feeling of calm that rushes over her after she cuts. Maria indicates that all of her negative feelings disappear right after she engages in self-injury. Tomas says the burning stops the negative voice inside of his head that says he is worthless, at least temporarily.

It is our job as helpers to assist the person in understanding the function of the behaviour and its context. This understanding lays the groundwork for clarity and provides the motivation to engage in treatment. Counsellors should remember that, often, young people do not understand all of the reasons why they self-injure. In the process of exploring their reasons for self-injuring together, we can model and teach new skills along the way.

CASE APPLICATION

KATELYN

In early sessions, Katelyn could only identify that she felt "more alive" after cutting, however, we were able to discover deeper links to past experiences. As we continue our work, she is able to understand the lingering impacts of trauma, the connection between how she needed to shut down and dissociate to survive, and the deadened feeling that is so common as a result of her early sexual abuse.

For Katelyn, sometimes self-injury is a means of "up-regulation" to counter shut-down, dissociative states and relieve a feeling of numbness. Katelyn describes that, prior to cutting herself, many times she feels almost as if she is a robot, and the self-injury behaviour reminds her she is alive, especially when she sees her own blood. At other times, it serves to "down-regulate" and settle her arousal and anxiety. During these times, Katelyn feels that the surge of adrenaline that causes her to feel wired will be replaced by feelings of relaxation.

MARIA

Maria, in contrast, connects her self-injury behaviour with a sense of self-nurturing as she tends to her wounds. Maria also describes in detail the function of down-regulation, the feeling of calm and peace that would warm her entire body after the initial feelings of panic and dread that precede her self-injury. In fact, she sometimes tends to her boyfriend's wounds as well and identifies that this was proof of how much they care for each other.

TOMAS

Tomas, who initially did not understand his compulsive need to burn himself at all, has come to see that he believes he had a need to punish himself, that he is deserving of physical pain, and that, somehow, it solves a "double-bind" scenario for him regarding to his father. As Tomas describes it, he is damned if he does and damned if he doesn't. The regulatory function for him is a little more complex, as he feels more himself when he burns himself, but he also feels lighter and calmer.

He wants to quit using marijuana, although he will alternate between saying he loves it and will never give it up and saying that he hates it and wants to quit cold turkey. Somehow, he feels a sense of relief when he burns himself, but he knows intellectually it doesn't seem to make sense. However, he can't deny that he feels better and calmer for a couple of hours after feeling the pain of his flesh burning, and thoughts of suicide are no longer at the forefront of his mind.

Once clients, their families, and their support systems are able to understand what purpose the self-injury behaviour is serving, they can begin the process of building new ways of thinking, understanding emotions, and finally acting with increased self-awareness.

Some of the more common functions of self-injury that can be found in Katelyn's, Maria's, and Tomas' stories may be summarized as

- influencing emotional regulation;
- helping to reduce suicidal ideation;
- reinforcing beliefs that lead to self-punishment or self-anger;
- serving as an anti-dissociation method;
- seeking nurturance and/or pleasant sensations.

COUNSELLING STRATEGIES

A solid therapeutic relationship is a great place to start in order to understand the functions of self-injury behaviour, which you may find out in the process of discovery together.

1) Hold a curious, non-judgmental stance
   - Begin the relationship by focusing on getting to know the youth or the adult as a person, rather than initially focusing on the self-injury behaviour.
   - Do not respond to revelations of self-injury with shock, anger, aversion, or disgust. Convey a sense of concern without overreacting. Advise about medical attention as needed.
   - Do ask about suicide but do not assume that the self-injury behaviour is an indication of a suicide attempt.

2) Start to build awareness of the cycle of self-injury
   - Communicate that each person's experience of the cycle is unique to them.
   - Help them to begin the process of separating what they are thinking and how they are feeling before, during, and after the act of self-injury. *See page 291 in the Resources section to map out the cycle.*
   - Explore the impact of relationships and environment. For example, when, where, and with whom do they self-injure? What is

the impact on their relationships when they self-injure? How do others respond?

3) Invite open discussion of what the client believes is the function of self-injury

> ➤ Ask questions about what the client sees as the benefits of the self-injury behaviour.

> ➤ Explore all of the common functions of self-injury so that the client can consider if any of them are a "fit" in their own situation.

When clients have built the habit of escaping from the present moment when difficulties arise, a safe container needs to be offered where empathy and understanding are present. It can be extremely alarming to contemplate giving up a behaviour that has served to calm them down and help make them feel "normal." As counsellors, we do this by being intentional about our presence, using compassion, and, very importantly, conveying a sense of trust in clients' abilities to explore what they believe is happening on the inside for themselves. Young people who self-injure have often built up a long history of ignoring or overriding their own needs.

CASE APPLICATION

KATELYN

During elementary school, teachers would often observe that Katelyn had difficulty paying attention and focusing on her schoolwork. She describes several instances when she "lost track of time" and had memory lapses that were mildly distressing. As she got older, these types of experiences became more frequent and were accompanied by a numb, deadened feeling. Katelyn became increasingly anxious that she was incapable of feeling anything – until she tried cutting herself. The intense rush she experienced was both exhilarating and reassuring. Katelyn now sees a connection between her tendency to dissociate and her desire to cut, and she feels a sense of relief knowing that she is not simply "crazy."

MARIA

Maria frequently speaks of being careful never to "rock the boat" in her family, for fear that someone else will suffer. It didn't really occur to her that she could choose a career other than medicine, even though the sight of blood makes her feel queasy and weak. She slowly uncovers some of her thought patterns and beliefs as she begins to feel permission to explore her own thoughts and feelings. One such recurring thought is "It's *not* okay to be weak. I must always be strong and never show my feelings." This was a common theme in her family.

She began to untangle the mess of thoughts, beliefs, and emotions, allowing space to assess them and decide whether she wants to claim them for herself. She can also choose to replace them with healthier ones. Maria has started to see the connection between caring for her wounds and wanting to seek care from others. She is beginning to see that wanting nurturance from others is actually acceptable, and perhaps there could be ways of communicating this that don't involve self-injury.

TOMAS

Tomas began to understand his own experience of the self-injury cycle when his wife, Lori, pointed out certain patterns of behaviour to him. She shared in a counselling session her observation that both his marijuana use and burning himself served as stress management tools for him and had become the only way he could cope on a daily basis. At first, it was inconceivable to Lori how this was serving in any way to make Tomas feel better. As she is able to learn more about the functions of self-injury behaviour, and specifically why Tomas may be engaging in the behaviour, Lori is able to participate much more meaningfully in his treatment.

2) WORK FROM A HARM-REDUCTION PERSPECTIVE

It is *not* helpful to demand that a person who is cutting, burning, hitting, or picking at wounds stop the behaviour immediately. Unfortunately, this can be the first response of those individuals who discover that self-injury is taking place. Harm reduction approaches accept that someone may need to self-injure at a given time and the focus should be on supporting that person to reduce the risk and the damage inherent in their self-injury. Harm reduction considers the overall context of the person engaging in the self-injurious or dangerous behaviour.

As helpers, we need to understand that the self-injury behaviour will likely continue until the client has other means of coping with distress, regulating their feelings, challenging some of the beliefs that support the act of self-injury, and gaining more effective communication skills. It is also important to understand that, sometimes, maladaptive coping strategies, such as self-injury, keep people alive by keeping suicidal ideation at bay. Often compulsive behaviour serves to regulate feelings that would otherwise become too threatening or painful. It makes sense that if a behaviour serves to regulate emotions successfully, there is incentive to continue the behaviour, and it can often feel as if *it is the only choice.*

Some of our clients may be living in unsafe environments, surrounded by violence, addictions, or chaos, yet this way of living has become normal to them. For clients who have deficits in getting their basic needs met, we must try to assist in filling those gaps whenever possible. Safety in the real world must precede building an internal sense that "everything is okay." The most successful outcomes in counselling are achieved when people have their survival needs met first. Clients then have energy and time to improve their psychological and emotional functioning.

COUNSELLING STRATEGIES

1) Focus on meeting survival needs

> ➤ Provide information about your client's legal rights and get outside agencies involved if the physical safety of your client is at risk.

➤ Advocate for your clients and connect them to services for income and employment, as well as survival needs, such as food and safe housing.

➤ Ask questions about how your client assesses their safety and what it means to them. Give them opportunities to be curious about their own intuition and boundaries. Help them identify how they can assess whether a situation or person is safe by listening to their own gut and using safe supports.

2) Encourage small steps toward reducing the self-injury behaviour

➤ Acknowledge the ambivalence that can come with change, such as the accompanying fear of coping without cutting, burning, or hitting, as well as the desire to stop. Allow your client to fully express all of the parts of self that may not always be in agreement.

➤ Normalize working at a slow pace toward making change, ensuring that the client has experiences of success early in treatment.

➤ Notice any signs that your client is using their increased awareness to make different choices, no matter how small.

➤ Validate the intention behind the behaviour to make the person feel better. Although causing other problems, this behaviour is also working *for* the client in some way.

3) Reinforce emotional literacy skills

➤ Emphasize that all emotions are acceptable.

➤ Provide coaching and roleplaying in order to increase knowledge and awareness of emotions and the messages they convey. *See page 283 in the Resources section for an emotion vocabulary list.*

➤ Encourage efforts to increase tolerance for discomfort and explore other strategies for coping with strong emotions and stressful events. For example, if your client tends to isolate themselves when they feel shame or sadness, encourage them to reach out to someone when they identify those emotions or simply spend more time with others rather than staying alone.

CASE APPLICATION

KATELYN

Katelyn has rarely felt truly safe, since she has been vulnerable to sexual abuse in her own home for so many years. Katelyn spent many years feeling almost as if she and her mom "shared a body." She says she struggled to separate her own feelings from those of others, and she could feel every emotion she sensed that her mom felt – and a lot of them were painful.

Katelyn faces the challenge of beginning to contemplate other ways of coping with emotions that are overwhelming her. As our sessions progress, I am careful to avoid causing an extreme flood of emotions that could trigger dissociation. However, I am still curious about the impact that cutting has on her feelings of numbness.

[Counsellor] "What do you notice in the moments just before and just after you self-injure?"

[Katelyn] "Before I cut, I often feel a ball of emotions is stuck in my chest. There are no words, and it feels like even though I know the feelings are there, I don't really feel them. Everything looks and feels grey."

[Counsellor] "And what happens to the grey after you cut?"

[Katelyn] "I feel a rush of aliveness, and the red colour of my blood gives me a feeling of relief. I really feel alive … not like I am living in black and white anymore."

Katelyn recognizes that not only does cutting make her feel calm, but it also actually makes her feel more alive. The numbness, or lack of emotion, often drives her impulse to see if she is still capable of feeling.

I decide to help her explore further by reminding her of the work she has done toward recognizing her own internal states.

[Counsellor] "What have you noticed since you have been paying more attention to your own feelings and identifying your emotions?"

[Katelyn] "It's kind of strange ... I'm so used to feeling every emotion that others around me feel. Sometimes I'm still not really sure of what I am feeling."

She looks down, and then up. We make eye contact, and I gently smile in recognition of her observation.

[Counsellor] "Yes, it takes time and practice to be able to recognize what is happening on the inside. Is there an example that stands out for you over the past week when you were able to focus internally and use what you notice in a positive way?"

Katelyn looks at me, at first with a puzzled look. Then a smile spreads across her face.

[Katelyn] "Yes! I was at my friend's house when another group of people came over, and it suddenly got very noisy. Instead of just sitting there trying to tune it out, I went outside, and the overwhelmed feeling started to go away."

I smile again and nod my head.

Katelyn has begun to see that in order to regain her sense of self, she needs to recognize her distress earlier, so that she does not enter into a dissociative state as quickly. By starting to focus on recognizing her *own* emotional states, rather than focusing on those around her, she begins to feel empowered and able to start making simple choices.

MARIA

When Maria discovered self-injury, she found not only a short-term solution to her mental anguish, but also a group of people who really seemed to understand her. In our first sessions together, she expressed fear that her family was going to force her to give up her new friends.

[Maria] "My parents don't like Carlo or any of his friends. They think he is a bad influence on me. What they don't understand is that I am just like him! He isn't a bad person. He just feels things deeply, like I do. They'll never get that, because they aren't like that."

Maria looks defeated as she sits back in her chair.

[Counsellor] "Sounds like you wish your parents understood you better and how you experience emotions. It seems like you feel that Carlo *gets you* in a way that you wish your family could."

[Maria] "Yes! They want me to change back into the perfect little girl. I don't want to lose them, but I can't turn my back on my friends either. They have been there for me, especially Carlo."

Maria's bond with Carlo and her other friends feels like a psychological antidote to the pressure she experiences within her family and from their impossibly high standards. This aspect of Maria's self-injury behaviour is what causes the most ambivalence for her as she considers giving it up. After we had established enough rapport, and I had acknowledged the value of the relationships she had made, I could gently invite her to consider her family's point of view.

[Counsellor] "Perhaps your parents have had a hard time recognizing the importance of your friendships, because they are so concerned about you hurting yourself. Maybe there is still a way to change things for yourself, as everyone who cares about you wants you to be safe, including Carlo and your parents."

Looking at me directly and clearly, she takes a deep breath.

[Maria] "I want to make the decision to quit self-injury myself, and when I make mistakes, I want to be able to get support rather than feel I have to hide it, like I did before, because my parents wouldn't let me see my friends again."

[Counsellor] "Yes, I'm glad to hear that you want to be able to be upfront and honest and receive support when you need it. Let's work together to make that happen."

TOMAS

Tomas relies on both self-injury behaviour and substance use to combat the discomfort he feels from his many years of violence and abuse at the hands of his father. During one of the sessions with both Tomas and his wife, the impact of Tomas' past on his marriage comes to the forefront.

Speaking directly to her husband, Lori turns to face him.

[Lori] "You have been using the drugs, and now burning yourself, to avoid all the pain your dad caused your family. It's time to let some of that pain go!"

I turn to Tomas to allow him to respond. He slowly lifts his head, looks at his wife, and speaks in a whisper.

[Tomas] "You're right."

With this awareness, Tomas is ready to face his painful past. He knows what he is doing now is hurting his family, and he wants to stop the pattern of using unhealthy behaviours to cope with his emotions.

Later, in an individual session, Tomas and I discuss the aftermath of his wife's statement.

[Counsellor] "Tell me about how things have been between you and Lori since your last visit."

[Tomas] "Her calling me out was actually a relief. I know that my past has caused problems in my marriage before, but now I feel that Lori does understand more about what I am going through. It has been easier to talk to her. She seems to have more patience."

With the support of his wife, Tomas can now risk talking about himself and how he feels.

3) INCREASE SAFETY IN THE SUPPORT SYSTEM

Helping to rebuild secure relationship experiences and foster attachment is often accomplished through family work and is a key piece of the clinical puzzle. When working with families, it's important to provide information on how to respond without overreacting, creating an environment where healthy communication can grow, and helping caregivers, family members, and others involved with the person to not inadvertently reinforce the self-injury behaviour.

There is a connection between the family environment and a lack of emotional validation, sometimes as a result of stress from socio-economic factors, mental health patterns in the family, the lack of a *good fit* between the temperaments of the caregiver and child, or the use of harsh discipline (Arbuthnott & Lewis, 2015). Therefore, an increase in healthy interactions and the ability to communicate effectively are essential for successful interventions to occur.

A counsellor must attempt to build a safety net so the person who self-injures can express themself and get their needs met. For young people, it is often necessary to help the family be an effective part of this. With adult clients, it may be a partner, other family members, or friends who serve as part of the support and safety network. Building on the previous principles, it is important to have a balanced focus between the behaviour and the function it serves without being overly focused on abstinence, especially in the beginning. Safety requires that people in the support system come to understand the behaviour as based on a positive need for engagement and attention, rather than as manipulative attention-seeking or overly dramatic behaviour.

COUNSELLING STRATEGIES

1) Help parents, partners, and other support people manage their own emotions

   ➤ Remind them not to respond out of *fear*. Education about our *fight, flight, or freeze* instinct helps foster understanding of the powerful impact of remaining calm and being fully present when someone else is in distress. The power of being a regulated, solid, and responsive role model cannot be overstated.

➤ Teach and practice breathing and other emotion-regulation strategies. Breath is one of the most direct routes to calm our nervous systems and process our emotions. Some people also benefit from other mindful awareness activities that involve using their senses or engaging in guided imagery. Also, activities involving movement, such as walking or martial arts, help people to restore their own emotional equilibrium. *See pages 285 and 286 in the Resources section for sample activity descriptions.*

2) Help caregivers and other support people provide an emotionally validating environment

➤ Coach parents, partners, or family members to be able to be present and notice what is happening for the client. For example, they could show interest in the emotions clients are feeling and send a message that those feelings are okay. Reinforce the idea that emotions are separate from behaviours.

➤ Provide genuine but respectful feedback on their communication skills. Offer gentle guidance about how to talk to the person and interrupt unhealthy communication patterns that may have developed over time.

➤ Encourage support people to give less attention to unhealthy or dysfunctional behaviours. Provide examples of how they can validate the person without reinforcing the self-injury behaviour, for example, by setting a regular time to spend time together and focusing on a shared interest or hobby. The need for time and attention from loved ones cannot be underestimated.

3) Treat underlying mental health needs

➤ Actively screen for mental health concerns for both the individual who is engaging in self-injury behaviour and their family members whenever possible.

➤ Collaborate with other professionals in healthcare and the school system or work setting when it is appropriate to do so.

The concept of safety is broadly applicable across many domains. Lack of safety – physical, emotional, and psychological – along with a lack of validation is a common thread interwoven in the stories of people who self-injure. When people experience trauma, they feel captive to their emotions, which often seem overwhelming, volatile, and intense. As discussed in the self-injury cycle, the feeling of strong emotions becomes linked with sympathetic arousal and physiological dysregulation. The ability to calm ourselves and turn down our stress response is learned from our parents and caregivers. Any difficulties that our primary caregivers may have had in modulating their own physiological states is passed down to us, as our nervous systems learn from theirs.

CASE APPLICATION

KATELYN

Katelyn's mother, Rhonda, was not overly enthusiastic about being involved in counselling early in the process. In our first session, Rhonda peered at me skeptically.

[Rhonda] "I don't really know why I need to be here. It's too late for me to undo all the mistakes I have made, which I am already well aware of. Katelyn needs to get her own act together."

Recognizing that Rhonda had felt judged in the past by other professionals, I was careful in my response.

[Counsellor] "It is true that Katelyn is becoming more independent and making her own choices. It is respectful of you to recognize that."

I paused to let the positive feedback sink in. Then I continued.

[Counsellor] "As parents, we don't always get it right, but it's my experience that our kids still benefit from our involvement, especially when our intentions are to keep them safe and healthy."

Eyes welling slightly, Rhonda sighed and continued.

[Rhonda] "I have fought really hard to stay sober, and I left that abusive jerk once I got my head on straight. I knew I had to do that for both Katelyn and me."

[Counsellor] "Yes, even though it wasn't easy. And maybe it took longer than you would have liked, but you were able to make choices to keep you and your family safe. That makes a big difference for Katelyn."

Once Rhonda was able to get past some guilt, she came on board, and she has been a key part of Katelyn's support system. She now sees the connection between her own recovery and the positive impact in her daughter's life. Staying sober through the support of her 12-step program and leaving her abusive partner has greatly contributed to increased stability and safety in both of their lives.

MARIA

Maria was greatly impacted by the bullying she experienced in middle school, her struggle to meet expectations in the dance studio, and her family's high hopes for her. These experiences reinforced her negative beliefs that she did not fit in or measure up. When Maria's mother, Carmen, learned of the impact that striving for perfection had on Maria, she was reminded of the difficulties in her family growing up with a sister who struggled with an eating disorder.

[Counsellor] "We have been discussing how members of the family recognize and process their emotions. What do observe about your own emotional regulation strategies?"

[Carmen] "I haven't thought it about really. I like to be busy, on the go. Sitting around navel-gazing always seemed to be a waste of time to me."

[Counsellor] "So it sounds like, up to this point, you haven't paid much attention to how you notice your emotions. What is like to pay attention to that now?"

Carmen shifts in her chair. She closes her eyes and then opens them as she begins to speak again.

[Carmen] "An image of my own mother flashed in my mind, dressed in her apron, immaculate as always. She had a pained look on her face but quickly forced a smile. She always used to say it was better to focus on tomorrow than dwell on yesterday. Keep going, no matter what."

Her eyes drift off sideways.

[Carmen] "Maybe that is why I have never stopped to pay attention to my own feelings. I've just had to keep up the appearance that everything is always alright."

[Counsellor] "Perhaps it is time to re-examine that pattern and whether it is serving you and Maria best in the present."

I wanted to acknowledge Carmen's efforts to be more present and attuned to her daughter's needs, as she discovered some patterns in their communication that needed to be addressed. She could let go of some old beliefs that were not serving them well as a family in the present day. She was also able to open up to the idea of getting further assessment for Maria regarding some concerning eating patterns that she had been ignoring and hoping would simply go away.

TOMAS

As well as his own experience of emotional and physical abuse from his father, Tomas was also exposed to domestic violence toward his mother from a young age. His lack of solid emotion-regulation skills, along with the recent loss of his mother, has sent his sense of safety into a tailspin.

In one of our sessions, I remind Tomas of what we have learned together so far.

[Counsellor] "Remember that anything that disturbs our sense of safety in the world and our ability to relax leaves us stuck in a *fight or flight reaction* and causes us to seek ways of restoring equilibrium."

Tomas straightened up in his seat. His eyes widened.

[Tomas] "I have always felt so guilty for how my drug use and self-injury has impacted my family. I didn't want to really see how it hurt them. I wanted forgiveness without facing it. But now I realize I need to forgive myself first."

[Counsellor] "Part of the repair process is certainly taking responsibility for your behaviour, but recognizing that that repair process must take place within yourself as well sounds as if it is empowering for you."

Tomas felt an enormous burden of guilt for how his behaviour was impacting his family. Part of the repair process was taking responsibility for the damage he had done, but it was also being able to *take in* the support of people around him. He was keen to start addressing some of his past experiences with his father's violence and open to the possibility that some of the symptoms he was attempting to treat through substance use and self-injury were actually a result of past trauma.

4) FOCUS ON DEVELOPING HEALTHY COPING BEHAVIOURS

People who have trouble with emotional regulation have a sense that they are better at coping with stress when they do not focus on what is happening in their body and mind. They feel the need to distract themselves by feeding their attention with strong impulses, and cutting, burning, picking, or hitting one's own flesh can certainly fill that role. We need to match the replacement behaviours to suit the primary function(s) that the self-injury behaviour is playing.

People who self-injure may experience a variety of different emotions – including anger and frustration, sadness, loneliness, and hurt – and sometimes the absence of emotion, which can also be distressing. After building awareness and increasing safety, clients' emotions surface powerfully, which is not uncommon when exploring past traumatic experiences. For clients, the next step is being able to manage and modulate the emerging intense feeling states appropriately. We can normalize this process and help clients to understand the flow of emotion and how to both tolerate the discomfort and build emotion-regulation strategies. At this stage of treatment, clients feel increased internal and external resources and a greater capacity for building safety into their lives.

COUNSELLING STRATEGIES

The capacity to manage and modulate internal states is a key focus in the counselling process, so that the person feels increased resilience and the ability to make different choices. The compulsion to engage in self-injury behaviour can then be reduced.

1) Teach and practice self-regulation skills

> ➤ Actively promote emotional regulation and self-soothing. Make it a regular part of each session and practice along with your client. Provide blankets, pillows, and sensory objects that they can use for comfort. This, along with practicing relaxation, imagery, and breathing exercises will boost their confidence in their ability to use these tools outside of the counselling sessions. *See page 293 in the Resources section for an example activity to build a coping tool kit.*

> ➤ Bring your language into the present to promote *here and now* awareness. Ask your client to look around the room and tell you what they notice with their senses (such as sight and sound).

When they discuss distressing events that occurred in the past, ask them how they are feeling about it now, rather than having them report what they felt in the past.

➤ Practice grounding exercises to help increase your client's capacity to remain regulated and connected to their body in the present. Be curious about internal sensations. For example, you can invite a client to notice how a chair is holding their weight and supporting them, while also paying attention to their breath or the room's surroundings, including you.

➤ Promote awareness of negative thinking patterns and the self-injury cycle. Your client can easily slip into old patterns in the face of stress and emotional triggers, so they need to be able to observe their own thinking patterns.

2) Use replacement behaviours when appropriate

➤ Promote the use of movement and actions in helping to regulate emotions. Many people benefit from activities, such as walking, martial arts, yoga, dance, or other forms of self-expression.

➤ Help clients to regularly practice being emotionally expressive. This can be done through expressive arts activities, such as writing, drawing in a journal, painting, music, poetry, or any form of creative activity that brings pleasure and enjoyment.

➤ Formulate a plan so that the alternatives to self-injury, such as breathing exercises, self-soothing activities, and contacts for support services and people, are readily available. Examples include phrases set as reminders in a smartphone or written onto business cards and placed strategically in the client's space.

3) Encourage the active use of a support system, both formally and informally

➤ Remind clients that avoidance is a common strategy in the face of stress and adversity, and that seeking help from others is not only okay, but also a behaviour that needs to be practiced. Talking to others that we trust helps us feel understood and less isolated.

➤ Normalize the necessity for us to need each other. Provide lots of information about self-help and support groups, mental health professionals, and appropriate online resources.

CASE APPLICATION

KATELYN

Katelyn has begun to journal more regularly, write poetry, and do sketch art. With some advocacy on my part, she has also been able to access a painting class. Her mother has started attending a self-help group and seeing her own counsellor, and she has been much more present in a healthy way for Katelyn. This has allowed Katelyn to focus on self-expression, her own wellness, and letting go of some of the old, unhealthy patterns wherein she acted like her mother's caregiver.

During an early session, I had asked her to create a "crystal ball" and to draw inside of it what she saw in her future. She looked at the blank paper for a couple of minutes and pushed it back at me, saying, "I see nothing in my future." After many sessions, she is able to articulate her goals differently. Now she says, "I want to graduate from high school and then start my own business creating cosmetics and body care products from natural materials."

MARIA

Maria's life has always been filled with structure and high expectations. During our counselling sessions, there is often a tension between wanting to be perfect and learning to let go and accept mistakes. While listening to me lead a relaxation exercise, Maria begins to giggle. At first, she automatically tries to stifle it. However, when we make eye contact, and I make a funny face, she erupts into a full fit of laughter. This is a turning point for her to feel increasingly comfortable with being silly and let her natural instincts take over sometimes. She continues to practice relaxation exercises with apps we find on her phone to guide her.

TOMAS

In earlier sessions, Tomas described his anger that was starting to feel "like a bomb ready to explode." About 10 sessions into our work, he describes a recent situation when his daughter was scared of him and said he was angry. He said back to her, "I am not angry! I will show you what angry is!"

As he repeats this story to me, we notice together how his hands curl into fists and his whole body starts to tense up. He reports feeling remorse that he reacted this way to his daughter, but he is unsure how to handle it.

I ask him to tell me how he learned to define anger. He says anger means yelling and saying hurtful things, and it usually involves violence. He is sure that his daughter was misreading his cues, as he had never raised a hand to her. This opens up a space for us to explore anger, including the gradations of the emotion. When I mirror back to him the facial expression, body language, and statements he had described, he realizes that, indeed, his daughter had accurately identified that he was angry.

Unpacking this incident together allows Tomas to acknowledge to himself that something isn't quite right. He is able to look clearly at a previously unconscious pattern. Irritation, frustration, anger, and finally rage and violence have been untangled from each other through our joint exploration within a solid counselling relationship. These changes are also supported by his ongoing practices of mindful awareness using breath, staying present in his body while running, and doing grounding exercises.

FINISHING THOUGHTS

Self-injury often leaves lasting scars, some that are visible, and perhaps some that are not. The scars can be reminders of past trauma and pain, or they may also serve as symbols of the ability to overcome adversity. This shift in perspective is also symbolic of the messages received from a person's support system as they learn to let go of a coping strategy that is harmful and to make healthier choices. The path to healing self-injury behaviour involves facing down shame, stigma, and isolation.

As a counsellor, I am consistently reminded of how the path to resilience is shaped by the ability to understand our emotional experiences and to safely express ourselves to those around us. The challenge of a change in perspective applies to anyone who has a person who self-injures in their life. The key is understanding that self-injury is primarily a way of coping with difficult emotions. Its functions can include restoring calm and comfort, expressing distress, releasing tension, reducing suicidal ideation, and, at times, grounding a person in reality. Effective interventions are accomplished by taking an individualized approach to treatment and a warm, empathic relationship with each person and their support system.

The roadmap to healing is unique for each person. Using the guiding principles in this chapter will hopefully contribute to understanding the diverse paths for people who have used self-injury behaviour as a means of attempting to temporarily feeling better. Many people have been able to discover increased confidence in managing emotions, more hopeful ways to look to the future, and, often, a new way to relate to the important people in their lives. This work is accomplished by all of us increasing our capacities for compassion and understanding.

ABOUT THE AUTHOR

Trish Harper, MSW, RSW

Trish has worked in many diverse mental health settings with families, youth, and children, providing direct practice for over 20 years. She is a Registered Social Worker who has a master's degree in social work, as well as an undergraduate degree in psychology, and she has completed professional training in trauma resolution therapy. Trish is a trainer with the Crisis & Trauma Resource Institute, and she has a small private practice that specializes in recovery from early adverse experiences, self-injury, trauma, anxiety, depression, and vicarious trauma.

REFERENCES

Arbuthnott, A. E., & Lewis, S. P. (2015). Parents of youth who self-injure: A review of the literature and implications for mental health professionals. *Child and Adolescent Psychiatry and Mental Health, 9*(35), 1-20.

Jarvi, S., Jackson, B., Swenson, L., & Crawford, H. (2013). The impact of social contagion on non-suicidal self-injury: A review of the literature. *Archives of Suicide Research, 17,* 1-19.

Klonsky, E. D. (2007). The functions of deliberate self-injury: A review of the evidence. *Clinical Psychology Review, 27*(2), 226-239.

Klonsky, E. D., & Muehlenkamp, J. J. (2007). Self-injury: A research review for the practitioner. *Journal of Clinical Psychology: In Session, 63*(11), 1045-1056.

Peterson, J., Freedenthal, S., Sheldon, C., & Andersen, R. (2008). Nonsuicidal self injury in adolescents. *Psychiatry, 5*(11), 20-26.

Shanker, S. (2016). *Self-reg: How to help your child (and you) break the stress cycle and successfully engage with life.* Toronto, ON: Penguin Random House.

Sutton, J. (2007). *Healing the hurt within: Understand self-injury and self-harm, and heal the emotional wounds* (3rd ed.). Begbroke, UK: How To Books.

Victor, S. E., Glenn, C. R., & Klonsky, E. D. (2012). Is non-suicidal self-injury an "addiction"? A comparison of craving in substance use and non-suicidal self-injury. *Psychiatry Research, 197*(1/2), 73-77.

CHAPTER SIX

SUICIDALITY

By Tricia Klassen

THERE IS A GREAT DEAL OF FOCUS IN THE CURRENT LITERATURE ON prevention, intervention, and postvention responses to suicide. But counsellors who work with individuals past the initial intervention stage are often left wondering which theoretical framework is most effective in addressing suicidality, resulting in a lack of confidence and feelings of professional vulnerability. Additionally, concern about suicide risk can distract helpers from focusing on therapeutic change and leave them stuck at the risk-assessment stage. Increasingly, frameworks focusing on resilience building as a buffer to suicide are informing clinical practice.

Suicide intervention tends to include three stages, which do not necessarily occur in a linear fashion. Helpers will first attend to immediate stabilization and safety and then undergo an in-depth risk assessment. If the individual is able to commit to living and to accept therapeutic support, ongoing management and active problem solving of contributing factors may be provided. In this third stage, helpers can feel the least prepared and may lack therapeutic direction. Due to concerns about safety, an emphasis on hospitalization and medication has traditionally been seen as most responsive. Until recently, the medical model has taken precedence in providing help to individuals who express suicidal ideation and behaviours. However, it is vital that helpers approach support of individuals at risk for suicide with a holistic and goal-oriented lens in order to assist with longer-term change.

Various clinical frameworks have been outlined in the literature that can be effective, but a strengths- and resilience-based approach that focuses on health and wellness can have the most enduring impact (Johnson, Wood, Gooding, Taylor, & Tarrier, 2011). This framework focuses on identifying existing areas of resilience and protective factors within individuals and their support systems. An emphasis is given to the development of new skills and resources to increase resilience and mitigate risk for suicide.

Resilience refers to an individual's ability to overcome adversity by relying on both one's internal and external resources. It isn't merely a quality someone is born with, but rather a quality that can be fostered. Resilience can be nurtured in many ways, however, the best way to approach it as a helper is to first recognize positive capacities that already exist. One of the best ways to help prevent suicide is to help foster resiliency in individuals, communities, and families.

SARAH

Sarah, age 15, was referred to me after she was seen by the local mobile crisis service due to suicidal ideation. Her mother had called the crisis line after the school guidance counsellor contacted her to let her know that Sarah had dropped a class and shared that Sarah said she "can't take it anymore, and what's the point of living anyway." Sarah had admitted to the crisis team that she has been having suicidal thoughts increasingly over the past year, due to pressures to excel in school and in her sports teams.

When I meet with Sarah, she shares that, despite typically high grades, she never feels her performance is good enough. She also shares that her parents have been unsupportive of her recent disclosure that she is a lesbian. Sarah has a history of anxiety and has been on an antidepressant for about a year. She has recently begun to lose weight, she is getting lower grades than usual, and she has demonstrated low energy on the basketball court. Sarah shares feelings of inadequacy and hopelessness. Although she is very hesitant to talk to a counsellor, she has agreed to attend sessions and has shared that she still has some will to live.

NELSON

At the age of 65, Nelson is recently widowed and is living alone. He retired two years ago from a federal government office job. At a recent appointment with his family doctor, Nelson shared that he is having increased difficulties sleeping and is feeling lonely and disinterested in activities that he once enjoyed. Upon further discussion with his doctor, he admitted that he has a gun at home that he has started to consider using to end his life. Nelson agreed to see me upon the recommendation of his doctor.

Nelson has some contact with an adoptive brother he grew up with after living his first few years of life in various foster homes. Although Nelson is uncertain of what happened in his early years in foster care, he has been told that there was violence and neglect in these homes. He has limited knowledge of his Indigenous culture and of the community that he was disconnected from so many years ago. Nelson shares that his wife, his work, and his role as a father have fulfilled him over the years. Nelson's children are both married and now live in different provinces. Nelson is embarrassed by his suicidal thoughts and always believes he is able to problem solve and work through whatever life throws at him.

Threads of resilience shine through for both Sarah and Nelson, despite the challenges and crisis-oriented states that they find themselves in. Sarah is a capable young woman who was able to find strength to go speak to her guidance counsellor about her struggles. Although Sarah felt a lack of support from her family, her mother immediately contacted a crisis service for help, which shows a commitment to helping Sarah. Nelson finds fulfilment through his work and his family and is accustomed to working out his problems on his own. In addition to these apparent strengths, both individuals are demonstrating a willingness to get support. The act of reaching out is a sign of resilience.

When individuals allow us to enter their worlds in a helper capacity, even briefly, one of the most important ways we can validate them is by acknowledging their willingness to show up. Questions like "What does it say about you that you are here today?" or "What do you believe it is that has led you to be willing to come talk with me?" can both pull out areas of strength and increase the working alliance. When people are willing to talk and work through their thoughts and emotions, it is a strong indication that their suicidality is more about managing deep emotional pain than the actual desire to end their life. By opening themselves up to the helping relationship, individuals show that they already have so much resilience to work with.

Working from a strength-based perspective requires that we acknowledge signs of strengths and capabilities, as well as build upon areas of resilience in the individual and their support system. Michael Ungar (2008, 2012) defines resilience as including both individual and collective capacities to identify psychological, social, cultural, and physical resources that promote well-being. Ungar emphasizes the collaboration between the individual and their "family, community and culture to provide these health resources and experiences in culturally meaningful ways." (Ungar, 2008, p. 225).

Our role becomes about approaching capacity holistically and working with the individual, and, if possible, their support system, to access internal and external resources (Ungar, 2012).

INSIGHTS AND GUIDING PRINCIPLES FOR COUNSELLING

Over the years, I have come to recognize that there are various elements I can focus on in the therapeutic setting that highlight and promote resilience in the individuals I work with:

1) **Build a secure circle of support**
    Build upon and access reliable support that facilitates hope and

connection, with an emphasis on the therapeutic alliance between yourself and your client.

2) **Highlight themes of purpose and meaning**
   Cultivate a sense of hope and intentionality through a focus on protective factors, reasons for living, and moving beyond safety to wellness.

3) **Strengthen emotional intelligence**
   Assist clients to increase their ability to perceive, appraise, and express emotions accurately and appropriately. Additionally, help build stronger emotion regulation skills to promote both emotional and intellectual growth.

4) **Develop skills**
   Strengthen clients' abilities to change their situation, express their needs, and improve their relationships with problem solving, communication, and conflict resolution skills.

An emphasis on these four elements is supported by Klonsky and May (2015), who have found that suicide risk can be decreased by focusing on improving connectedness (circles of support), increasing hope (strengthen a sense of meaning), reducing pain (strengthening emotional intelligence), and increasing capacity (building on healthy coping strategies).

1) BUILD A SECURE CIRCLE OF SUPPORT

Social connectedness has been found to be a key protective factor in reducing risk for suicide. This can happen through family connection, support, and cohesion, healthy relationships with other peers and adults, and a sense of belonging in one's school, work, and community. Research has found a connection between resilience and a strong social network. The relational stance between helpers and individuals they support can have a much greater impact on positive outcomes than any other variable. Segal, Egley, Watson, and Goldfinger (1995) found that clients who were being assessed for suicidal risk in a hospital emergency room were more likely to avoid hospitalization and attend follow-up appointments when hospital staff used an interpersonally sensitive approach.

Our early relationships with caregivers largely determine the degree of resilience we carry with us throughout our lives. Attachment theory highlights the role of early caregivers as providing an internal working model for later relationship patterns. When caregivers are nurturing, calm, and attuned to children, they promote the development of organized and regulated brains where one can trust others and themselves. Our nervous systems are built for this connection, as humans access their social engagement systems by reaching out to connect with others as a way to cope with stress.

When we don't have caregivers who meet these needs for protection and nurturing, we must rely on our own built-in survival patterns in our sympathetic nervous system. This system signals danger, prompting the mobilization of our fight, flight, or freeze response. This mobilization can lead to stress and over-activation of the nervous system on an ongoing basis. Individuals who experience suicidality tend to have a very high tolerance for physical trauma and physical pain through the experience of dissociation and disconnection and a very low tolerance for emotional pain (Orbach, 1994).

Thus, childhood abuse or developmental trauma is one potential risk factor for suicidality. Research demonstrates that both physical and sexual abuse are highly correlated with suicidality. We know that many individuals who experience suicidal thoughts have not experienced trauma or abuse, however, the experience of disconnection is still often present.

Nelson has very little memory of early patterns in his relationships with caregivers. However, he is able to describe how difficult it was to initially develop trust in the parents that eventually adopted him. Over time, Nelson was able to feel safe with his adoptive family, an experience that he has had with few others. When Nelson met his wife, Cecile, he was able to develop the same trusting relationship with her that his adoptive family had built with him. However, when Nelson lost Cecile very rapidly to cancer, he experienced an intense degree of panic and feelings of loss of control, which very quickly brought him to believe that suicide was the only way out.

In the cases of Nelson and Sarah, the biosocial model can help explain the potential impact of one's environment on the development of suicidal tendencies. This model explores the vulnerability of individuals who are biologically predisposed to high sensitivity and emotionality and who experience their environment as invalidating. Invalidating families tend to expect behaviours beyond the child's capabilities and punish negative behaviours rather than helping the child learn new behaviours (Brown, 2006).

Although Sarah was raised in a home where her parents showed her love and had her best interests in mind, she experiences her parents as invalidating and rejecting of her when she does not perform at the level that they expect from her. Sarah has learned from a young age that her emotions are too big and her reactions too strong. She has learned over time to keep her thoughts and feelings to herself and at the same time internalizes her parents' expectations as her own.

COUNSELLING STRATEGIES

The most important focus of our work with individuals who experience suicidality becomes the development of a strong therapeutic alliance, as well as the strengthening of their informal support system, which will sometimes include family members.

1) Ensure that the clinical relationship becomes central to the counselling plan

> Clearly define your role so your client knows what to expect and find out what your client's hopes, goals, and preferences are for the therapeutic relationship and counselling plan. The cultivation of trust and mutual respect is paramount from the first meeting onward, and will only occur if the individual feels a connection with you.

> Validate the individual's thoughts and feelings, even related to suicide. When individuals with suicidal ideation feel heard and experience some normalization of these kinds of thoughts, they

are often able to move out of a place of shame, and their suicidal thoughts may become less intense. Talking about suicidality can decrease stigma, encourage expression, and increase their perception of themselves as strong and even as a potential support or advocate for others who are having similar struggles.

➤ Recognize that withdrawal from counselling is common for individuals who feel an ongoing sense of hopelessness, who are emotionally exhausted, and who fear experiencing yet another relationship as rejecting and painful. Normalize the experience of ambivalence (both to stay alive and to attend counselling) and ensure that a risk assessment and safety plan is an ongoing priority. *See page 295 in the Resources section for an assessment checklist.*

2) Explore past and current family dynamics and strengthen family supports when possible

➤ Explore their attachment history and interpersonal relationship patterns and look for opportunities to do reparative work. You may find that a visual aid like a genogram or structural map, which shows people and relationship qualities (strong, distant, conflictual, and so on), is helpful in identifying the relationship dynamics between family members.

➤ Recognize that the individual's family may be experiencing a variety of emotions related to their family member's suicidality, including shock, devastation, fear, disbelief, guilt, or indifference. Part of your role may be to provide support and education about suicide, as well as to assist in establishing healthy interaction patterns. Family and parental reactions to the issue of suicide can either increase stigma or provide needed relief and openness for the client.

3) Look for opportunities to expand and strengthen your client's larger social support system

➤ Assess existing formal and informal supports by creating a map together that includes the people involved and visually depicts their strengths or strains using symbols or colours that resonate for your client. An exploration of various levels of relationships (such as acquaintances, friends, relatives, or co-workers) can help identify gaps but can also emphasize already existing supports, both utilized and under-utilized.

➤ Actively work with the individual to strengthen their sense of belonging and connection to potential and existing supports. This may include inviting supports to a case conference, accompanying them to their first visit to a potential resource, researching possible support services, and assisting them to strengthen and better sustain existing relationships. Focus on resources that highlight the individual's interests, strengths, and values and that increase hope and meaning.

➤ Ensure that you work collaboratively with other support services. A combination of informal, formal, and crisis and emergency services should be identified and clearly defined for the client in a safety and wellness plan where the individual knows who they will contact under which circumstances. *See page 297 in the Resources section for a safety and wellness plan.*

CASE APPLICATION

SARAH

Sarah is initially very guarded, as she is accustomed to having her thoughts and feelings disregarded. In the past, her parents viewed her as dramatic and attention seeking when she shared strong emotions. Sarah is not open to having her parents attend her sessions initially, so the reparative work is largely done through the client-counsellor relationship, with a focus on counsellor attunement and validation. Much of our initial session is used to develop trust and allow Sarah to define what is important for her to focus on and what she would like to gain from our time together.

As Sarah becomes more comfortable in sessions, I approach her relationship with her parents with increasing interest, with the hope that Sarah will become more curious and consider different perspectives and possibilities. Circular questions assist this process.

[Sarah] "I went into my room because I had started to yell and my mom was getting frustrated with me. I felt so alone, but I couldn't tell her how I was really feeling."

[Counsellor] "What do you think your mother would have said to you in that moment if she had recognized what you needed from her?"

[Sarah] "I don't know. She usually gets frustrated when I get upset."

[Counsellor] "What does you being upset usually look like to others?"

[Sarah] "Umm ... I yell, so I guess maybe angry?"

[Counsellor] "And what are you actually feeling? Is it anger?"

[Sarah] "Well, no. I usually yell when I feel rejected or insecure. I guess that's how I felt that day."

[Counsellor] "Have there been times when you told your mom you felt rejected or insecure?"

[Sarah] "I guess that's what I told them when I shared I'm gay."

[Counsellor] "How did your mom respond to you that day?"

[Sarah] "She told me that she didn't want me to feel rejected or left out."

[Counsellor] "What does that tell you?"

[Sarah] "I guess that she might be really worried about me being lonely."

Through discussions like these, Sarah begins to become curious about whether her parents may be able to approach her differently, and she agrees to consider inviting them to a session. In the meantime, we explore other support options to determine what her circle really looks like.

[Sarah] "My biggest concern is that I won't be accepted at school, and others will think I'm not the person they thought I was."

[Counsellor] "Is there someone in particular that you are concerned will feel this way?"

[Sarah] "Well, I guess my best friend Josie."

[Counsellor] "What gives you the impression that she may not accept you anymore?"

[Sarah] "She can be hard on me. She was upset when I didn't show up for basketball a few weeks ago."

[Counsellor] "Why do you think she was upset?"

[Sarah] "I think she was disappointed in me. She always says she thinks I am so good at everything."

[Counsellor] "So how do her hopes for you fit with how she may react if you tell her you are gay?"

[Sarah] "I don't know. Maybe she would be disappointed."

[Counsellor] "What kinds of things tend to lead her to be disappointed in you? If you think about some of these situations?"

[Sarah] "Well, probably when I don't try hard enough."

[Counsellor] "What do you think that says about how Josie feels about you?"

[Sarah] "That she cares about me and wants me to be happy."

Sarah and I explore other potential supports, including several peers, her guidance counsellor, and her aunt. Sarah and her parents provide consent for me to talk with her guidance counsellor, who invites Sarah to attend a wellness group she is starting up and helps get Sarah connected to the Gay-Straight Alliance group in her school.

I am able to emphasize areas of strength and resilience at each session, and I notice that she continues to attend sessions, is building trust with several adults in her life, has good relationships with peers, and is naturally gifted and interested in most of her academic and sport activities.

NELSON

Despite Nelson's hesitation to seek support and his tendency to work out his problems on his own, he is clearly committed to attending sessions as he promised his doctor he would. Nelson is independent but pragmatic and focuses on keeping his word. His goal is to not need support and to be able to return to managing on his own. Our work together focuses largely on examining Nelson's relationship history and exploring the value of independence, but also the potential benefits of inter-connectivity, feelings of belonging, and trust.

[Nelson] "I don't know what's wrong with me. I know how to be independent, so it makes me feel weak that I feel this way."

[Counsellor] "Nelson, what are you feeling? Tell me more about that."

[Nelson] "I don't really know how to explain it. It's like I don't matter anymore."

[Counsellor] "When you felt like you mattered, what was that like?"

[Nelson] "Like I was there for someone else, and they were there for me. And that I had skills that I could use."

Nelson recognizes that he is grieving the loss of his attachment figures (his wife and his adoptive parents), as well as the loss of his sense of identity as a productive income earner. Nelson struggles to admit that he feels lonely and isolated and is not accustomed to reaching out to his brother or his children.

As we work together and Nelson learns about the neurobiological role that his early attachment experiences play, he is able to better understand where his feelings of panic and anxiety come from, and to understand that these physiological responses are greatly contributing to his thoughts of suicide.

[Nelson] "Whenever I think of reaching out to friends or my kids, I get all uncomfortable."

[Counsellor] "What does that discomfort feel like?"

[Nelson] "It sounds weird but kind of nervous."

[Counsellor] "Have you always felt that way around others?"

[Nelson] "Never Cecile. But yeah, I guess that's how I felt around a lot of people."

[Counsellor] "When is the earliest you recall feeling that way?"

[Nelson] "Right from when I was young. I felt that way around my (adoptive) dad the most, I think."

[Counsellor] "Any idea why you felt that way around him?"

[Nelson] "He had pretty high expectations, I guess. I wasn't sure what to expect from him."

[Counsellor] "How may your experience with your dad have impacted the way you feel around others?"

[Nelson] "Well, maybe I feel worried that I won't measure up to others. I didn't think about it that way – I just noticed that I had nervous feelings."

Through these discussions, Nelson is able to better understand where his feelings of panic and anxiety come from and to understand that these physiological responses are greatly contributing to his thoughts of suicide. Nelson is starting to become more open to strengthening his relationship with his brother and reaching out to his children. He also is beginning to consider the potential value of some kind of reconnection to his biological culture and community. I acknowledge his ability to problem solve and manage independently as a sign of resilience and simultaneously a more balanced life that incorporates connection and meaning.

2) HIGHLIGHT THEMES OF PURPOSE AND MEANING

Individuals who consider suicide tend to experience a lack of hope that often comes from the inability to find a larger sense of purpose, intentionality, and meaning in their lives. Many of the risk factors for suicide are related to a sense of individual and environmental discouragement and hopelessness. Individuals are more at risk for suicidality when they feel they do not have anything to offer, do not have a strong sense of personal identity, are not engaged in meaningful activity, and are not connected to meaningful values, belief systems, or a sense of cultural identity. Nelson became at risk for suicide when his roles as a husband and employee were taken away from him, stripping him of his sense of personal identity and of a general sense of utility and purpose. Additionally, he always struggled to make sense of his cultural identity, as he had limited exposure to his biological roots throughout his life.

Similarly, many family and community risk factors may exist that stem from a sense of emptiness and discouragement, including a family history of suicide, abuse, and substance use, disconnection from culture and spirituality, community epidemics of suicide, community marginalization, and lack of control over resources.

In addition to risk factors, protective factors tend to buffer individuals from suicidal thoughts and behaviours. Protective factors can be defined as characteristics that tend to mitigate or eliminate risk and increase health and well-being. Many protective factors include themes of self-pride and achievement, and a connection to a purpose beyond themselves. Individuals are less likely to view suicide as an option if they have a strong sense of identity, perform well in school and work, are socially integrated in their communities, have responsibilities to others or a cause, have cultural and spiritual connections, love to learn, and have a sense of self-worth and confidence.

Sarah appeared to be successful and to have every reason to be confident and proud, due to her school and sports achievements. However, Sarah was not engaged in activities or causes that had personal meaning and value to her. She was not yet comfortable with her sexual orientation and had no ties to peers within the LGBT2SQ+ community. Her school and sports activities held limited meaning for her, as there was no sense of contribution to the larger community or to social and environmental causes that were important to her. She was inundated with pressures to perform in academics and sports and had no energy or space to explore areas of meaning and interest.

COUNSELLING STRATEGIES

Building resilience in individuals who experience suicidal thoughts and behaviours should include exploring existing themes of meaning and assisting individuals to strengthen and develop interests and activities that increase a sense of meaning in their lives.

1) Explore both risk factors and protective factors

    ➤ Although we tend to be good at exploring risk factors, it is just as important to assess and emphasize protective factors that are present or can be strengthened for individuals. Protective factors can include positive relationships and supports, interests, skills and areas of success, cultural and spiritual beliefs and values, future hopes and goals, and a sense of belonging and connection. Everyone has at least some protective factors present in their lives, and it's our job to help explore and highlight them.

    ➤ One of the ways we can help make protective factors meaningful for individuals is to explore their identified reasons for living. Protective factors are the more objective aspects of an individual's situation, where reasons for living demonstrate what is particularly meaningful to the individual. This is not only a key component of the crisis suicide intervention stage, but also must be referred to and built upon throughout the therapeutic process. Wenzel and Jager-Hyman (2012) recommend the construction of a "hope kit" (p. 127) that holds items and mementos that remind the individual of their reasons to live, as those reasons may not be as accessible to individuals when they are in the midst of experiencing suicidal thoughts.

2) Help strengthen the individual's sense of personal identity

➤ Spending time exploring potential reasons to live is a natural way to start building upon various aspects of personal identity. Someone who has suicidal thoughts, however, tends to be focused on their pain, sense of hopelessness, and failures or deficits. Our role is to ask questions that evoke an increased sense of purpose and positive sense of self. Questions like "What does your love of your cat say about who you are as a person?" and "What would you like people to know about your decision to become a vegetarian?" lead individuals to make a link between their thoughts and interests and their larger sense of identity, purpose, and potential role in their community.

➤ Assist the individual to find ways to invoke a greater sense of meaning in their lives in a practical way. Their pursuit of a greater sense of meaning and purpose lends itself not only to a stronger sense of self-identity but also to being more involved in meaningful activities and possessing a sense of utility, responsibility, and contribution. For example, individuals who take action to become involved in social causes that help others tend to gain an increased sense of meaning from life. This may include helping a neighbour, volunteering at an animal shelter, helping at a soup kitchen, or becoming involved in causes through one's community centre or faith community.

CASE APPLICATION

SARAH

It is easy to get to know Sarah as she develops more trust in me, and she is relieved to have someone to talk to who is interested in her as a person. Sarah has regular thoughts of suicide, however, she becomes future-oriented as soon as she has the opportunity to express herself. Sarah readily identifies reasons she thinks about dying, including the ongoing pressure she feels to perform and her parents' lack of validation and acceptance of her interests and sexual orientation. Once it is clear that I understand how impactful these experiences are for her, she is able to share various reasons for living, which include her dog and cat, her role as a support to her friends, her teammates' reliance on her on the basketball court, and her interest in art. It is clear that there are lots of protective factors at play, however, these factors need to be strengthened, so that she is able to gain a larger sense of meaning in her life.

Through open and circular questioning, I am able to help Sarah see that she is a capable and compassionate person who has so much to give, but who also deserves to surround herself with support and acceptance. She schedules a meeting with her guidance counsellor and parents to review her second semester schedule so she can take an art class, she starts to attend meetings of the Gay-Straight Alliance group, and she starts to talk to her friends about her own struggles, rather than merely being the friend that everyone comes to for support.

NELSON

Nelson admits to feeling very alone since the loss of his wife, and he says that he considers death because he no longer has a partner or a sense of connection to his family. He also feels useless and as if he is lacking purpose. I explore with Nelson some potential reasons to live.

[Counsellor] "What about your children? How does thinking about your children affect your thoughts about ending your life?"

[Nelson] "Well, of course I should stick around for my children and grandchildren. And my brother ..."

[Counsellor] "Do you have any other family?"

[Nelson] "Not really. But I recently met my biological cousin. He grew up on the same reserve that I was born on."

[Counsellor] "How interesting. What was it like to meet him?"

[Nelson] "I guess it got me thinking about my family and my culture."

[Counsellor] "Has meeting him impacted your thoughts about living or dying at all?"

[Nelson] "I don't know. It has piqued my curiosity ..."

Nelson cares about his family members, but he has been raised to value independence and solve his own problems, and he feels uncomfortable reaching out to his children. We draw upon his perceived role as a father to help him reach out, exploring what role he could play in his family's lives to support them, and how that might provide him with a sense of meaning.

[Counsellor] "So what do you think makes you the most uncomfortable about reaching out to your children for support?"

[Nelson] "How could I do that? It's my job to take care of them."

[Counsellor] "It sounds like you take that responsibility very seriously. How do you tend to show them that you take care of them?"

[Nelson] "Well, maybe that is where I have failed in the last few years. Neither live in the province anymore, so I don't really offer them much of anything anymore."

[Counsellor] "It sounds difficult to help out when they live so far away. Do you still talk?"

[Nelson] "They don't call like they used to. Since Cecile died ... she was always the one who talked on the phone."

[Counsellor] "What would it be like to start to call them yourself?"

[Nelson] "I'm not sure what to talk about on the phone."

[Counsellor] "What are you most comfortable talking about?"

[Nelson] "Well, I'm curious if Chris ever figured out how to fix that tiller …"

When Nelson starts communicating more with his two children and asking about their lives, he discovers that his daughter and her husband need a few home renovations but don't have the money or time to get them done. He tells his daughter that she shouldn't pay to have the work done when he can do it, and he schedules a trip to visit them for three weeks. He also agrees to meet up with his biological cousin and is considering going to some traditional Indigenous ceremonies that he has been invited to attend. He figures it can't hurt to learn more about his biological culture and to find out if he connects to any part of it.

3) STRENGTHEN EMOTIONAL INTELLIGENCE

Emotional intelligence has been defined as a key protective factor against suicidal ideation and behaviour. This concept refers to the ability to understand, appraise, and express emotions accurately and appropriately, to use emotions to guide one's thinking, to use emotional knowledge effectively, and to regulate emotions to promote both emotional and intellectual growth. Emotional intelligence has been described as an element of resilience, as those who can understand and express their needs tend to have an internal locus of control and the capacity to have their needs met.

Individuals who experience thoughts of suicide tend to have a very difficult relationship with their emotions. When we revisit the concepts of attachment theory and biosocial theory, we recall that early experiences with caregivers teach individuals whether or not to both trust and express their emotions. From this perspective, suicidality can be seen as a skills deficit issue, as individuals need to learn skills to label, tolerate, and regulate emotions that were not learned in childhood.

Sarah displays the general ability to communicate her thoughts and feelings with adults who provide validation, however, she is not able to express her emotions very readily to her parents or her peers. Sarah has some ability to express herself, but she really struggles with managing and coping with strong emotions.

Nelson, on the other hand, has a very limited relationship with his emotions. It does not occur to him to consider his feelings, as he tends to approach situations from a cognitive and rational perspective. So, although Nelson is having thoughts of suicide, he is unable to understand and express the emotions that have contributed to these thoughts.

Dialectical behavioural therapy (DBT) is a well-researched form of cognitive behavioural therapy that can be effective in developing emotional intelligence, or emotional regulation, for individuals with suicidality (McMain, Korman, & Dimeff, 2001). Although DBT in its entirety is an intense and multifaceted treatment model that will neither be available to nor appropriate for all individuals who experience thoughts of suicide, the behavioural skills emphasized by this model include an emphasis on emotional experiencing.

COUNSELLING STRATEGIES

In order to promote the development of greater emotional intelligence, we can focus on assisting individuals to identify, tolerate, and regulate their emotions more effectively. This can be done through an emphasis on behavioural skills like emotional regulation, distress tolerance, and mindfulness strategies.

1) Model regulated states as a helper with your clients and their families, if possible

   ➤ Notice your own body and whether you are in a calm state. Speak at a moderate pace, relax your body, breathe slowly, and keep your environment quiet and peaceful.

➤ Model a healthy relationship with emotions. Find opportunities to talk about different emotions, share your own emotions as appropriate, and provide healthy messages about emotions, including all emotions being acceptable to feel and share.

2) Help clients learn to manage their emotions when they feel suicidal through the development of emotional regulation strategies

➤ Teach your clients that suicidality is largely a state of physiological over-arousal and that their nervous system sends out false alarms that signal danger when there is none. Often suicidal thoughts start when the body becomes activated due to early negative experiences and predispositions to anxiety and depression.

➤ Emphasize that suicidality often occurs due to difficulty with experiencing various levels of emotion. When individuals are used to being stuck in intense emotions, it can be difficult not to over-respond to typically less upsetting types of situations. Do scaling exercises on various levels of emotions (such as annoyance, irritattion, disappointment, feeling upset, anger, or rage) and then practice various case scenarios that tend to elicit certain levels of response. For example, a friend needing to cancel plans tends to be a disappointing experience rather than an experience that leads to anger.

➤ Various emotional regulation exercises can be used, such as engaging in opposite actions to one's typical response. For example, if your client identifies that they tend to isolate themselves when they are sad, encourage them to reach out to a support instead.

3) Help clients learn to ride the wave of emotions when they feel suicidal through the development of distress tolerance and mindfulness

➤ Help individuals understand the value in connecting with their five senses to learn to self–soothe. An example of using one's hearing, smell, and tactile senses may be attending a yoga class where

one is soothed by gentle music, essential oils, and the comforting positioning of their body.

➤ Explore distraction techniques that can assist your clients to engage in activities until their intense emotions subside. This may include concentrating on enjoyable activities, invoking a competing emotion, or using thought-stopping techniques.

➤ Help individuals learn to manage problems through developing an understanding of *radical acceptance.*[1] An individual who lost their job can be encouraged to move from "that's not fair" to "it's frustrating, and I don't agree with their decision, but I accept that I must now move forward."

➤ Incorporate breathing exercises or other body-regulating activities into your work to teach clients how to regulate their bodies, as well as mindfulness exercises that promote stillness and silence, presence in the moment, self-acceptance, compassion, and non-judgment.

CASE APPLICATION

SARAH

Sarah greatly benefits from understanding how her early experiences of feeling invalidated have resulted in her tendency to ignore and hold in emotions. Through these discussions, she is also able to shift her perception somewhat from believing that her parents do not care about her feelings to an understanding that her parents care very deeply but struggle with emotional expression.

Sarah begins to learn how her body experiences emotion, and she is able to learn how to notice signs of stress and then use various strategies to move into more regulated states.

[Sarah] "Everything just feels, like, mad all the time."

---

1. Radical acceptance is the total acceptance of one's situation, regardless of other feelings or thoughts about it. This state can assist to decrease one's suffering as one experiences greater inner peace.

[Counsellor] "Are you mad all the time?"

[Sarah] "No! I'm usually just insecure. I don't know why I act like I'm mad when I feel that way."

[Counsellor] "What does your body feel like when you feel insecure? Where do you notice changes in body sensations?"

[Sarah] "Um, probably in my muscles. My arms feel tight. And in my head – I feel kind of panicked and I can't even think. I feel like my head is going to explode."

[Counsellor] "That sounds like anyone's body would feel when they are stressed or overwhelmed. Have you heard of the fight or flight system?"

[Sarah] "Yeah, I think I heard of that in science. What does that have to do with being insecure?"

[Counsellor] "Well, let's figure out if it does. What is happening for you when you are insecure? Let's think of an example."

[Sarah] "Uh, I notice the way someone is acting and think they don't like me anymore."

[Counsellor] "Okay, when you think someone doesn't like you anymore, how does that affect your thoughts and feelings?"

[Sarah] "I guess I start to panic that I won't have friends anymore and that I'll be alone, and that's when I feel my arms and fists get all tight."

[Counsellor] "So your body is responding to your thoughts. Your body is telling you that there is a threat, so your nervous system is moving out of its window of tolerance and into a fight or flight response. Does that sound like what might be happening?"

[Sarah] "Yes, I think so. Maybe my yelling is my fighting and my going into my room is my flight?"

[Counsellor] "Sounds like it! So, your body needs help moving out of the fight or flight response and moving back into a state of calm. How do you think you could become calm again when you are so activated?"

[Sarah] "Well, my basketball coach taught us how to do some breathing exercises when we're frustrated on the court. Maybe that would help."

Sarah is also able to learn how to level her emotions more appropriately, becoming aware that even though her body tends to give her signals of threat, often her initial intense reactions are not appropriate to the situation.

[Sarah] "I felt so embarrassed! I don't think I could face her again."

[Counsellor] "On a scale of zero to 10, zero being totally fine and 10 being completely humiliated, how did you feel when you tripped in the hall?"

[Sarah] "At least nine. It was terrible!"

[Counsellor] "So, tripping in the hall was almost the most humiliated you could ever be? Could there be anything worse?"

[Sarah] "Ha, well, I guess I could do a lot of embarrassing things."

[Counsellor] "Okay, let's figure this out. Let's think of a word that means the most embarrassed level of the emotion and one that means just slightly embarrassed. Let's make a scale to figure out those different levels."

[Sarah] "Alright. Well, slightly embarrassed could be feeling silly, and I like your word for very embarrassed – humiliated."

[Counsellor] "Okay, now let's fill in some levels in between, going from silly to humiliated."

[Sarah] "Um, okay. Well, after silly would be sheepish, and then ... "

We continue until the scale is filled in.

[Counsellor] "Great. Now that we have six levels of embarrassed, let's think about which situations may fit with these different levels of emotions. You said tripping in the hall is a nine and is humiliating. Do you still want to put that example at the highest level?"

[Sarah] "Well, now that I see the scale, I would probably put it somewhere in the middle."

Sarah notices that when she begins to express her emotions rather than hold them in, they don't become so intense. She also says she has been having fewer suicidal thoughts.

NELSON

Nelson has a limited emotional vocabulary. He understands that he feels sad and lonely and lacks purpose, however, he does not understand fully that his suicidality is based on deep emotional pain. Much of our sessions focus on exploring confusing emotions and putting them into a context. Over time, he is able to identify that he carries a lot of resentment towards his adoptive family for not understanding the desire to be connected to his culture of origin, and so he learned to ignore his own needs and focus on what others expected. Nelson starts to work through some of these emotions, connects to the concept of radical acceptance and mindfulness, and starts to use various mindfulness and visualization exercises when he begins to feel overwhelmed.

4) DEVELOP SKILLS

One of the protective factors in buffering against suicidal risk is a strong sense of competence and optimism in coping with life problems. Most individuals can learn problem solving, communication, and conflict resolution skills if given the opportunity. Suicide tends to be about escaping pain rather than about dying. Individuals who express suicidal thoughts often can't see any way out, as they don't know how to express their needs, they can't figure out how to change their situations, or they don't know how to improve or mend their relationships. A large part of the supporting experience must be focused on addressing areas where individuals are stuck and helping them believe that there is a way out.

An initial impression of Sarah was that she had a lot of skills as well as resources in her life. However, it became apparent that she struggled with the problem-solving skills that were needed to both process her experiences and work through challenges. As well, she didn't know how to share her struggles with her parents and teachers.

A cognitive behavioural model of suicide suggests that individuals consider suicide when they see no solutions to problems that create pain. It is critical for helpers to focus on identifying solutions to problems that clients perceive as unsolvable, reducing negative thought patterns and cognitive distortions, improving problem solving skills, and assisting to reduce perceived emotional pain (Matthews, 2013). Assertive communication and conflict resolution skills are part of the problem-solving process.

Nelson prides himself on his ability to solve problems. Yet he has been so accustomed to working out challenges independently that he perceived reaching out to others and expressing his needs as a sign of weakness and incompetency. For a long time, Nelson did not feel a sense of connectedness and believed that in reaching out to others he would impose himself as a burden. Nelson claims that he did not have a genuine desire to die, but rather that his inability to work out how to move forward was prompting his thoughts of suicide. He experienced a significant sense of isolation and lack of meaning in his life. However, he believed that he was unable to change these circumstances.

Using a cognitive behavioural approach, we worked on Nelson's ability to identify negative belief patterns that were rooted in both childhood experiences and his recent loss. Over time, Nelson has developed the belief that he is only of value if he contributes practically and requires nothing from those around him. This has led him to ask nothing of anyone and to ensure that he could always "fix" everything. Recently he has found himself thinking, "I am useless," and "Everyone would be better off if I wasn't here."

COUNSELLING STRATEGIES

A cognitive behavioural model presents skill deficits in individuals who consider suicide as based largely upon cognitive rigidity. Individuals who feel stuck are unable to generate more hopeful solutions than ending their lives. The following ideas can be helpful in supporting clients to learn new skills, identify and challenge cognitive distortions, focus on goal development, and expand their coping strategies.

1) Implement a psychoeducational component into your approach

   ➤ Provide information and normalization of mental health and suicide to the client and, if possible, their family, in order to decrease stigma and promote knowledge.

   ➤ Teach about effective communication skills that may include an emphasis on basic social skills, conflict resolution, and highlighting the difference between passive, assertive, and aggressive communication.

2) Identify the impact of thought patterns on one's emotions and behaviours

   ➤ Identify and map the individual's automatic thoughts that occur before, during, and after suicidal thoughts and/or behaviours. Pay close attention to unhelpful thoughts, assumptions, and core beliefs. An example of this mapping is a chain analysis exercise, which can help individuals assess the chain of events that occur when they struggle with suicidal thoughts and behaviours and then explore alternative solutions and more adaptive responses. *See page 298 in the Resources section for a sample chain analysis and instructions.*

   ➤ Identify underdeveloped skills, such as problem solving, communication, and conflict resolution.

   ➤ Ask the individual to go through the sequence of events of a recent episode of suicidality and assist the individual to replace automatic thoughts and potential behaviours with alternative thoughts and behaviours that highlight skills learned in sessions.

➤ Apply new thinking patterns and skills to potential future scenarios so that the individual has an increased chance of being able to activate more adaptive thought patterns and responses.

3) Develop a goal-oriented approach to increase motivation and problem-solving skills

➤ Assess readiness for change and implement a cost-benefit analysis. In addition to exploring an individual's reasons for living, we must also acknowledge and validate their reasons for wanting to die. This honouring of their current cognitive and emotional state is necessary in order to help the individual start to explore alternative ways of thinking and to recognize the value of making some cognitive shifts.

➤ Utilize a graded exposure technique to assist individuals to start to envision hopes for change. This process involves breaking down a larger goal into smaller, more manageable steps, and then tackling increasingly difficult steps over time.

4) Identify both existing and potential coping strategies

➤ Build coping strategies into a safety plan early in your work together. Often, individuals leave counselling with a commitment of what not to do but do not feel equipped enough with strategies of what to do.

➤ Assist with the development of a coping "tool box" that utilizes a holistic approach to health and wellness (cognitive, physical, emotional, spiritual, and relational strategies). This can include a list of coping strategies, cognitive behavioural practice exercises, and instruction cards that motivate individuals to complete a specific goal ("When I feel overwhelmed, I will …"). Emphasize all the positive coping strategies that are already being used, as the individual may not be able to recognize that they are already coping better than they realize. *See page 293 in the Resources section for instructions to build a coping kit.*

CASE APPLICATION

SARAH

Sarah's mom phoned me several months after Sarah and I had completed some work together to share that Sarah would like to come see me just to let me know how she is doing. Sarah's mom also thanked me for helping Sarah develop more confidence and a stronger sense of identity, which allowed her to start communicating with her parents more openly. Sarah arrives at my office with a relaxed smile and proceeds to tell me about the Pride Week that she was helping organize at school. She shares that she has joined the Gay-Straight Alliance at school as an ally, and is working towards coming out to many of her friends and family by starting to become more open with them in general.

Through our work together, Sarah has been able to identify that her automatic thoughts tend to centre on fear of rejection, not meeting others' expectations, and not being accepted if she comes out as a lesbian. She's starting to understand how those assumptions and limiting thoughts are impacting not only her feelings, but her behaviours as well. Sarah says that she occasionally has fleeting thoughts of suicide, but that she's able to quickly identify the messages she's giving herself, as well as find a more accurate emotion than *suicidal* and then find an appropriate level of emotion for the situation.

NELSON

Nelson comes to see me occasionally, but he is often busy visiting family and taking on casual employment. He has also been getting to know some family and members from the Indigenous community in which he was born. Nelson needed to learn how to reach out to others and how to identify and express his thoughts and needs. He was recently able to share some of his childhood experiences and newfound knowledge about his culture and community with one of his daughters. He noticed that he felt okay visiting his daughter's family without having any projects to work on, and he found a sense of satisfaction from having conversations and getting to know his grandchildren better.

Nelson is practical and finds that building healthy coping strategies into his days is the best way to manage stress, combat negative thought patterns, and avoid returning to a place where suicide becomes an option.

[Counsellor] "So, what would you say are the primary changes you have made in your daily routines?"

[Nelson] "Well, I find that it can still be really difficult to get up in the morning, because I initially feel tired and unmotivated. So I keep practicing those energizing exercises you showed me on my computer, and then I go for a walk. I always tell myself I'll just go down the driveway, but once I get that far, I figure I may as well keep going. Yesterday I walked for an hour!"

[Counsellor] "How does that impact your day?"

[Nelson] "I feel more energy and not so down. I have started to use that time to plan what else I'll do for the rest of the day."

[Counsellor] "And what kinds of things do you tend to plan?"

[Nelson] "I have started doing projects around the house again, and I've started to make sure that I talk to or see at least one person every day. I use those visualization exercises you suggested, too. I have a picture of Cecile in my wallet, and sometimes I'll take it out and think about some of our best memories together. Using my senses, like we talked about. I think I feel the closest to her when I listen to that Louis Armstrong song."

[Counsellor] "Do you still have thoughts about dying at times?"

[Nelson] "I'm not going to lie – sometimes I feel really down still. Especially when I feel lonely. But I have too much responsibility in my life to even think about ending my life. The yard won't mow itself, and my kids are waiting for my next visit. I guess you can say that I feel kind of thankful these days for what I still have."

FINISHING THOUGHTS

The experience of suicidal thoughts and behaviours can be extremely painful and confusing for an individual, and also for their family, friends, and professional helpers. The task of assessing safety and affecting change can feel like a daunting one for counsellors. Assessing risk and planning for safety must always be the priority, however, the majority of individuals who experience suicidal thoughts are seeking relief from pain and are able to move out of crisis when given appropriate support.

In my role as a helper, I have found that a model of support that assumes and builds upon strength and capacity is the most effective approach in helping individuals to move past suicidality. Individuals who experience suicidal ideation will most optimally heal when they feel interpersonal connection, develop increased meaning in their lives, create a healthier relationship with their emotions, and build a stronger sense of optimism through learning how to find solutions to problems.

ABOUT THE AUTHOR

Tricia Klassen, MSW, RSW

Tricia is a Registered Social Worker and holds a master's degree in social work and a bachelor of arts in psychology and developmental studies. She is a trainer with the Crisis & Trauma Resource Institute and is a compassionate therapist who specializes in suicide intervention, self-injury, anxiety and depression, and neurodevelopmental issues. Tricia has a profound belief in the resiliency of the human spirit, particularly in conditions of relational attunement, connection, and support.

REFERENCES

Brown, M. Z. (2006). Linehan's theory of suicidal behavior: Theory, research, and dialectical behavior therapy. In T. E. Ellis (Ed.), *Cognition and suicide: Theory, research, and therapy* (pp. 91-117). Washington, DC: American Psychological Association.

Johnson, J., Wood, A. M., Gooding, P., Taylor, P. J., & Tarrier, N. (2011). Resilience to suicidality: The buffering hypothesis. *Clinical Psychology Review, 31*(4), 563-591.

Klonsky, E. D., & May, A. M. (2015). The three-step theory (3ST): A new theory of suicide rooted in the "ideation-to-action" framework. *International Journal of Cognitive Therapy, 8*(2), 114-129.

Matthews, J. D. (2013). Cognitive behavioural therapy approach for suicidal thinking and behaviours in depression. In R. Woolfolk & L. Allen (Eds.), *Mental disorders – theoretical and empirical perspectives* (pp. 23-43). Retrieved from https://www.intechopen.com/books/mental-disorders-theoretical-and-empirical-perspectives.

McMain, S., Korman, L. M., & Dimeff, L. (2001). Dialectical behavior therapy and the treatment of emotion dysregulation. *Journal of Clinical Psychology, 57*(2), 183-196.

Orbach, I. (1994). Dissociation, physical pain, and suicide: A hypothesis. *Suicide and Life-Threatening Behavior, 24*(1), 68-79.

Segal, S. P., Egley, L., Watson, M. A., & Goldfinger, S. M. (1995). The quality of psychiatric emergency evaluations and patient outcomes in county hospitals. *American Journal of Public Health, 85*(10), 1429-1431.

Ungar, M. (2008). Resilience across cultures. *The British Journal of Social Work, 38*(2), 218-235.

Ungar, M. (Ed.) (2012). *The social ecology of resilience: A handbook of theory and practice.* New York, NY: Springer Science + Business Media.

Wenzel, A., & Jager-Hyman, S. (2012). Cognitive therapy for suicidal patients: Current status. *Behavioral Therapy, 35*(7), 121-130.

CHAPTER SEVEN

SUBSTANCE USE

By Amber McKenzie

SUBSTANCE USE IS A VAST AND MULTIFACETED TOPIC. SUBSTANCE USE problems range from being no problem to the user, to degrees of problematic use, to addiction. Not everyone who uses substances or even abuses them will develop addiction (see Figure 7.1).

Addiction is a profound and complex problem that has a destructive impact on a person's life. When a person is caught in the turmoil of addiction, they have crossed into a pathological pattern of use over time related to several different problems (American Psychiatric Association, 2013). An employee who occasionally misses a deadline or day at work, or a student who binge drinks on the weekends and engages in some high-risk behaviour, may have a mild to moderate substance use problem. On the other hand, someone with a severe substance use disorder or chronic addiction may use substances nearly all day every day, need an increasingly larger amount of them to get the desired effect, and experience withdrawal symptoms if they do not use. In addition, they may struggle to maintain employment, have high absenteeism at work or school, and spend a great deal of their money on substances.

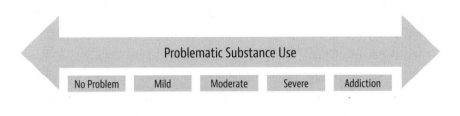

Figure 7.1
Problematic substance use continuum

The word "addiction" is generally associated with compulsive and habitual substance use, in which a person has little choice about if they are going to use or not. Addiction often comes with urges, cravings, and obsessions that drive the person to use substances. People who have more difficulties with problematic substance use and are further down the continuum usually have several failed attempts at quitting or reducing their use.

At the other end of the spectrum is normal use, which also varies from person to person. A person with normal use has a large degree of control over their choice to use substances and could take or leave the substance or stop when they've had enough. These are people that would absolutely be able to stop using or reduce their use if a life circumstance warranted.

The greater the impact of the substance use problem, the more likely the person also has emotional difficulties and may experience feelings of shame, guilt, remorse, anger, sadness, or anxiety. The individual may demonstrate other concerning behaviours, such as no longer spending time with friends, changing the people they spend time with, or experiencing problems in their friendships. The person may spend increasing amounts of time using the substance or need more of the substance to reach the desired level of intoxication.

BEN

Ben was 17 years old when he came to see me. He grew up in a home with his mother and younger brother. His father left when he was three, and they have not seen each other since. He often looks at his father's

Facebook page, where he learned that his father lives in a car and uses methamphetamine, crack cocaine, and alcohol. From a young age, he learned that his mother drank each evening while watching television. She was generally attentive during the day, but once 7 p.m. arrived, she did not want to be disturbed. Ben remembers when his mother would drink only one bottle of wine in the evenings. He recalled that, one time after his mother's ex-boyfriend physically assaulted her, she went to the liquor store and bought a bottle of vodka and drank the entire thing. Over time, his mother began to drink more and more vodka in addition to her evening bottle of wine. By the time he was 13 years old, he was putting his younger brother to bed and then going to check on his mother. Most nights, he covered her with a blanket after she passed out.

Ben has always had a hard time in school. From early on, he struggled to sit and pay attention in class. Teachers were hard on him, and he often felt embarrassed and ashamed. When he got his report cards, he dreaded going home, because he knew his mother was going to scream at him. He felt defeated, because no one seemed to understand that he was trying. One day a substitute teacher made a snide comment about his inability to sit still. Ben felt the tears welling in his eyes and went to the washroom. In the washroom were three other kids he knew sharing a 375ml bottle of vodka. They asked him if he wanted a sip, and he said yes. Ben remembers the glorious sensation of the alcohol running down his throat and the warming in his belly. After a few more sips, he was oblivious to the pain he felt only moments before.

In my office, Ben sits slouched over and speaks slowly. He tells me he feels horrible and has lost most of his friends, because they do not drink the way he does. He explains his frustration with his ex-girlfriend who told him he's an alcoholic and has left him. He is adamant he is not an alcoholic and stated he would never come back to counselling if I called him an alcoholic. He drinks at least 750ml of vodka each day, and often that is not enough. A psychologist once told him that his drinking is probably contributing to his depression and urged him to stop, but he continued to drink despite this. He shared that he would like his life to be better, but is not sure that he wants to stop drinking entirely.

ALISON

Alison is 41 years old. She comes from a loving, intact family system with no history of substance use problems. When she was 19 years old, she started drinking, smoking marijuana, and occasionally using cocaine with friends. She liked to indulge on the weekends. When she was in university, she would drink to excess, and she regularly blacked out while drinking. After graduation, she started a successful business career, and she stopped drinking and using drugs in a problematic fashion.

About six months ago, her son got into a great deal of trouble at school, and then her nephew passed away. One night, she decided to have a beer with her husband. The following evening, she had a bad day and decided to have another beer, and that beer turned into six. The next morning, she was hungover at work, and a colleague offered her some cocaine to help her get through the day, and she immediately knew she was in big trouble. This quickly turned into the pattern of drinking six to 12 beers a night and using cocaine all day at work.

In the last three months, Alison and her husband have been fighting most evenings. He tries to talk to her about her substance use. She explains that she feels so bad when he brings it up that she shuts down and goes to the bedroom without explanation. He often follows her and tries to make up, but she refuses to talk to him. She knows that she is in the wrong but cannot bring herself to face him. To make their problems worse, in the last six months, she has rapidly spent $12,000 dollars of their savings on alcohol and cocaine.

Alison sits slumped over in my office and talks in a sombre voice. She explains she has a problem with alcohol and is afraid of where her drinking has led her in such a short time. She talks about the embarrassment and shame she feels that she cannot seem to solve this problem on her own, and that it is really difficult for her to tell me the truth about what she does with alcohol and cocaine. She said to me, "Do you know how many times I've tried to quit drinking and using cocaine this week? Seven times. Do you know how many times I failed? Seven times. I feel like such a loser. I'm just hopeless, aren't I? I feel broken inside." With tears trickling down her face, she asks, "Do you think you can help me stop drinking and using cocaine?"

INSIGHTS AND GUIDING PRINCIPLES FOR COUNSELLING

Ben and Alison each have different circumstances that may have contributed to their problematic substance use. In addition, they have a unique genetic makeup and mental factors that have likely contributed to their current issues.

Substance use disorders arise from a mix of many interwoven risk factors. Some of the risk factors may include:

➤ having a family history of addiction or substance use problems;

➤ predisposed vulnerability to developmental, cognitive, social, emotional, or behavioural challenges;

➤ exposure to trauma, which could mean the direct witnessing of an event or learning about the traumatic experience of someone one is close to; multigenerational trauma or cultural trauma; childhood neglect, maltreatment, or abuse;

➤ living in a home with some kind of family relational problem, which could take the form of a chaotic and unpredictable environment, domestic violence, or chronic, hostile communication;

➤ other psychological problems, such as anxiety, depression, or post-traumatic stress;

➤ difficulty with regulating challenging emotions like anger, sadness, fear, shame, guilt, or remorse.

The complex blending of risk factors can make understanding the nature of the problem challenging. Recovery from a substance use problem or addiction is often convoluted, as there may be many factors that need to be addressed in addition to use reduction or abstinence.

Substance use problems vary in nature and complexity. As such, counsellors will routinely meet people at different stages of the problem. Some people will be seeing the counsellor for unrelated issues and may be completely oblivious or in denial about their problematic use, whereas others will have a great deal of insight into their problem and a willingness to actively work on change.

Finding agreement on a goal is a grounding mechanism in which both the individual and the counsellor know what they are trying to achieve. To do this, it is important to be clear on the goals of the client and the goals of the counsellor. Goals are often set after understanding the factors that keep the problem in place and the specifics of that individual's substance use problem.

Once goals are established, a number of counselling interventions can be helpful. As people reduce their use or abstain from substances, they usually encounter challenging symptoms. Individuals often need counselling to work through intense urges to use substances, to help manage emotions, and to recognize triggering thoughts.

Working through these challenging related factors can have a powerful impact on recovery. Though setbacks in the counselling process and relapses into old problematic substance use behaviour are often part of treatment, creating a plan to overcome these obstacles facilitates forward momentum. In my experience working with clients like Ben and Alison, I have found the following framework helpful for guiding recovery:

1) **Develop a trusting and respectful relationship**
   This is the foundation for client comfort, active participation, and helpful connection.

2) **Establish the goal**
   Work to identify key issues that will need to be addressed in order to achieve the treatment goal. In addition, the choice between abstinence or harm reduction will need to be addressed.

3) **Manage urges, cravings, thoughts, and emotions**
   Identify the internal triggers that lead to the problematic use.

4) **Manage relapses and re-evaluate goals**
   A challenge in substance use treatment is the high likelihood of relapse. Recognition and management of obstacles allows for imperfect progress towards the goals.

1) DEVELOP A TRUSTING AND RESPECTFUL RELATIONSHIP

Just as it is difficult for Alison to share the nature of her alcohol and cocaine use due to the shame and embarrassment she feels, many individuals may have a hard time being open about their use. Engagement thrives in trusting and respectful relationships (McCrady & Epstein, 2009; Miller & Rollnick, 2013). Creating a welcoming atmosphere leads to a co-operative relationship. This might take the form of simple things, such as smiling, saying hello, and offering the client coffee and water.

People decide within minutes if they are willing to work with their counsellors. They can discern quickly whether they think their counsellor will approach problems in a demanding or collaborative fashion. In most cases, people want to be given options and have a sense that their voice will be heard. Clients want to have some degree of control in the relationship, and if they feel listened to and understood, they are more likely to show trust.

The label that the counsellor assigns to a problem may also impact the counselling relationship. It is important to think critically about using labels such as *alcoholic* or *addict*, which carry a great deal of stigma. Using them can often imply blame or criticism (Sanchez-Craig, 2013; White & Epston, 1990), impact the client's self-esteem, and damage a counselling relationship. Only qualified professionals should make diagnoses of mental disorders, including substance-related disorders.

Some groups, such as Alcoholics Anonymous, assert that it is important for members to identify with the term *alcoholic* (Alcoholics Anonymous, 2001). In contrast, other theories emphasize that having a problem with substance use may be only one of the many stories that makes up a person's identity and need not be integral to who they are.

The counsellor can create a non-judgmental atmosphere by using effective listening skills and communicating understanding and empathy to the client (Miller & Rollnick, 2013). It is critical to understand what is important to the client and what are they looking for. Problematic substance use can become all-encompassing, and it is essential to see who the person is outside of this problem. This can be achieved by using strategic open-ended questions. It's important to stay away from rhetorical questions that often appear open-ended but seem judgmental and directive. Examples of helpful open-ended questions are

➤ "What is your goal?"

➤ "What are you hoping I can help you with?"

➤ "What do you think the best approach for you would be: abstinence or reducing your intake?"

➤ "What do you think your ideal substance use looks like?"

Examples of rhetorical questions that look like open-ended questions but are not include

➤ "Surely, you don't actually think that would help, do you?"

➤ "Don't you think you should _____?"

➤ "A person who really wanted to try to be in recovery would try _____, right?"

Balanced thinking about a client and the nature of their problem includes considering both the nature of the problem and the nature of the person outside of their problem. Balanced views of a client can be communicated by highlighting things the client is doing well or by affirming their efforts to change. Statements you might be able to use to communicate this to your client are

➤ "I can see you are gaining a lot of insight into your problem";

➤ "It must have taken a lot of courage to share that with me";

➤ "This problem has impacted several areas of your life, and this must have been hard on you."

COUNSELLING STRATEGIES

Paving the pathway to engagement in a counselling relationship requires that the client feels seen, respected, and safe. Strategies to help create this foundation include:

1) Developing collaboration and trust

➤ Rather than telling your client they can trust you, focus on creating an environment that creates trust. Also, be mindful of the limitations you have in your ability to keep things confidential. In some cases, professionals have mandatory reasons why trust or confidentiality would be broken.

➤ Consider how to be collaborative with your client. People are likely to respond if they have some degree of control over the process. Think about how you can give the client choices.

➤ Question your use of labels. Think about where the client may be at on the substance use continuum (Figure 7.1) before assigning a label. Be sure to think about if you have the required training to assign a label to a client's problem.

2) Showing empathy and understanding

➤ Carefully reflect your client's thoughts and feelings back to them or paraphrase the content of what they have said. This allows for the client to feel heard and understood.

➤ Strive to understand the problem from the client's point of view.

➤ Become a masterful question-asker. This paves the way to the client sharing the problem from their point of view. Use curious, open questions. Be careful to stay away from rhetorical questions.

3) Getting to know the person outside the problem

➤ In your own mind, actively consider the client in a balanced way. It may be helpful to consider the positive attributes they possess or the places in their life where they are still engaging in health-promoting behaviour. Balance this consideration with the areas of their life negatively impacted by their substance use.

➤ Explain to the client the things you can see that they are doing well and the places you are seeing success in their life. In some cases, this is challenging. Counsellors may need to look at small actions, such as that they have maintained their housing or are brushing their teeth. In cases where the problem is not as pervasive, it is generally easier to look for positives.

➤ Affirm the client's effort, vulnerability, and willingness in the counselling process.

CASE APPLICATION

BEN

Ben sits upright and speaks with a harsh tone as he explains that all the adults in his life blame him for his problems and tell him he needs to grow up. He tells me he isn't sure about counselling and is tired of people telling him what to do, and that he believes counselling will be more of the same.

[Counsellor] "So you think I'm going to tell you what to do. Help me understand, what about coming to counselling is the most troublesome to you?"

[Ben] "It doesn't matter what I do. Everyone thinks it's my fault."

[Counsellor] "It makes you mad that no matter what you do, you get blamed?"

[Ben] "Yes. I want to be able to talk about what is going on in my life without being put down."

[Counsellor] "It must be really hard to try to reach out for help, because you think you're going to be criticized."

[Ben] "Yeah, exactly."

[Counsellor] "I'm glad you told me what usually happens when you reach out."

At the end of the exchange, Ben is leaning slightly forward in his chair. His voice has become softer, and he seems comfortable in our conversation.

ALISON

Alison has come to her first session eager to do anything to that would help her be the mother she wants to be. She knows she must stop drinking and using cocaine. She pleads for help and asks what she should do. She is teary eyed and stares at the floor after explaining that she keeps trying and cannot get clean and sober.

[Counsellor] "I hear that you have repeatedly tried to quit this pattern of use and, despite your best efforts, you can't seem to quit. Is that right?"

[Alison] "Yes, that's right. I just can't seem to stop using."

[Counsellor] "What do you think it is that draws you back to using even after you decide not to?"

[Alison] "That's easy. I love the high the cocaine gives me. Then I'm so sped up when I get home at night, I need the beer to help me wind down and get to sleep."

[Counsellor] "You seem to have some insight into the problematic patterns that keep you stuck. Why don't we work together to help you out of this rut?"

She looks up at me, scrunching her forehead together, and I can see that she is deciding if it is okay to hope for something to be different.

2) ESTABLISH THE GOAL

The far-reaching continuum of substance use problems can make determining a reasonable goal challenging. The more risk factors and circumstances that hold the problematic use in place, the more difficult it can be to set realistic and achievable goals. The negative impact of a substance use problem often weaves itself into several areas in the individual's life. Some of the areas that may have been adversely impacted are physical health, emotional regulation, psychological functioning, family relationships, spiritual connection, social relationships, financial difficulties, and workplace or school effectiveness. It is often helpful to include exploration of multiple aspects of the individual's life when determining the goal (Daley & Marlatt, 2006; McCrady, 2014; McCrady & Epstein, 2009).

Collaboration between counsellor and client is important for goal setting. In most cases, people know what their goals are. In addition, counsellors often have their own goals for the client in mind. It is important to unite the two fronts to keep the collaborative, trusting, and respectful relationship intact.

Initially, setting goals can often be overwhelming and intimidating. In some cases, it is easy to develop long-term goals, while in others it's difficult to plan for down the road. Goals can be changed or modified as circumstances evolve over time, and they must be good matches with both the interventions used and the client's readiness to change. To assist the client with goal setting, the counsellor should consider what is going on in the client's world, both externally and on the inside.

It is useful to generate both long- and short-term goals. Short-term goals allow for incremental successes and building blocks to achieve the final long-term goal. Goals should be specific, realistic, probable, and measurable, so it is clear whether the goal has been achieved. Looking at the full picture of the impact of the client's use on their life may assist to create goals. You may systematically work through different domains of a client's life, such as what their physical recovery, emotional recovery, psychological recovery, social recovery, and spiritual recovery could look like. It is often helpful to map out the full nature of the problem and all of the problem areas before deciding where to focus. Tools such as goal setting worksheets can be helpful in this process.

CASE APPLICATION

With both Ben and Alison, I found it useful to chart their goals in a worksheet. *See page 300 in the Resources section.*

BEN

Ben and I noticed that most of his long- and short-term goals are in the social sphere of his life, and that was where he felt the most need for change. Early in the treatment process, he was unsure about making goals directly related to his substance use. *See page 195.*

ALISON

Alison identified that the greatest pains she felt were around her family. She talked about her joy of being a mother and her feelings of despair. Despite this being a key area, she thought she would be too raw to start there. We worked with what she thought she could manage. We identified the long-term goal of abstinence. She also wanted to look at other goals related to finances, her relationship with her husband, and her thoughts. *See page 196.*

Clients will be more motivated to commit to goals that match their own values. One way to understand what might be important to your client is to explore their values to help imagine the impact of their problem through their eyes and experience. Then it is possible to generate their

Substance Use Goal   Abstinence ☐   Harm Reduction ☒

I'm not sure about this yet.
I don't want to stop drinking.

Long-Term Goal	Short-Term Strategies to Achieve Goal
(What kind of use by what date – be as specific as possible)	(Concrete plans, tasks, or strategies that will help achieve long-term goal)
➤ Not feel horrible inside anymore.	➤ Ask counsellor about not feeling horrible.
➤ Be able to go to the bar with my buddies when I turn legal age.	➤ Ask counsellor about how to make my life better and get to go to the bar when I'm of legal age.
➤ Be able to drink like my friends do.	
➤ Find out what my options are.	➤ Actually listen to what the counsellor says.

Life Domain Impacted	Long-Term Goal	Short-Term Strategies to Achieve Goal
(Physical health, emotional regulation, financial, workplace, family relationships, spirituality, and so on)	(Be as specific as possible)	(Concrete plans, tasks, or strategies that will help achieve long-term goal)
Friends	Get them back. Get rid of the people that stab me in the back.	1) Reach out to Jamie and see if he will let me know why we stopped hanging out. 2) Stop hanging out with people who use me.
Girlfriend	I want a good girlfriend who is nice and smart.	1) Go to school. 2) Talk to girls at school.
School	Graduate.	1) Go to school. 2) Talk to guidance counsellor about my options.

Substance Use Goal   Abstinence ☒   Harm Reduction ☐

Long-Term Goal	Short-Term Strategies to Achieve Goal
(What kind of use by what date – be as specific as possible)	(Concrete plans, tasks, or strategies that will help achieve long-term goal)
I want to get my life back on track. I think I need to be 100% clean and sober to do this.	➤ Throw out all alcohol and cocaine in the house. ➤ Commit to my husband that I am giving up the alcohol and drugs. ➤ Start identifying triggers that make me want to drink alcohol and use cocaine.

Life Domain Impacted	Long-Term Goal	Short-Term Strategies to Achieve Goal
(Physical health, emotional regulation, financial, workplace, family relationships, spirituality, and so on)	(Be as specific as possible)	(Concrete plans, tasks, or strategies that will help achieve long-term goal)
Financial	I would like to replace the $12,000 I have spent on alcohol and cocaine this year.	1) Allocate 30% of each pay cheque to savings. 2) Set up automatic withdrawal on my bank account to have the money come out each month without me noticing.
Relationship	I would like to be best friends with my husband again.	1) Explain why I would shut down and go to the bedroom. 2) Apologize.
Thoughts	To be able to focus my mind so that my thoughts about using don't take me over.	1) Ask my counsellor, because I've tried everything and I can't seem to make it work. 2) Do what my counsellor suggests.

treatment goals based on this shared understanding. Questions that may be helpful to ask are

> ➤ "Tell me about which areas of your life matter most to you. If your substance use changed, how would this be different?";

> ➤ "What are your top five values? How do you express these? Does your present level of substance use help or hinder your lived expression of these values?";

> ➤ "What is different between your current level of substance use and your goal of substance use?"

The counselling process may be approached in different ways, depending on your context. You may take a directive focus, in which you as the counsellor decide where you and your client will start. This could be appropriate in residential treatment, intensive day treatment, or when the client has told you they will do best if you take the lead. You may also want to collaborate with your client. This approach often works best in outpatient counselling relationships.

It is ideal to empower the client to make healthy choices while the counsellor provides options, expertise, guidance, and support. Lastly, you might decide you want to follow your client's lead and ask them where they would like to start. This could be useful in cases where your role is not to provide too much guidance and you are a support person in the client's life, or in cases where you have a client with whom you are still working to build a trusting and respectful relationship.

In some cases, it may be very clear where the counselling process should begin. In other cases, there may be multiple starting places based on the information gathered. Alternately, there may be no clear idea with the best way to proceed. When it is not clear where to start, you may need to broaden the picture until it becomes clear. It may be helpful to explore potential places to start and then just choose one. Once you pick a goal, it is important to focus on it until that person develops some level of competence or mastery within that area before moving on to the next.

Every client will be at a different stage in choosing their goals and what they are actually willing to do. Research in the area of change has well-illustrated common stages that people move through as they struggle to let go of unhealthy patterns of behaviour and work to adopt new ones (Prochaska, DiClemente, & Norcross, 1992). These stages range from holding no intention to change, although other people in the client's life may wish it (precontemplation), to openly exploring their own reasons for moving toward change and beginning to put a plan in place (contemplation and preparation), to actively integrating the change into many parts of their life (action and maintenance), until finally the old behaviour no longer holds any pull on the person (termination). Each of these stages requires a different approach from us as the helper to best partner with our client to have the greatest chance of success.

For clients who are actively ready to change, like Alison, goals will be about actively reducing use. For clients who are in denial, not yet thinking about changing or are thinking about changing but not ready to plan to change, different goals will need to be set. Alison is a very motivated client who is actively ready to change her use. Her goals are to throw away her substances and stop using. We will be looking at plans, strategies, and tasks that will empower her to continue to say "no" to drugs and alcohol.

Ben's goals will focus on raising consciousness and awareness around the impact of his substance use problem and re-evaluating how the substance use impacts his life. Ben is not ready to stop. It would likely be premature to insist on a goal of stopping his use or reducing while he is not clear he wants that. Rather than trying to force change in his substance use, I need to think about setting goals that match his readiness and work to raise his consciousness around how his use creates problems for him. For example, one of his goals is that he does not want to feel horrible anymore. It may be useful to ask careful questions about how his use may increase the horrible feelings or if he uses to get rid of the horrible feelings. This could eventually guide him to want to reduce or quit using because of the insights he has generated.

COUNSELLING STRATEGIES

Generating goals can be done in a variety of ways. There are a number of tips to approach goal setting, outlined below.

1) Explore the impact
   ➤ Start with what the client is most willing to share. Establish a relationship with the client that is based on promoting self-confidence and dignity. Being an empathetic and supportive listener helps to generate trust, which allows the client to share the more challenging aspects of their story, as they feel comfortable.

   ➤ Remain curious and approachable. Keep in mind that understanding the impact of the substance use problem will involve hearing incidents that are potentially shameful or embarrassing. Secrecy and silence are typical reactions to shame. Clients may expect condemnation or rejection after sharing some of their incidents (Brown, 2013; Greenberger & Padesky, 2016). Be careful to monitor your own reactions to the stories clients share.

   ➤ Pay careful attention to the different life domains that have been impacted by the substance use problem. Ask thoughtful questions that encourage sharing about multiple life domains, including physical, emotional, intellectual, social, and spiritual areas.

2) Choose initial goals
   ➤ Choose goals you are reasonably certain the client can achieve. If the client's confidence in their ability to carry out the goal is low, pick a goal that they think they can complete. Goals should be somewhat challenging but obtainable (Higgins, Sigmon, & Heil, 2014; Sanchez-Craig, 2013).

   ➤ For physical recovery, obtain a clear picture of what the change in substance use looks like for them. It is critical to understand if the client's physical recovery goal is harm reduction or abstinence. If it is reduction, it is important to be clear and specific about under which conditions and how much of a substance they want to use (Sanchez-Craig, 2013).

➤ Prioritize goals that are going to be most influential in the client obtaining recovery. Progress may be sabotaged if the most acute issues are not worked on first. Look at the other life domains impacted by the substance use to determine what other goals need to be worked on to support physical recovery from the substance use (Daley & Marlatt, 2006).

➤ Identify the long-term and short-term goals. Take the long-term goal and break it down into a couple of short-term goals. These short-term goals should be the building blocks that support the long-term goal. Recognize that achieving long-term goals can seem like a daunting task, so it is okay to set initial goals that can be modified later. When selecting both long- and short-term goals, be specific, realistic, and define how they will be measured. *See page 300 in the Resources section for a goal-setting worksheet.*

3) Select goals that fit the client's life

➤ Seek to see the world through the eyes of your client. Tune in to your client's inner reality. Try to understand their beliefs and values and how their goals support who they want to be.

➤ Use future-oriented questions to help uncover intentions. Questions are a key part of helping your client generate their own goals and solutions. Examples could include: "If you went to school tomorrow and everything was different – you have stopped using, and your social relationships were unfolding beautifully – what would be different about you?" or "You have quit using drugs, and you overhear your husband talking about you. What are the positive things you would hear him saying about you?"

➤ Match goals, tasks, plans, and strategies to where the client is at in their change process. Be deliberate in choosing steps that align with what the person is willing to do at that time.

3) MANAGE CRAVINGS, URGES, THOUGHTS, AND EMOTIONS

The mental and emotional state of someone with a substance use problem is usually in rough condition when they choose to reduce their problematic use or quit altogether. When they finally make the commitment to change, there are several barriers, triggers, and habits that could come up along the way and could draw the client back into their problematic use.

To make this profound change in problematic substance use patterns, the counsellor should identify the internal and external triggers that may lead the client to relapse into old problematic substance use. Once the triggers are identified, you will have the opportunity to work on problem solving, enhanced coping, and improved emotional regulation. It is useful to move away from *why* the behaviours started, and rather focus on the present factors that hold the problematic use in place. Identifying the urges, cravings, thoughts, and emotions that keep the unhelpful patterns in place is useful in creating lasting change.

Cravings and Urges

Cravings are strong longings or desires to use a substance. Cravings exist on a continuum from subtle and sneaky to overt and intense. Often, they are more evident early in the change progress and become less prominent as the change persists (McCrady & Epstein, 2009). An urge, on the other hand, is the mindset of intention to consume the substance after the craving has occurred (Daley & Marlatt, 2006).

Cravings and urges are triggered by both internal and external cues (see Figure 7.2). External cues are often situations, people, places, experiences, or objects. For example, a client might see a friend they often drank or used drugs with. Internal cues refer to thoughts, memories, emotions, and physical sensations associated with their substance use and any reminders of it.

Ben and Alison both found it useful when I visually mapped out the connections of how triggers can lead to cravings and urges. We explored this with each of their unique triggers, cravings, and urges.

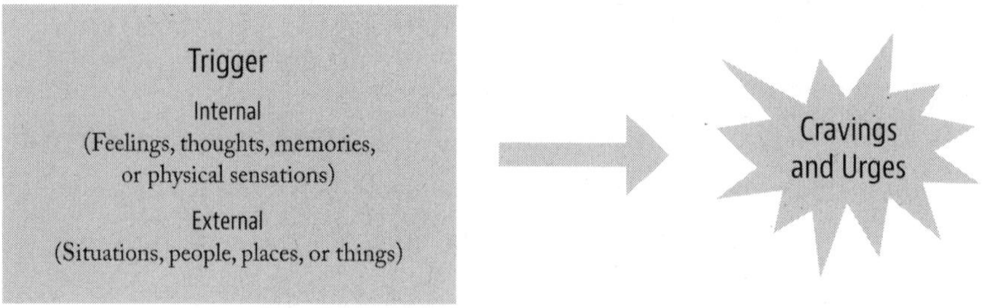

Figure 7.2
Triggers toward cravings and urges

Thoughts

When people are caught in the grips of problematic substance use, a great deal of conscious and unconscious thought is devoted to obtaining and using the client's substance of choice. Whether clients are abstaining or reducing their problematic substance use, they will continue to have triggering thoughts that will lead to cravings and urges. Conscious thoughts include the things we intentionally think about, and unconscious thoughts are those that flow through our mind all day with or without awareness that thinking is occurring. When working with substance use problems, it is helpful to have people identify their thoughts that lead to use.

For example, Alison often had thoughts like, "If I just had a bump of cocaine, it would be so much easier to complete this project," and would then develop the craving to use. We worked on creating counter thoughts, so that she did not develop the urge to go through with it.

On the other hand, with Ben, who was not ready to give up his use, we worked to identify the thoughts that brought about cravings and urges but did not actively develop thoughts about how to stop them. The purpose of identifying his triggering thoughts was to help him see how his unhelpful thinking (that consequently led to his problematic use) got in the way of his goals. I asked curious questions about other things that may be more helpful to do instead of using or how his use could cause problems in certain situations.

For example, on a number of occasions, Ben had worked up the nerve to ask out a good-natured girl who prioritized school and did not drink. He was able to identify his thoughts prior to the date. His thoughts were that if he had one drink, he would feel more comfortable meeting up with the girl. In most cases, after he had one drink, his mind would convince him that having more drinks would help the situation. He would have multiple drinks, and he would get very drunk. He would show up to the date, and the girl would not want to see him again, because she was not into dating someone who got this drunk, especially while finishing high school. I worked to link how his problematic use got in the way of achieving his goal of having a girlfriend who was nice and smart and used this information as motivation to change.

There are many problematic using thoughts that people get stuck in. It can be helpful for clients to identify the common themes, so that they have a baseline for how to cope and focus on creating constructive and adaptive thinking (Daley & Marlatt, 2006; McCrady & Epstein, 2009). Examples of problematic substance use thoughts are:

➤ *Problematic thought:* No one will ever know if I have this one

    _____.

➤ *Problematic thought:* I'm going to do an experiment and see if I can have _____.

➤ *Problematic thought:* I won't be able to socialize if I don't have a

    _____.

➤ *Problematic thought:* I deserve a reward. I've had a hard day.

The next step is to help the person generate alternative thoughts for their critical thoughts that lead them to problematic use. Clients benefit from learning to focus their thoughts to refuse problematic substance use (Higgins, Sigmon, & Heil, 2014). *See page 301 in the Resources section for a worksheet.* Alternative thoughts that include refusal for the above statements could be:

➤ *Problematic thought:* No one will ever know if I have this one
_____.

   • *Alternative thought:* No, I am working towards my goal. I will know.

➤ *Problematic thought:* I'm going to do an experiment and see if I can have _____.

   • *Alternative thought:* No, this is just my rationalization to get back into my problem behaviour.

➤ *Problematic thought:* I won't be able to socialize if I don't have a
_____.

   • *Alternative thought:* Socializing might be hard at the beginning. I am choosing to socialize without _____.

➤ *Problematic thought:* I deserve a reward. I've had a hard day.

   • *Alternative thought:* I do deserve a reward. What can I choose that will help me achieve my goals? (Daley & Marlatt, 2006)

Emotions

Emotions are universal to human experience. Emotions can be particularly troubling or very welcome, depending on what they are. They can be difficult to identify and label. When the client can recognize their emotions, they can make sense of their experience and, in turn, soothe themselves.

In Ben's case, he identified that he does not want to feel horrible anymore. It would be helpful to know what he means by horrible, because different emotions are best coped with in different ways (Greenberger & Padesky, 2016). If *horrible* means he feels *sad*, a coping strategy may be to go out and do a pleasurable activity like skateboarding or making a meal he enjoys. Whereas if *horrible* means *anxious*, engaging in relaxation strategies would be more appropriate.

Alison talked about shutting her husband out and wanting to be best friends again. She has been able to identify that feeling *lonely* is a trigger for her drinking. We worked on identifying the feeling, accepting the feeling, and problem solving about the feeling. Her problem solving leads her to approach her husband more often for conversation and hugs. As she does this, she feels *connection* and the triggering emotion – *loneliness* – is less of a problem for her.

It is helpful to stay away from thinking of emotions as good or bad, and rather distinguish between the various emotional states and different degrees of similar emotions (see Figure 7.3). Different emotions require different coping strategies to assist in emotional regulation. Using a list of emotions can help people begin to think about and differentiate what they are feeling (Greenberger & Padesky, 2016). I gave Alison and Ben a word list as a reference in sessions when I was asking them about their feelings, and we worked on using accurate emotional language to describe their emotional states.

Happy	Grateful	Content
Sad	Hurt	Betrayed
Joy	Excitement	Hope
Afraid	Worry	Terror
Anxious	Anticipation	Panic
Angry	Irritated	Enraged
Embarrassed	Regretful	Disgust
Love	Connection	Lust
Lonely	Forgotten	Isolated
Shame	Humiliated	Guilty

Figure 7.3 *Emotions list showing variations*

COUNSELLING STRATEGIES

Managing cravings, urges, thoughts, and emotions can be perplexing and challenging. Here are some strategies to start the process.

1) Identify and make a plan for the management of cravings and urges

➤ Remember that cravings and urges are natural and will be present, especially at the beginning.

➤ Help your client learn to identify their cravings and urges. Work with them to recognize the signs and sensations associated with specific cravings and urges. Often when clients do not understand what is happening to them, the cravings and urges can feel over-whelming. Help to give it a name and normalize the experience.

➤ Help your client to identify both the internal triggers (their thoughts, feelings, behaviour, and physical sensations that lead to cravings and urges) and external triggers (situations, people, places, and objects), and generate coping strategies for the triggers.

2) Identify and manage substance using thoughts

➤ Invite your client to notice their thoughts in a non-judgmental way. Encourage them to be a curious observer of the things that natu-rally flow into their mind. Pay attention to patterns in thoughts.

➤ Notice the thoughts that evoke strong emotions in your client. Help the client recognize the connection between their thoughts and their emotions that trigger the desire to use substances. Strong emotions can be used as clues to help clients identify trig-gering thoughts that lead to substance use. Ask your client about which thoughts trigger the cravings and urges.

➤ Once the most influential thoughts have been identified, work with your client to develop alternative thoughts they can practice telling themselves. Help them remember the benefits of not using, the risks that accompany the using, and that they do not need to act on their thoughts. Encourage them to use assertive language in their coping statements, such as "I choose not to drink," or "No, this is not an option for me. Using cocaine will cost me my job."

➤ Practice, practice, and more practice. Once alternative thoughts are identified, practice these thoughts with the client. Consistent and repeated guidance to use the alternative thoughts by the counsellor encourages similar behaviour in the client. Plan with your client about when they can practice these thoughts.

3) Identify and manage emotions

➤ Invite your client to tune in and notice their emotions and thoughts. If they seem to struggle to identify or talk about feelings or thoughts, provide a vocabulary and educate them about emotions and thought patterns. Encourage the client to be as specific as possible in discerning which emotion they are having.

➤ Collaborate to identify specific strategies that will help the client through the feeling. Remember that what helps one client settle, soothe, or regulate an emotion may be different from what helps another client. Check in to see what the client may already do to manage their feelings and see if you can build upon the helpful strategies they already have. Often, teaching strategies to manage emotions is useful. Talk about and decide on times they can practice these strategies. *See page 302 in the Resources section for an emotion identification worksheet.*

CASE APPLICATION

BEN
I have met with Ben a few times, and Ben has made it clear that he does not know exactly what he wants to change but he likes having someone to talk to. He is not ready to commit to making a change in his substance use, but is open to understanding what is happening inside him.

Ben explains that he feels horrible inside and that he does not know what to do. He talks about being hit with waves of sensations that incapacitate him when his mother screams at him. He describes starting to tremble, experiencing numbness and tingling, and then chest pain. He tells me that he asked one of his friends one day while drinking if this ever happened to them. His friend gave him a strange look, which made Ben feel crazy.

[Counsellor] "That must have been hard to tell your friend about trembling, numbness and tingling, and chest pain, and have your friend give you a strange look. It makes sense you would question yourself after sharing something like that. I'm glad you told me, because I think we can make sense of this. Are these sensations part of the *horrible* you keep telling me about?"

Ben looks at me a bit quizzically and nods yes. He describes his sensations as taking him over.

[Counsellor] "Let's talk about what emotions accompany these sensations. Do you know what emotions you are feeling when you have those physical sensations?"

[Ben] "Yeah, horrible."

[Counsellor] "Why don't we see if we can be a little more specific? Let's try to identify the emotion you have when you hear your mom screaming."

[Ben] "I think she's coming for me again. I just get my guard up."

[Counsellor] "This sounds like you're afraid, scared, or anxious to me. How does that fit for you?"

[Ben] "Yeah, exactly. I'm scared of her."

[Counsellor] "So, the emotion we are working with here is 'scared.' Let's look at how we can help you identify that emotion in the future and some ways to cope with that. What do you think about that?"

ALISON

Alison has committed to give up drinking and to give up using cocaine entirely. She has decided she is going to quit for now and later evaluate if she wants to drink or use again in the future. At this point, she is certain that if she keeps going down this path, she is going to lose everything. She questions how on earth she is going to stop thinking about drinking and using cocaine, because it always seems to be on her mind.

[Counsellor] "It seems like you are most worried about managing your thoughts about drinking. Let's talk a little bit about your thoughts and see if we can find some strategies to help you stay on track. How does that sound to you?"

[Alison] She leans in and says, "Yeah, anything."

[Counsellor] "Tell me some of the thoughts you are struggling with."

[Alison] "I know that when I think about using cocaine, I tell myself it's okay, because other people do it at my workplace, so it's not that bad, and that I don't do it at home. Somehow those thoughts make it okay."

[Counsellor] "It sounds like you have a pattern of rationalization. What do you think?"

[Alison] "Absolutely. I rationalize my using all the time."

[Counsellor] "Can you think of any other rationalizations that lead you to use?"

[Alison] "Yes, after I put my children to bed, I tell myself I deserve a reward."

[Counsellor] "Okay, we have three rationalizing thoughts here: 'Other people do it so it's okay,' 'I don't do it at home,' and 'I deserve a reward.' Let's come up with some assertive alternate thoughts you can practice telling yourself when you notice that these thoughts are popping into your head. Now, once we've developed these, it will be important that you practice them many times a day."

4) MANAGE RELAPSES AND RE-EVALUATE GOALS

A challenging part of working with this population is that quite often clients drop out of counselling, relapse, do not improve, or regress substantially after counselling. Many clients with substance use problems are in denial, have little or no motivation to change, or are defensive – characteristics that lead to poor results. Setbacks are to be expected and are a normal part of the treatment process. But as long as the client does not drop out, they can return to the place they were before the setback and continue to make progress (Prochaska, DiClemente, & Norcross, 1992). It is useful to create relapse prevention plans to mitigate the risk by building on the guiding principles already explored in this chapter.

It is important to re-evaluate goals as clients progress. Setting goals and generating plans, tasks, or strategies to achieve those goals is an ongoing process. In Ben's case, he moves from thinking about the problems he has in his life to actually choosing to reduce his use. At this point, we specifically talk about when he plans to drink, what he plans to drink, and how much he plans to drink.

Alison decides to remain sober. Social situations and how she relates to people without drinking are ongoing challenges for her. Our goals become finding a new peer group and becoming comfortable at social gatherings without drinking. At work, her new goal becomes saying "no" to projects she does not have time for. She knows that working long hours is a trigger for her cocaine use, so, as a result, working long hours can no longer be part of her life.

COUNSELLING STRATEGIES

High relapse rates and regression are predictable obstacles and normal parts of the progression through the stages of change. Identifying and working through these challenges provides a basis for making inopportune and flawed, yet creative, progress throughout the treatment process. To help create forward momentum during setbacks, consider the following strategies:

1) Recognize client resistance as a normal part of the treatment process

   ➤ Some clients will be in a place of resistance, rejection, or opposition to the treatment process. Become aware of what this stage looks like in the clients you work with. Rather than trying to force change, choose motivational interventions to help clients see why they would benefit by making changes.

   ➤ Manage your own expectations for the counselling process. Remember that it is normal to see potential in your client and anticipate what they could be. Work to be aware of when these hopes are not in alignment with where the client is at in the present. Work with where the client actually is, not where you would like them to be.

2) Re-evaluate goals after a relapse or a progression in treatment

   ➤ Notice when a client's goals no longer match their circumstances. This may occur due to natural forward progression and an increased motivation to change or due to regression or relapse.

   ➤ Check in with the client to clarify the goals you are working towards. Think about fine-tuning already-established goals, plans, tasks, and strategies to achieve the goals rather than generating an entirely new treatment plan.

   ➤ Establish immediate and short-term goals that allow for quick progress and generate forward momentum.

3) Create relapse prevention plans

   ➤ Talk with the client about the nature of substance use treatment and the value of creating relapse prevention plans.

   ➤ Work to normalize relapse while simultaneously being careful not to give permission to relapse.

➤ Collaborate with the client to identify their strengths and weaknesses. Ask the client about the unique factors that might cause them to relapse.

➤ Incorporate the client's strengths into the relapse prevention plan and validate the resourcefulness and grit they can use to overcome setbacks. Supplement their list with more general strategies for managing cravings, urges, thoughts, and feelings.

CASE APPLICATION

BEN

Ben arrives late to the session. His speech is abrupt and short. He starts out by saying he did not want to come today. I attempt to engage him and ask why he does not want to be here. After four minutes of sitting in silence, he says he thinks he is probably my worst client and a fraud because he has not even decided whether he wants to quit using. Ben has moved back into a resistant place that he has not been in for a number of weeks.

[Counsellor] "Ben, it sounds like you're afraid to get started, because you are afraid you are not doing it right."

[Ben] "I never do anything right. It's like I know what I should do, but I never do it. Just like how you told me to decide if I want to reduce my use or try for abstinence. I just don't know if I want either."

[Counsellor] "Let's go back to your goals sheet. You were sure about not wanting to feel horrible and wanting your social life back. Let's review how you have been doing in these areas."

He glares at me and pauses before speaking.

[Ben] "But you asked me to decide on one goal, and I couldn't even do that – I failed."

[Counsellor] "I hear you. You think you have failed again. I agree that you did not do what I asked you to do. On the other hand, I see that you have made progress in other areas. Do you think we can explore what is getting in the way of you making this decision and try to break it into small steps, like we did with some of the other goals you achieved?"

[Ben] "I don't think it's going to work. Do whatever you want." [Ben lets out a big sigh.] "Okay, fine, let's try to break it into small parts. That has worked."

[Counsellor] "Okay, how about our first task is to make a pros and cons list of reducing your use and a pros and cons list of abstaining completely. Let's get all the information and then see what you think. If I do this with you, will you give me the best answers you can?"

[Ben] "Yeah, I can answer the questions if you ask them."

ALISON

Alison comes into my office and begins to rapidly tell me that she has failed, as tears slide down her face. She talks about the embarrassment she feels as she explains that she stayed late at work three days in a row, and, on the fourth morning, she used cocaine to stay awake at work. She is confused, because she knows she does not want the drug in her life anymore, but she feels an overwhelming pull to keep using cocaine for a few more days.

[Counsellor] "It sounds like your old pattern of working long hours and then using cocaine to help you stay awake has crept back in. I also hear that you know you don't want to use cocaine, but there is a part of you that isn't willing to give it up yet."

Alison slouches and tenses her jaw.

[Alison] "I know you are going to tell me to stop with the cocaine, but I have three more nights of work left, and I don't know how I'm going to get through them without it."

[Counsellor] "It sounds like it would be really hard to get through those nights without it. Prior to those six months you were using cocaine, you still worked a lot of long hours. How did you make it through the long hours then without using?"

[Alison] "I just sat down, resigned to the fact that I would not be able to put my children to bed, and got down to business. Once I started working, I would get into a workflow, and it would all get done."

[Counsellor] "What would it take for you to get back to that same resigned state about not getting to put your kids to bed, get working, and move into your workflow?"

[Alison] "I haven't thought about it. I guess I already am in the resigned state. I keep telling myself that I need the cocaine for the workflow. Now that we're talking about it, I can see that is not true. I know that to get into the workflow, I just need to sit and get working. It comes by doing the work."

[Counsellor] "When can you let go of the cocaine again and use your old method of getting into your workflow?"

[Alison] "I don't want to, but I can do it today. I think I can use my assertive alternative statements to help me against the triggering thoughts, too."

[Counsellor] "Okay, let's write out this plan we have just generated. That way, if you are experiencing cravings and urges, you can pull it out and remind yourself of what we just talked about."

FINISHING THOUGHTS

The loss and harm caused by severe problematic substance use often generates a dark cloud of despair and desperation. Many people still hold onto their problematic use because of the social ease it creates, the softening of harsh feelings it offers, or the blissful oblivion it can offer them. Even though the person may know their problematic use harms them, it is crucial to remember the important purpose that substance use has served in their life and that it may be hard to give up.

As a counsellor, it can be hard to understand why someone holds onto their problematic use when it is so evident that it is causing incredible destruction. It is important to remember the life circumstances that keep the problematic use firmly in place. Like any big storm, the clouds part from time to time, or the sun might shine down momentarily, and these are the moments that we as helpers look for, strive to hold onto, and remember for our clients and ourselves. For some people, the clouds may be all-encompassing, dark, and heavy, whereas for others, the sky may be slightly grey with a great deal of light peeking through. No matter where the person is at, celebrate the small changes and bits of light until the sun overtakes the sky.

I have found that when I strive to meet the client exactly where they are, not where I would like them to be, this is when our most collaborative bond is formed. At that point, we can face the chaos of the problematic substance use together, using the strategies I have outlined above. We then move away from powerlessness and fear to power and freedom.

ABOUT THE AUTHOR

Amber McKenzie, MSc, CPsych

Amber is a psychologist who has a master's degree in marital and family therapy. She is a trainer with the Crisis & Trauma Resource Institute and also works as a therapist. In her clinical practice, she provides treatment to children, adolescents, and adults experiencing addictions, mental illness, and other psychological difficulties. In addition, Amber does a great deal of work with couples and families. She believes in the inherent strengths within her clients and in their abilities to be integral parts of the healing process.

REFERENCES

Alcoholics Anonymous. (2001). *Alcoholics anonymous* (4th ed.). New York, NY: Alcoholics Anonymous World Service, Inc.

American Psychiatric Association. (2013). *Diagnostic and statistical manual of mental disorders* (5th ed.). Arlington, VA: Author.

Brown, B. (2013). *The power of vulnerability: Teachings on authenticity, connection, and courage* [Audiobook]. Retrieved from Soundstrue.com

Daley, D. C., & Marlatt, G. A. (2006). *Overcoming your alcohol or drug problem: Effective recovery strategies: Workbook* (2nd ed.). New York, NY: Oxford University Press, Inc.

Greenberger, D., & Padesky, C. A. (2016). *Mind over mood: Changing how you feel by changing the way you think* (2nd ed.). New York, NY: Guilford Press.

Higgins, S. T., Sigmon, S. C., & Heil, S. H. (2014). Drug use disorders. In D. Barlow (5th ed.), *Clinical handbook of psychological disorders* (pp. 588-616). New York, NY: Guilford Press.

McCrady, B. S. (2014). Alcohol use disorders. In D. Barlow (5th ed.), *Clinical handbook of psychological disorders* (pp. 533-587). New York, NY: Guilford Press.

McCrady, B. S., & Epstein, E. E. (2009). *Overcoming alcohol problems: A couples-focused program. Therapist guide.* New York, NY: Oxford University Press, Inc.

Miller, W. R., & Rollnick, S. (2013). *Motivational interviewing: Helping people change* (3rd ed.). New York, NY: Guilford Press.

Prochaska, J. O., DiClemente, C. C., & Norcross, J. C. (1992). In search of how people change: Applications to addictive behaviors. *American Psychologist, 47*(9), 1102-1114.

Sanchez-Craig, M. (2013). *Saying when: How to quit drinking or cut down* (3rd ed.). Toronto, ON: Centre for Addiction and Mental Health.

White, M., & Epston, D. (1990). *Narrative means to therapeutic ends.* New York, NY: W. W. Norton & Company, Inc.

CHAPTER EIGHT

LGBT2SQ+ CENTRED APPROACHES

By Marion Brown

ACROSS TIME AND PLACE, PEOPLE WHO IDENTIFY WITH A RANGE OF gender identities and sexual orientations have faced an almost universal history of exclusion, discrimination, and violence. Gender identity, gender expression, biological sex, and sexual orientation are all aspects of how each person experiences and expresses themselves. They entail gender, as well as a person's focus and degree of attraction toward others for sexual, romantic, and emotionally intimate relationships. These ideas are simultaneously distinct and interwoven with each other, with endless possible variations because of the vast spectrum of human experience. Inherent in this spectrum is the notion of fluidity and movement in gender identity, gender expression, sexual attraction, preference, desire, and expression.

In this chapter, our intention is to be inclusive and acknowledge that each person has their own understanding and choice for language that captures and reflects who they are. We have chosen the acronym LGBT2SQ+,[1] which stands for lesbian, gay, bisexual, transgender, Two-Spirit, and queer, as well as an expansive inclusion with the use of "+." We recognize this is

---

1. See the glossary at the back of the book for definitions of the various terms that appear in this chapter.

not a comprehensive acronym; we use it in recognition of the necessary ongoing conversation exploring the evolution and diversity of language and its meanings. Getting to know your local community and the meaningful choices of people you work with is part of an affirming LGBT2SQ+ approach and is explored more in this chapter. In my community, the term queer is held as a positive, reclaimed word, and therefore, I use it interchangeably with LGBT2SQ+. Although a diversity of sexual orientations and gender identities has been present throughout human history, the social systems of Western civilization – including family, education, religion, medicine, and justice – rest upon the assumption of and preference toward heterosexual union and cisgender expression. These are communicated through formal structures as well as informal social practices.

Examples of formal structures include curricula, policies, funding decisions, and laws. Informal social practices include the way a school has always cast its annual musical or the way a physician assumes that a female who says she's sexually active requires birth control. Experiences with social service organizations, including individual, family, and group counselling, have too often mirrored the ignorance and insensitivity of the wider world. In the face of hostile surroundings within home, work, neighbourhood, and community, LGBT2SQ+ people have demonstrated profound psychological, social, and political resilience.

This chapter is written with a focus on building one's capacity for LGBT2SQ+ centred practice – a practice that considers the unique and specific experiences of LGBT2SQ+ clients to inform *how* we practice. Doing so begins with an understanding that there are not inherent issues and illnesses related to being LGBT2SQ+ that lead people to come for services, supports, and counselling. LGBT2SQ+ people often seek out services, supports, and counselling as a result of living in a society that privileges heterosexuality and cisgender identity and excludes and pathologizes ways of being and living that do not subscribe to these identities. In other words, this chapter does not focus on how LGBT2SQ+ people can or should change. Rather, it focuses on how helpers need to integrate analyses of heterosexism and cisnormativity into their skills and strategies so they can be allies in shifting the conditions that oppress the lives and potentials of LGBT2SQ+ people. It is important to note here that we are all socialized within the structures of heterosexism, heteronormativity, and cisnormativity. This focus on integrating our analyses, then, applies to all who come to this work, regardless of sexual orientation and gender identity.

TAY

Tay is 16 years old, the youngest of three children, and identifies as gender non-binary, saying labels of sexual orientation and gender expression just don't fit. Tay uses the pronouns "they," "their," and "them." This is frequently a choice for people who identify outside the gender binary of female (she) or male (he).

Tay is mixed race, of Lebanese and Italian origin, and lives with their parents who immigrated to Canada before Tay was born. Tay has never "come out." They've always expressed themselves according to how they feel, dressing according to a range of clothing and accessorizing styles, and engaging in activities of their choosing. Tay is used to lots of parental redirection regarding what they wear, how they talk, and the things they do. However, recently, things have become more tense, as Tay has begun high school and is dressing in ways their parents say is wrong and behaving in ways they say will make them be the weird kid who gets left out, bullied, or worse. Tay is feeling anxious about how mad their parents always seem to be these days. One of the teachers at Tay's school referred them to my private practice.

JAKE

Jake is a 60-year-old man with a loving partner named Rob, a good job teaching at the local high school, and close connections with friends and family. He's been involved in Pride events for several years, often performing with his jazz band for one of the musical showcases. One night after a gig, Jake was leaving the venue a little after the rest of the band and was jogging up the street to catch up with the group. As he was crossing at an intersection, a car came up behind him and careened around the corner, catching his back foot and sending him flying forward onto the pavement. As the car screeched away, he heard voices laughing and yelling, "Serves you right, you fucking faggot!"

I met Jake and Rob three weeks later. They described the incident and stated that both of them were feeling unsafe in their neighbourhood and that Jake was having difficulty sleeping. Jake had also not returned to work. He started drinking daily as a way to manage his anxiety and stopped responding to friends and family who were worried about him.

As practitioners, both in direct counselling positions and in the many roles of therapeutic support that comprise social service organizations, we hear stories and we immediately begin to unpack what might be happening for people. We meet someone and start to hear their story, and we start placing their story in a psycho-socio-cultural framework – our *thinking* processes kick in. Some of what we hear we may take as facts and other aspects we tend to speculate about, working from our hunches as well as our assumptions based on life experiences and what we have learned.

All of these assumptions rest within a lens that is shaped by our values and beliefs, which lead us to understand the world in certain ways. These contribute to who we are – our *being*. Our work in the helping professions also requires us be engaged in *doing*. It's not enough to only analyze and consider, for our role is to actively provide support. Our work includes a unique combination of thinking, being, and doing, where *we* are the primary therapeutic tools. As we start considering what is happening for Tay and Jake, this framework of thinking, being, and doing can guide our approach.

In the domain of thinking, we can draw upon particular theories and understandings that queer theory reveals to us, starting with the predominance of binary categorizations in Western thinking. This is the either/or labelling that classifies a person as male or female, heterosexual or homosexual, as though each category is exhaustive and mutually exclusive. We see this also in the distinctions upheld between a "helper" and a "helpee" or between being "able-bodied" or "dis-abled," as though we can't be both.

A problem of binary thinking is that we come to believe that there are always and only ever two options, and they are always polar opposites. Unpacking binary thinking can also help us see that what we take to be "givens," such as gender, gender roles, sexual orientation, and the presumption of heterosexuality over other sexualities, are actually just socially constructed to be valid. They were and are upheld as truths by powerful, influential people and, subsequently, critical masses of people. However, they are ideas that don't have any inherent basis in fact or truth. When we interrupt and deconstruct these mainstream, dominant ways of thinking, we can open up possibilities for flexibility in how people understand themselves and others and possibly even adjust what we value in our society.

Thinking, then, leads us to focus on the "being" of people – what makes them who they are. Engaging in LGBT2SQ+ centred practice means a unique focus on identity, since there are individualized components of queer identity as well as collective components. Each person expresses their own unique blend of both these components. Applying the thinking of LGBT2SQ+ centred practice leads us to understand each person's being as a valid expression of the self, as different yet equal manifestations of the human experience. LGBT2SQ+ centred practice also leads us to question what else could be socially constructed and upheld as true. It helps us to see that efforts at social change and activism are likely required to interrupt mainstream thinking. This is the realm of doing: displacing the ideas of presumed and preferred heterosexuality and cisgender expression and including a range of sexual orientations on the spectrum.

An LGBT2SQ+ centred approach is an interrelationship of thinking and being and doing, each shifting and being shifted by the others. This conceptual grounding is necessary before getting to practice principles, because the pull back to the dominant idea of working with *those people* – people who have been labelled as deviant and disordered – can be strong. It is the othering of queer ways of being that has led most LGBT2SQ+ people to seek therapeutic support in the first place, as the stories of Tay, Jake, and Rob reflect.

INSIGHTS AND GUIDING PRINCIPLES FOR COUNSELLING

The following practice principles are generated from the wisdom of the people I've worked with and tested through my experiences in the field.

1) **Do your own work first**
   What do you need to learn about, examine within yourself, and reflect upon in order to be genuinely invested in this work?

2) **Recognize the power of language**
   To what degree do your words reflect the thinking, being, and doing of LGBT2SQ+ centred practice?

3) **Focus on the messaging of your workplace**
   Who does your office reflect and attract?

4) **Develop relevant programs**
   What services and supports can your agency create to be responsive to the needs of LGBT2SQ+ people?

5) **Bring your sharpest skills**
   How can you activate empathy and validation, mobilize strengths and insight, and connect with and politicize individuals and communities?

1) DO YOUR OWN WORK FIRST

In frontline counselling and support roles, the relationship is the central vessel for engagement and change, and who we are in the relationship is the anchor. We are professionally obligated to be competent and self-aware, responsibilities that are keenly important in LGBT2SQ+ centred work.

There is an inherent vulnerability to seeking services and coming to meet with a professional. We cannot add to that load by doing our learning on the backs of people in need. For example, cisgender counsellors cannot still be figuring out what they think and feel about people who are transgender as a clinical encounter begins. Nor can it be expected that clients carry the full weight of educating clinicians regarding hormones and medical procedures, for example.

The counselling relationship is a shared endeavour where all parties come with contributions. To approach it otherwise is to reinforce a binary of "them" and "us," which undermines the likelihood that everyone will be a recipient of some form of therapeutic/social/health service at some time in our lives. We need to do our own work first, digging deep to explore what values and assumptions underpin our ways of seeing the world and being in the world. We need to take time to do our own unpacking and unlearning first. This means working to understand the social construction of our gender identities and our sexual orientations and the ways social systems maintain gender normativity and heteronormativity.

We also need to think about the relationship of sexual orientation and gender identity with the other identity markers that we know shape a person, particularly racialization, socio-economic status, and ability. We can deepen our knowledge and understanding by reading first-person narratives, cutting-edge texts, and activist blogs, by going to lectures and community events led by LGBT2SQ+ groups, by watching documentaries, and by connecting with people and resources well established in this field. This is not value-neutral work. Since we are aiming for congruence among what we think, who we are, and what we do, we need to sort out that alignment first.

COUNSELLING STRATEGIES FOR SELF OF THE HELPER

1) Spend time self-reflecting

> Examine the origins of your beliefs and assumptions about bodies, genders, and sexual orientations. Where did they come from? Who was influential in shaping them? Are you drawn to scientific authority or personal experiences for explanations? How fixed are your beliefs and assumptions? What contributes to how fixed they are? What might influence or shift your beliefs and assumptions?

2) Engage with material that features first-person stories

> Watch documentaries, read books, attend theatrical expressions, and attend activist events. Hear the detailed stories of pain and triumph in the lives lived by LGBT2SQ+ people. Make notes on recurring themes. Read broadly and seek out opportunities to discuss your reactions, feelings, and thoughts about the material you engage to develop your professional analysis.

3) Be in queer spaces

> Now that you've thought some things through, move to the level of authentic doing and being. Attend LGBT2SQ+ events and seek out speakers, activism, and the arts. Never rush it, yet *as it becomes aligned with your values,* come to be known as a practitioner who can be counted on to be queer-positive, informed, and well resourced. LGBT2SQ+ people talk with one another and recommend services and practitioners as a result of the uncertainty that professionalized relationships will be safe for them. Being engaged with the LGBT2SQ+ community and having partnerships with LGBT2SQ+ organizations and practitioners is an important component of one's clinical skill set.

CASE APPLICATION

TAY

In working with Tay, I needed to have sorted through my own understandings of gender and sexual orientation. I needed to reflect on my values, biases, and assumptions – as they apply to me, and how they influence how I am with others – before I met with Tay. This groundwork ensures that I can simply *be* with Tay's self-expression and not fall prey to the pathologizing of LGBT2SQ+ identities by theorizing about what trauma may have occurred that led to their way of being. Perhaps there are traumas in Tay's life that I will come to learn about, unrelated to gender identity, however, my first step was to welcome Tay's way of being and expressing themselves as valid, good, and true.

I also need to know – from reading, from podcasts, and from attending public events – that members of the current young generation are moving away from self-identifying by existing labels and the traditional models of "coming out" that were predominant in the 1970s, eschewing labels and "old school" theories of identity development. Rather, they are embracing understandings of identity and desire as fluid, rather than fixed.

JAKE

I've seen Jake's band perform at Pride events, and I know he is a well-respected teacher at the high school. I've heard both youth and parents talk about him and the impact of his role as an out gay teacher. I've read books on the private-public tensions for gay men across the decades, including Tom Warner's 2002 *Never Going Back: A History of Queer Activism in Canada* and Gary Kinsman and Patrizia Gentile's 2010 *The Canadian Cold War on Queers*. I understand that for gay men of Jake's age, there is a push and pull between being out and proud yet also knowing that public scrutiny, harassment, and violence are always just around the corner.

A colleague of mine studies the lingering effects of the AIDS hysteria of the 1980s and the ongoing regulation of gay men's bodies. We regularly talk about the false illusions created by the media, and success of certain television shows and personalities, and we question the degree of inclusion in our town. This foundation helps me contextualize Jake's experiences as an active member of many queer-oriented events and organizations, the community he has felt there, and how shaken his sense of security has become since the incident.

2) RECOGNIZE THE POWER OF LANGUAGE

Ah, language. It is hard to know when we get it right, but we certainly know when we get it wrong. Language is regularly evolving with changes in meaning and application. As a central tool of our trade, we need to be vigilant to the impact of what we say, how we say it, and, most of all, how it lands.

Investment in the thinking, doing, and being of LGBT2SQ+ centred work means that we take time to listen to the impact of words. "That's gay" is still one of the most reviled insults in schoolyards today. It's typically taken to mean that something is stupid or disgusting. It is a rejection, with moral, derisive undertones. It doesn't matter that the person who said it didn't intend to be offensive to LGBT2SQ+ people – it is the impact that matters. There is an impact for the individual and an impact in terms of the culture that is created when discriminatory and hurtful language like this goes unchecked.

It is unlikely that someone in a helping role is going to say, "That's gay" in the company of a client. Yet it is this type of phrase that we need to understand for its history and connotation, for the ramifications that have been catalogued by activists over the years, for the meaning it has for LGBT2SQ+ people as a collective, and ultimately for the queer person sitting with us.

While we may not say these words, do we interrupt when they're said? Moreover, do we use other words or assumptions, perhaps intending to be supportive, not realizing that they carry similar negative impact, such as "I don't even see you as lesbian – I just see you as a person," or "Are you going to get a sex change?" Perhaps we engage in a line of questioning that presumes that sexual orientation is the cause of all presenting issues. Or maybe we value the coming out process to the point where we encourage it as a critical accomplishment.

These are examples of ways that we can engage in microaggressions, which are the casual dismissal of or denigrating remarks or behaviour toward a person or group of people. On the surface, they may seem harmless, however, there can be a cumulative effect of creating an atmosphere of negativity or invisibility for the person or group (Shelton & Delgado-Romero, 2011). The fact that we don't recognize them or don't mean to offend does nothing to minimize their effects. Let's use our primary instrument – the spoken word – to lift up and liberate, to be micro*progressions* in this work.

This is active work with our colleagues, as well. Do we take a stand when we hear derogatory comments and assumptions among our co-workers? Once we have come to a new level of consciousness ourselves, we need to consider what it would take to become a leader in shifting the workplace culture and actively challenge stereotypes and prejudices that we hear around us.

Part of this work means knowing our local context, knowing the histories and meanings of terms in that context, and deciding what positions we will take in relation to language. For example, some communities, influenced by queer theory and queer activism, have reclaimed use of the term "queer" as a matter of personal and political action and use it interchangeably with terms like LGBT2SQ+. Choices like this are based in part on breaking away from a list of discrete identities in favor of words that challenge binary constructions of gender and sexual orientation. Yet, for many, LGBT2SQ+ or other acronyms remain preferred. Many articulate and impassioned perspectives can be found for choices in naming identity and expression. Engaging resources and others' perspectives can help us figure out our own priorities and politics in relation to understanding and language. At the same time, foundational to our work as helpers is to centre the experience of the person with whom we are working, and we can do so by asking what terms they want to use and want us to use in talking with them.

COUNSELLING STRATEGIES

Given that so much of our work rests upon the use of language, we have daily opportunities to refine our skills in this area.

1) Use words that reveal awareness of a spectrum of gender expressions and sexual orientations

   ➤ Make a habit of introducing yourself with your name as well as your pronoun, such as "Hello my name is Marion, and my pronouns are *she and her*." This sets the stage for asking for the same from others.

➤ Cast aside the grammar lessons of your elementary school, and embrace use of "they" for a singular person who identifies outside the gender binary. You're in good company in doing so. The American Dialect Society's word of the year in 2015 was the singular "they" (American Dialect Society, 2016). The singular "they" provides us with an accepted alternative to making an assumption and reinforcing the gender binary of "he or she" when referring to an otherwise unidentified person.

➤ Other pronouns regularly in use are "ze" and "hir." Ze is pronounced like "zee" and is also spelled zie and xe; it replaces she/he/they. Hir is pronounced as "here" and replaces her/hers/him/his/they/theirs. An example is "Ze was late for school, because ze missed hir bus." The people you work with likely have other ideas. Ask and then use the pronouns people tell you they would like you to use.

➤ Asking for someone's "preferred" pronoun insidiously suggests that this pronoun doesn't reflect who they "really" are, and that it masks their "true" identity. Our pronouns are not a matter of preference – they are a matter of accuracy.

➤ If you're asking about the love interest of a client, don't default to the assumption that love interest is of a different sex. You could simply ask if they have a partner.

2) Review all paperwork and documentation for consistent attention to inclusive language

➤ While it may be standard procedure to ask for gender and/or sex identification on your forms, ask yourselves why you do. There are many times when our default assumptions about required information prove unfounded.

➤ As you revise forms and policies, have conversations with your colleagues about your new ways of thinking that are stimulating recognition of a wider range of ways of being and prompting new ways of doing.

3) Be provisional rather than definitive in talking about gender expression and sexuality experiences, identities, and possibilities

   ➤ Using phrases such as "your sexual interests right now" or "I currently identify as …" suggests a fluidity in attraction and sexual activity, as well as identity and self-expression. They signify understanding that a label or term that fits at one point in time does not necessarily fit at another point in time. They communicate to your client that you do not expect that what they say to you today – about who they are and how they feel – will forever remain in place.

   ➤ Talk about examples of how all words and concepts are socially constructed. Invite a conversation about how we can apply different interpretations to commonly used words and where/how we can reshape meanings within language. For example, pink triangles were a marker used by the Nazis to target people suspected to be lesbian or gay. Now the pink triangle has been reclaimed as a marker of honour, with Pink Triangle Day celebrated on February 14 to counter heteronormative expressions of love and romance.

CASE APPLICATION

TAY

When I met Tay for the first time, I said my name and that my pronouns are "her and she." I could see a flicker of awareness in Tay's eyes that something was different about this introduction. They then said their name is Tay, and when I said "nice to meet you," I also said "what pronoun do you use?" which was when I learned it is "they."

Reflecting on the first principle of doing my own work, I remember when I first started meeting people who used "they," and how I felt some dissonance from my usual use of "they" for the plural. It tripped me up several times, and I had to remind myself it was not a group of people being referenced, but one person. Over a short time, however, and with a conscious commitment to support the politics of non-binary gender identity and validate the being of non-binary people, it didn't take long to become smoother in my speaking and writing, and ultimately, my thinking. I've reflected often that some socially constructed language conventions are simply more rooted than others, but they were all just decisions someone made long ago and are not more right than any other word choice.

JAKE

In our first meeting, Jake and Rob talked openly about their relationship of 24 years, their friends, family, and work experiences, and what they've seen in terms of public "tolerance" of gay men in their town. They think they don't stand out, and they haven't wanted to. They have lived through times before sexual orientation and gender expression were protected characteristics under provincial human rights legislation and have seen friends lose jobs, be harassed by police, and be denied apartment rentals because of being LGBT2SQ+.

Jake has seen significant social and political changes over the years, as well as changes in language. He "came out" as a "homosexual" when he was a teenager, and those were important markers for him. At the same time, I am deliberate in framing questions in ways that encourage the exploration of meaning and impact of words. For example, I asked Jake, "What did it mean to you when you were 18 to call yourself gay? Is it the same as what it means to you now?" When he told me that he used to be shocked to hear gay men use the term "queer" but isn't now, we talked about the movement to purposefully and methodically attach new meanings of resilience and solidarity to a previously derogatory term. We talked about the work of activists in leading this movement, and how the shift seems more difficult for elders in the community compared to the young people. We speculated that perhaps the discriminatory residue is more difficult for older folks to shed, in comparison to the young.

3) FOCUS ON THE MESSAGING OF YOUR WORKPLACE

This principle applies to the concrete working practices of offices and organizations and beckons us to pay attention to how the physical environment and space shapes social relations. In your agency or in your private practice, examine the unspoken messages about who belongs there. What images are on the walls? Who and what do they prioritize? Who works at the agency or with you? Which identities do they represent and reflect? Is your office located in an area known for being queer-friendly? Might you be located in a place that is not queer-friendly? What are the implications?

As noted earlier, LGBT2SQ+ people often talk with one another about their experiences with professional settings and services – including social service organizations – because of the wealth of examples where the very people who ought to have been helpful and supportive have instead reacted based on assumptions and myth. Subsequently, all counsellors, therapists, and social support persons may be considered suspect until and unless demonstrated otherwise. This suspicion exists for good reason: in order to survive, queer people have highly developed antennae for homophobia and transphobia.

All organizations and offices reveal themselves before a person ever opens their mouth. Our surroundings communicate both overt and covert messages of welcome and inclusion. Variables to consider are location and accessibility of a building. The identity markers of office personnel – for example race, gender expression, and ability – can be interpreted as a reflection of who is expected to make use of the services. Images on the walls reflect these assumptions and associated priorities. This principle increases our awareness of passive messaging in our environments.

COUNSELLING STRATEGIES FOR STRUCTURES

1) Think about how you can take into consideration the meaning, relevance, and impact of office decisions for people who identify as LGBT2SQ+

➤ This is not a homogenous population, of course, and we must also be mindful of reducing such a rich range of identities to simplified characteristics based on our assumptions. However, through the implementation of the strategies of principle 1, you will have engaged in an active learning process of unlearning heterosexism and cisnormativity and developing insights from your engagement with people and community events. Consider how to apply them to your surroundings in ways such as having poster campaigns regarding International Day Against Homophobia, Transgender Day of Remembrance, World AIDS Day, as well as Transgender and Pride flags. Creating a "Wall of Fame" that highlights LGBT2SQ+ people is a collaborative strategy that creates more positive visibility. *See page 303 in the Resources section for additional ideas.*

2) Collect and display posters that reflect a range of identities and expressions

➤ There are great resources online that provide many examples or templates from which to develop your own images and slogans.[2]

3) Advocate for inclusive hiring practices

➤ Seek and employ people who identify as lesbian, gay, bisexual, transgender, genderqueer, Two-Spirit, or non-binary.

4) Hold a focus group or circulate an anonymous survey

➤ Seek the feedback of LGBT2SQ+ people on the accessibility of your agency in terms of location, personnel, services, and approaches as well as their experiences with you.

---

2. Good sources are Syracuse Cultural Workers (www.syracuseculturalworkers.com) and Egale Canada Human Rights Trust (www.egale.ca).

CASE APPLICATION

TAY

I want queer youth to feel comfortable in my workspace, so the posters on the walls depict a variety of young people – pierced, tattooed, all colours and expressions of the rainbow. When I worked at a counselling centre a few years ago and we needed a new front reception person, we advertised among the LGBT2SQ+ serving organizations and groups, as well as in the pro-queer publications around town, and we hired a 22-year-old who identifies as genderqueer. I think it made a difference for Tay when they came through the door to know they are represented in our agency, not just as clients, but also as staff.

JAKE

The new young receptionist may not have been the face that felt most welcoming to Jake and Rob, had they been receiving services there. They grew up in a different time, and their priorities have been to fit in, not to stand out. The posters on the walls that may resonate with them are those celebrating same-sex marriage and advertising the radio documentary *Remembering Stonewall* (Isay, 1989). Clearly, Tay, Jake, and Rob reflect different demographics. While they have a bedrock of shared history, the social and political conditions they navigate are distinct. It is my professional responsibility as well as my commitment to queer activism that I regularly seek feedback from all clients about the match between surroundings and services offered and client needs and experiences.

4) DEVELOP RELEVANT PROGRAMS

Whatever our role is in the helping professions, we ultimately want to provide a valuable service. This means thinking through what is relevant and meaningful to the population(s) with whom we work. In order to do so, we need to both develop population-specific programs and services as well as build LGBT2SQ+ centred clinical capacity into generic programs and services. In this way, we can retain allegiance to the reality that there are unique components of the lives and experiences of LGBT2SQ+ people, which need particular attention, and there are overlaps with other identities and needs that also require consideration. This is a both-and approach that reflects the thinking of LGBT2SQ+ centred approaches. We can identify and deconstruct the binaries that lead us to think we can only ever do one of two things, not both.

Ultimately, we need to ask what it would take for our workplaces to both refine our *doing* – specific approaches, skills, and services with queer people – and our *thinking* – our analyses across a range of approaches, skills, and services with all people.

COUNSELLING STRATEGIES FOR RELEVANCE

1) Consult broadly with population-specific organizations in your area and check online for well-established organizations endorsed by queer people and communities

   ➤ For example, learn about LGBT2SQ+ initiatives, such as inclusive curricula in schools, trans youth summer camps, and same-sex parenting groups, and consider offering these in your setting.

2) Develop an LGBT2SQ+ positive collection of resources, such as books, pamphlets, videos, magazines, and documentaries

   ➤ Consider what material would be of most benefit for those you serve and fit in your agency mandate. A visible collection of resources that is focused on LGBT2SQ+ people, interests, and issues signifies a clear commitment to expanding exposure and integration among all people. *See page 304 in the Resources section for additional ideas.*

3) Review the material you have gathered from the people with whom you've consulted and map out where, when, and how you can apply

the insights of your population-specific learning into all your approaches and services

► For example, consider how prompting reflection on gender role expectations could be useful for the cisgender heterosexual couple you are working with regarding trust and communication in their relationship, or how talking about how to support gender-creative kids can be relevant for all parents, not only those who come in talking about their trans child.

4) Consider developing joint programs

► Collaborate your agency or private practice and those that specialize in programs and services working specifically with LGBT2SQ+ people. Where might you work together and extend the reach of both organizations? How might such an alliance contribute to the societal shifts that ease the pressures and constraints of sexual orientation and gender expression upon everyone?

CASE APPLICATION

TAY

Being new to high school, Tay is daunted by feeling far more exposed and visible than expected, and at the same time excited to participate in their first Gay-Straight Alliance (GSA), which just started last year. I've been to GSA conferences as a volunteer adult advisor, having gone through the training put on by the local queer youth agency. In my work with Tay, I draw upon the training, specifically the importance of social connection with other queer youth and the connection of personal troubles to socio-political forces in our lives. We also talk about how the messages parents receive include a focus on helping their kids fit in, even sometimes being referred to as pro-social parenting skills.

[Counsellor] "Part of my role in talking with you, Tay, is to try to make connections between your personal experiences and the pressures put upon teenagers and parents, and all of us, really, that are generated by bigger messaging from society about who we all should be and how we should live. We've talked about that in relation to identifying as gender non-binary – how that is a completely valid identity and expression – and yet you feel the pressures of society telling you to be and act according to cisgender ways. Well, I want to raise the possibility that your parents might be feeling some pressures, though different, too. I know you've talked about struggling in your relationship with your parents, feeling not understood by them and feeling as though they want you to dress and act in ways that make you feel boxed in. That is a tough spot to be in, because I know you also love your parents and want to feel close to them. What do you think might be happening for them that's contributing to them making the choices they are?"

[Tay] "I don't know. They've always been on me, ever since I was little – my mum wanting me to wear my hair long and put on shoes that are pointy and sparkly. But now it's getting worse, and they're mad at me all the time. They say I'm going to regret not making friends in high school and not doing usual girl things. They can't see that I *am* making friends, and I don't *want* to do usual girl things."

[Counsellor] "Yes, I can see that you must be getting tired of some of those things, since you've been hearing them since you were little. Wow. That's a long time and can take a toll. I can also see how it feels like they are mad at you. I wonder also if your parents might be feeling protective of you and worried for you, but maybe it is coming across as being mad. Sometimes parents feel pressure to have kids who present as 'regular' and who don't make waves. This is sometimes especially the case for parents who may feel like they are under a watchful eye because they moved to North America in the last while. I know you don't want to be 'regular', and you like making waves! I get that and respect it. Yet for your parents, it might feel like they will get in trouble somehow – with friends, or co-workers, or bosses. Could that be?"

[Tay] "Maybe, but man, they are so on me! I swear they are the most suffocating parents ever."

[Counsellor] "That's a great word for describing how it feels. I wonder if other people your age ever feel that way – like they're being suffocated by parents?"

[Tay] "No one has it as bad as me."

[Counsellor] "That would be an interesting thing to talk about – with some of your old friends as well as new ones. In fact, it would be interesting to raise it with your queer friends, sort of in comparison with straight and cis friends. I think the pressures are on all teens, for sure, and it's a time of tension with parents for many of you. And yet, given all the societal messages that expect everyone to be cis and straight, I wonder if it is even more so for queer youth. What do you think?"

This discussion can help build understanding of Tay's parents' concerns and priorities. It can also help situate Tay's experience as both unique and also found within broader societal pressures that weigh upon most teens and their parents. Many teens want to express who they are, and many parents are concerned about societal reactions or longer-term implications. Attending the GSA events helps make these connections between personal and collective experiences.

JAKE

Jake has experienced a direct threat to his physical safety that is having significant emotional and psychological results, and Rob has also experienced this trauma indirectly. As a counsellor, I've studied the aftereffects of assault and victimization, and I incorporate techniques for these as well as for anxiety and panic attacks into my work with Jake. Further, I know of a local support group for people who have experienced violence, and after several sessions, I assess that Jake and Rob would benefit from the peer sharing and support that such groups provide. Several considerations contributed to this assessment:

➤ Jake has returned to his baseline patterns of sleeping and eating. Both Jake and Rob have spoken of this.

➤ Jake is, by personality, somewhat of an extrovert and has typically been comfortable processing his experiences, thoughts, and emotions out loud.

➤ We have moved from a focus on this singular event in Jake's life to a range of experiences he has had that are both challenging and affirming.

➤ Jake and Rob are regularly practicing techniques for managing panic and anxiety, including grounding activities that focus on breath and visualizations.

➤ Both Jake and Rob have previously been involved in activist circles in their community, which has politicized their experiences of being gay men in light of societal pressures. We have talked about how sharing their experiences may bring awareness to other participants that they might not previously have considered, which can lead to expanded empathy and consciousness.

Targeted homophobic attacks, however, carry an additional, unique layer of vulnerability, so I pair group participation with ongoing one-on-one work that continues to contextualize the attack within the societal practices of homophobic hate speech and violence.

5) BRING YOUR SHARPEST SKILLS

The skills needed in LGBT2SQ+ centred therapeutic encounters are foundational skills for all good counselling work. It is our professional and ethical obligation to bring our best skills with everyone with whom we work. We need to

- create the conditions that invite a person to tell their story;

- be genuine, engaged, and responsive;

- ask questions and initiate conversations that probe at meanings of experiences, help to reveal insights, challenge interpretations taken as truth, and consider alternative perspectives;

- deconstruct assumptions and arrangements that we may take for granted, for example, regarding what makes a "good" person or what are "worthwhile" activities, regarding how people achieve social status, and regarding how we can counter dominant values;

- prompt analysis of social, political, and economic forces in people's personal lives;

- link personal circumstances with societal and systemic explanations; and

- connect people with relevant collectives, communities, and supports.

The historical and contemporary contexts are unique when we consider the lives of LGBT2SQ+ people. They add an additional layer of complexity. Throughout history, legal, medical, educational, and religious institutions were designed to formally exclude gay and lesbian people, and a fuller range of LGBT2SQ+ identities was completely invisible. The Diagnostic and Statistical Manual (American Psychiatric Association, 2013) – the standard classification system for mental health diagnoses – classified homosexuality as a psychiatric pathology until 1973. In addition, unlike other social prejudices, homophobia and heterosexism are most often first learned and experienced in the family home. Beyond the home, discrimination, exclusion, and/or violence are experienced regularly in the social institutions of school, athletics, youth clubs, medical care, religion, and most cultural customs.

In the absence of inclusive, responsive supports, it is not surprising that many LGBT2SQ+ people internalize the societal judgment and condemnation and that some struggle with mental health and addictions. For example, a US-wide study reported that lesbian, gay, bisexual, and trans youth comprise 40 percent of the homeless youth population (Durso & Gates, 2012). Another study reported that suicide rates among lesbian, gay, bisexual, and trans youth are four times greater than for non-queer youth (Zhao, Montoro, Igartua, & Thombs, 2010). It's true also that there have been improvements over the past two decades in the areas of media representation, legal protections against discrimination, and protections against harassment. Yet, the effects of prejudice and marginalization continue to impact the lives of LGBT2SQ+ people with chilling consequences.

COUNSELLING STRATEGIES

1) Give time and space for the stories of exclusion, discrimination, and violence that LGBT2SQ+ people experience

2) Validate the capacity of LGBT2SQ+ people to navigate the exclusions and hostilities with strategies that draw upon their strengths and solutions

3) Make connections between personal experiences and the societal attitudes, customs, and stereotypes that allow for discrimination toward and exclusion of LGBT2SQ+ people

4) Become familiar with the degree to which internalized discrimination can impact health

CASE APPLICATION

TAY

In their 16 years, Tay has witnessed a wealth of dismissive, degrading, and discriminatory comments and behaviours toward non-binary people. They've read blogs, listened to podcasts, overheard people talking on the bus and at family BBQs, heard news reports, and had guest speakers come to their schools detailing incidents and issues. Some of these sources have addressed the ways that LGBT2SQ+ people analyze the issues, resist the internalizing effects, cope through struggles, combat the prejudices, and build communities of support, celebration, and pride. My job is to listen to all of it, probe for meaning for Tay, and help prompt application of these learnings in their life. Attending to the volume of harms as well as the stories of resilience has been crucial, not only for our therapeutic relationship, but also for the clinical issues we are working on.

[Tay] "You asked me how I feel about all of this, and the answer is shitty. My parents are pissed all the time, and it's never going to change. I'm a disappointment to them – a freak they can't understand. I just cannot be what they want me to be. They look at me just like those ladies on the street and like that teacher at school. It's everywhere. So my parents are no different. They're embarrassed and ashamed of me, and I know it."

[Counsellor] "That's a heavy load to carry, Tay. We've talked other times about how helpful it can be to separate *who you are* from what you are feeling, and how doing so can help to keep it from taking over the way you see yourself and feel about yourself. When you were talking just now, what's the overwhelming feeling?"

[Tay] "Shame. A big, shitty ball of shame."

[Counsellor] "Okay. Shame. And it's big. How about we call it 'the big shame?'"

[Tay] "Okay."

[Counsellor] "Okay. I've got some clay here, and we're going to create a ball of clay that represents the big shame. Let's try to create it to look like how it feels to you … Now, every time we talk about the big shame, we're going to get out this ball, put it on the table, and talk to it, think about it, and consider it as one piece of what is happening here and as something that does not capture all of who you are. See how we can move it from your hands to the table? I suggest that we start thinking of it as moveable and shifting – from inside of you to outside of you. This way we can sit and look at it like this and also get up and move around it, talking about it from a variety of perspectives and viewpoints."

All our conversations are structured in ways that externalize "the big shame" and how it operates, what it believes, who and what supports it, and also what destabilizes and counters it. This practice of externalizing the problem is a narrative therapy technique (Morgan, 2000). It helps to see the problem not as located within a person – in this case Tay – and not as a deficiency or identity that sums up their total being such that they become problem-saturated. Rather, externalizing can help to frame the problem as the problem, a de-personalized phenomenon that can be isolated and analyzed according to a range of perspectives.

JAKE

Working with Jake through the trauma of being victimized has prompted many of the same reflections as discussions with Tay, except that Jake has personally known many people directly impacted by those news reports and societal exclusions. His reflections lead in a different direction now, because he is realizing that the experiences he has had, along with those of his friends and acquaintances, have been layering up within him. The incident of violence he experienced served as a tipping point, revealing just how deeply scarred he has been from years of absorbing the homophobic slurs, exclusions, and dismissals. He is now feeling weighed down with angst and despair, as well as unsure how he can regain his confidence and return to his routines.

My role in this work is to balance several approaches: joining Jake in critiquing the structural and systemic conditions that have had profoundly damaging effects on queer people, including him, and drawing upon this personal-political connection as a potential mobilizing energy for Jake to join with others in social justice pursuits. I also engage Jake in telling the many stories of LGBT2SQ+ people overcoming adversity and living rich, rewarding lives.

We also work specifically through Jake's personal trauma, including its manifestations of panic and grief. For panic, I ask him to jot a few things down every time he feels a physiological sensation such as a racing heart, churning stomach, and sweats. These include

> - a full description of the bodily sensation, as though explaining it to someone from outer space or painting a picture to someone without vision;
> - where was I? What were the weather conditions (if outside) or surrounding conditions (if inside)? Was I alone? With others?;
> - what immediately preceded the experience?;
> - the mantra that we have talked about as having meaning for him: "I stopped looking for the light. I decided to become the light."

For grief, Jake journals the range of feelings he experiences – a stream of consciousness, unedited volume of rage, love, fear, joy, hope, and more. He writes letters to people to express feelings and share thoughts, only rarely sending them, as that is unnecessary for this purpose. He also writes letters to the issues of homophobia, hate, and social exclusion – another version of externalizing – working through his analysis of their impact on him.

These techniques mobilize Jake's strengths, connecting to his personal traits as well as the resources of support within his environment. Ultimately, the work is to attach new meanings to past experiences so that Jake can integrate his traumatic experience and continue to live his life in ways that feel fulfilling to him.

FINISHING THOUGHTS

Social service workers and counsellors have a critical role to play in addressing the social and political inequities that burden the health, well-being, and wholeness of LGBT2SQ+ people. This work extends from micro levels to macro perspectives. It begins with the self and a focus on the words we use, grows to the level of organizational structure, and comes to rest in the clinical skills we use. We have the opportunity to influence how LGBT2SQ+ people experience services and systems of care, and we often have the power to reduce or remove barriers that marginalize and oppress this population.

The reach of heterosexism, homophobia, and transphobia extends through all societal institutions and social practices, and right into our heads. It's a combination that requires particular attention to how we think about the issues, how they impact on people's ways of being, and how we do our work, not only with queer-identifying people, but also with all people. Once we can see the constraining effects of socially constructed identity categories and their behavioural expectations, the thinking, being, and doing of LGBT2SQ+ centred practices becomes relevant across all populations.

ABOUT THE AUTHOR

Marion Brown, PhD, RSW

Marion holds a PhD in social work and is a Registered Social Worker in private practice and a Professor of Social Work at Dalhousie University. She has worked in various positions, from frontline to supervisory, in both clinical and community-based settings. In addition to her responsibilities at Dalhousie, and training with the Crisis & Trauma Resource Institute, Marion has a small private practice where she works with individuals and families who are facing barriers related to mental health, addiction, poverty, discrimination, violence, and relationship conflict. She has a particular passion for working from an LGBT2SQ+ centred perspective.

REFERENCES

American Dialect Society. (2016, January 8). 2015 Word of the year is singular "they." Retrieved from http://www.americandialect.org/2015-word-of-the-year-is-singular-they

American Psychiatric Association. (2013). *Diagnostic and statistical manual of mental disorders* (5th ed.). Arlington, VA: Author.

Durso, L. E., & Gates, G. J. (2012). *Serving our youth: Findings from a national survey of service providers working with lesbian, gay, bisexual, and transgender youth who are homeless or at risk of becoming homeless.* Los Angeles, CA: The Williams Institute with True Colors Fund and The Palette Fund.

Egale Canada Human Rights Trust. (n.d.) Retrieved from www.egale.ca

Isay, D. (Producer), (1989). *Remembering Stonewall: A radio documentary on the birth of a movement* [Audio file]. Retrieved from https://archive.org/details/pra-PZ0146

Kinsman, G., & Gentile, P. (2010). *The Canadian cold war on queers: National security as sexual regulation.* Vancouver, BC: UBC Press.

Morgan, A. (2000). *What is narrative therapy?: An easy-to-read introduction.* Adelaide, Australia: Dulwich Centre Publications.

Shelton, K., & Delgado-Romero, E. A. (2011). Sexual orientation microaggressions: The experience of lesbian, gay, bisexual and queer clients in psychotherapy. *Journal of Counseling Psychology, 58*(2), 210-221.

Syracuse Cultural Workers. (n.d.) Retrieved from www.syracuseculturalworkers.com

Warner, T. (2002). *Never going back: A history of queer activism in Canada.* Toronto, ON: University of Toronto Press.

Zhao, Y., Montoro, R., Igartua, K., & Thombs, B.D. (2010). Suicidal ideation and attempt among adolescents reporting "unsure" sexual identity or heterosexual identity plus same-sex attraction or behavior: Forgotten groups? *Journal of the American Academy of Child & Adolescent Psychiatry, 49*(2), 104-113.

CHAPTER NINE

GRIEF

By John Koop Harder

ONE OF MY EARLIEST MEMORIES OF PERSONAL LOSS WAS MY EXTREME disappointment in not making the A-level hockey team. As a nine-year-old child growing up in Prince Albert, Saskatchewan, hockey was *everything*. I had played on the B team the year before and assumed the natural process was to advance to the A team. I remember hearing of the team roster divisions and keeping it together until I got to the parking lot, where I burst into tears. Remaining on the B team for me was utter failure. My father sat with me in the car and noticed the coach walking by and invited him in. Both my coach and my dad sat with me as I cried. In the end, I was still sad, but I felt better. Looking back, this experience demonstrated a number of things to me:

➤ Loss comes in many forms.

➤ Experiencing loss sucks!

➤ Supports can make it better.

➤ The loss itself does not change, but the meaning given to the loss can shift.

These learnings continue to influence me as a therapist working with others' grief, as well as working through my own experiences of loss.

MIKE, THE BROWN FAMILY, MARY, AND KEVIN

Stories shape our lives. Throughout this chapter, I will introduce some of the people that have shaped my understanding of grief. These are some of the stories you will hear and examples of various life situations that can involve grief.

MIKE

A young man in his mid-20s, working through the childhood chaos resulting from the emotional, physical, and sexual abuse he experienced at the hands of his father.

THE BROWN FAMILY

A family going through normal family life transitions, loving and caring for a daughter with severe disabilities, and anticipating both possibility and limitation in her future.

MARY

A woman reshaping her life from one organized by alcohol, having survived horrors in her childhood at a residential school, and the subsequent chaos and the aftermath that led to the suicides and early deaths of family and friends.

KEVIN

A father grieving the death of his one-month-old son.

Loss and grief are normal, natural, and needed aspects of life. The very act of living and loving is a vulnerable process. We cannot know love without loss. One of the constants in life is change. When there is a change to a valued relationship, there is a loss, which can include grief. Despite this long-standing relationship with loss, it is a difficult relationship.

INSIGHTS AND GUIDING PRINCIPLES FOR COUNSELLING

In my work as a counsellor, I am often asked about strategies to move past the grief. Grief is uncomfortable and painful, and it takes time and effort to deal with it. However, if grief was a container and we had the opportunity to look into it, we would see that it could teach us about what is important in our lives and the world around us. One of my key learnings on grief is to not rush away from it. Turn towards it. Press into it. Get to know it. Carry it with you. Learn from it.

As helpers, we can assist others in their grief responses if we are informed by a basic understanding of grief. The following guiding principles inform how I work with individuals and families experiencing diverse stories of loss and grief.

1) **Get to know grief**
   Define grief, loss, and mourning as part of the person's story.

2) **Explore the meanings around loss**
   It is important to be curious about the person's own meanings associated with loss. Sometimes the meaning is more significant to the person than the loss itself.

3) **Explore life in the aftermath of loss**
   Curiosity is also key for understanding the common and unique ways people may feel the impact of their loss.

4) **Respond to grief**
   Thoughtful, intentional, and active support is important.

5) **Understand grief as a process**
   Grief does not follow a prescribed model.

6) **Reflect on stories of loss and resilience**
   Experience is the greatest teacher. Understanding other's experiences of loss and resilience can help better equip us to support others.

1) GET TO KNOW GRIEF

Our relationship with grief is lifelong and may ebb and flow in intensity. Because of this, getting to know grief is a complex, ongoing undertaking. The terms *loss*, *grief*, and *mourning* are often used interchangeably. They contain some similarities and some differences. As helpers, it's good to familiarize ourselves with the common terms.

Loss

I define loss as a change in a valued relationship. Some common examples may include

- ➤ death;
- ➤ decline or loss of ability/potential;
- ➤ divorce, separation, relationship break-up;
- ➤ loss of a job;
- ➤ change in health;
- ➤ loss of financial security;
- ➤ selling of a family home or other significant/sentimental property;
- ➤ theft.

The notion of loss is not confined to physical losses, but also includes the psychological. Loss can be about change or absence, such as infertility, an acquired brain injury, struggles with dementia or mental illness, and/or the absence of innocence or joy. With any loss, issues of previous losses may rise to the surface. This can complicate grieving.

Although there is no official handbook on loss, there are often general assumptions made around legitimacy or hierarchy of losses. Some losses are given more merit than others. Death and divorce are typically seen as more serious and impactful, whereas the loss of a pet or a possession may be seen as less so. No such hierarchy exists. The event of the loss is less important than the meaning the person gives to it. As helpers, remaining curious about these varied meanings is key in providing helpful support.

Grief

I define grief as the normal and natural package of emotions (such as sadness, anger, fear, or guilt) that accompany the loss of something or someone valued. Grief is a complicated process.

Sometimes clinicians categorize grief as *normal grief* or *complicated grief*. Normal grief is culturally influenced and changes with time – and it is normal. However, some losses place additional obstacles/complications to the process. Complicated grief is sometimes defined as occurring when the grieving process steps outside what is considered normal. Complicated grief can include traumatic reactions, preoccupation with the loss event, issues of isolation, self-blame, and persistent distress.

Mourning

Mourning is the process through which we express the complex emotions and experiences related to the loss.

COUNSELLING STRATEGIES

1) Name the experience

   ➤ Rather than imposing my clinical terms on the person's experience, it is important to help them express and personalize their own experience of loss and grief. A starting point in my work with people in their grief is exploring several important questions:

   • What do you call this experience of loss? Do you have a name for it?

   • What does it look like? (I often have people sketch a drawing of their grief or sculpt it with clay or Play-Doh)

   • What does it sound like? Does it have a soundtrack?

The richness of the responses can be profound and illuminating. Some of the responses I have heard include

➤ this experience is soul murder;

➤ this has been hell;

➤ I call it The Abyss;

➤ my grief soundtrack is Pink Floyd's "Wish You Were Here."

Loss creates chaos, whereas the process of naming creates a sense of control/ownership. In addition, such a line of questioning separates the person from their grief, allowing for a better understanding of the relational elements. Sometimes words cannot do justice to the experience or speaking them aloud can be too painful. Providing creative outlets of expression, such as art or music, can ease the process and can be an additional access point in conversation.

2) Interview grief
➤ One engaging and innovative intervention when dealing with strong emotions can be to imagine/enact a conversation with that feeling or dynamic (such as anger or an addiction). This often yields interesting, new, and helpful insights and learnings. In particular, role play can be a helpful tool. Ask the client(s) to take on the role of Grief, and then interview Grief with gentle curiosity and compassion. Or take on the role of Grief yourself and ask the client to be the interviewer.

CASE APPLICATION

A CONVERSATION WITH GRIEF

[Counsellor] "Hello, Grief. Can I call you Grief? Or what would you prefer to be called?"

[Grief] "People know me by many names. Some know me as Sorrow, Despair, or The Blackness. But you can call me Grief if you want."

[Counsellor] "Tell me a bit about yourself. What keeps you busy?"

[Grief] "I am extremely busy. I'm well known in all walks of life. In fact, everyone knows me and spends time with me, whether they like it or not! With such a social calendar, I have very little down time."

[Counsellor] "Being so widely known, I'm wondering how people view you?"

[Grief] "Unfortunately, I am often shunned and avoided. People think I'm out to cause pain and misery wherever I go."

[Counsellor] "Does that fit for you?"

[Grief] "Definitely not. Sure, sadness and sorrow are part of me, but it isn't everything. I don't think people can have love, joy, or happiness without me. Tolstoy put it best: 'Only people who are capable of loving strongly can also suffer great sorrow, but this same necessity of loving serves to counteract their grief and heals them.'"

[Counsellor] "That is a great quote. So, it sounds like you've gotten a bad reputation. How do you want to be known?"

[Grief] "I kind of fancy myself as a teacher. You (and everyone else) can learn a lot about yourself, what is important in life, and what is valued by spending some quality time with me. If I may quote Lord Byron, 'Sorrows are our best educators. A person can see further through a tear than a telescope'. The thing is, the lessons learned by hanging out with me are difficult. A person needs time, patience, courage, and, most importantly, supports."

[Counsellor] "A teacher? Do people often see you this way?"

[Grief] "Some do, but most people do their best to avoid me. If people take the time to get to know me, some do begin to welcome me. Say, have you heard this one from Jerry Seinfeld? According to most studies, people's number one fear is public speaking. Number two is death. Does that sound right? This means, to the average person, if you go to a funeral, you're better off in the casket than doing the eulogy!"[1]

[**Counsellor**] [Laughing] "I don't think many people would expect you to have a sense of humour!"

[**Grief**] "Yes, I like to hang out with Laughter. I find we work well together."

[**Counsellor**] "I'm getting to see a different side of you here. But let's face it – it's not all learning and laughter. Do you ever find problems follow you?"

[**Grief**] "Yes, unfortunately. Sometimes I am just too much to bear, and people just turn off."

[**Counsellor**] "What do you mean 'turn off'?"

[**Grief**] "They turn off as a way of coping. Some turn to drugs or alcohol, others lose themselves in their work, or in gambling and so on. A visit from Addiction becomes a reality for some. For others, 'turning off' looks more like Depression. Sometimes Anxiety creeps in. The unfortunate thing is, I am still *there*. These things just tend to pause or cover over the pain of the loss."

[**Counsellor**] "So these are friends of yours – Addiction, Depression, and Anxiety?"

[**Grief**] "I wouldn't really call them friends. But they sometimes follow me around and tend to get in the way of things."

[**Counsellor**] "That sounds complicated. As you know, I work a lot with people in their relationship with you. Do you have any advice I could pass to them?"

---

1. Callner,1998

[Grief] "Tell them that I am part of their lives. You have known me since birth and will continue to know me until you die. We have a lifelong relationship, whether you want to acknowledge it or not. Take the time to invest in and consider our relationship. When you do, I wouldn't be surprised if you are the better for it. Reflecting on our relationship may also help prepare you for the next time I come to visit."

[Counsellor] "Thank you Grief for taking the time to meet today. I'm assuming we will meet again ..."

[Grief] "It's only a matter of time! See you soon."

3) Keep a grief journal

➤ Attention to the rhythms of grief and how it ebbs and flows in intensity can give a sense of control and may reduce some of the anxiety associated with grief.

➤ On a daily basis, the person can track the intensity of grief on a scale of one to 10, including when it was at its lowest and highest points and what they were doing/experiencing at that time.

Date	Least Grief-Intense Moment/s (1-10)	Activity	Most Grief-Intense Moment/s (1-10)	Activity	General Intensity of Grief (1-10)
6/12	4	Going for a run	8	Going to bed alone	6
6/13	3	Supper with friends	7	Breakfast alone	5
6/14	4	Playing guitar	8	Looking through pictures	6

Figure 9.1 *Grief journal*

➤ This exercise is valuable, because the person is not being asked to do anything other than observe and record. Although it may not seem like much, it can be very difficult to do on one's own. At times, I will walk through this exercise with clients in our meetings, taking time to reflect back on the past week.

➤ This strategy can offer an increased sense of control as the person reflects on the intensity of grief and connecting that with what they were doing at the time. It can also provide key insights that might inform them as the process of grief continues.

4) Create a lifeline

➤ Life happens. Life is joy, and life is loss and many other experiences as well. A strategy I sometimes use with people is to create a lifeline, chronicling joys and losses, highs and lows. This strategy works better for those later in their grief journey (it's not as appropriate when the loss is still raw). This exercise is influenced by James and Friedman's work (2009), which describes the usefulness of chronicling a timeline of loss. I have found it more helpful to include the life-giving experiences along with the difficult. *See page 305 in the Resources section*

➤ A lifeline drawing can be a visible acknowledgement of the client's ups and downs in life and can be kept for private reflection and learning or shared with others. Recently, my 12-year-old son came home from school having completed a similar timeline in his Grade 7 English/Language Arts class. It's a great illustration of what the lifeline can look like (see Figure 9.2, shared here with his permission) and demonstrates how this tool can be used very effectively with children as well as adults.

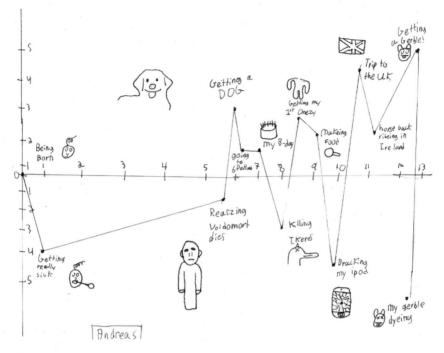

Figure 9.2 *Sample image of a lifeline drawing*

2) EXPLORE THE MEANINGS AROUND LOSS

We are all meaning makers. As such, people can endure the same loss and yet experience grief in very different ways. In order to understand the personal meaning of the loss, it is helpful to understand the various influences that will shape grief and its meaning.

CASE APPLICATION

MIKE

I met Mike early in my career as a counsellor. His story stands out and continues to influence my practice. When I met him, he was in his mid-20s and was seeing me to work through the childhood chaos resulting from the emotional, physical, and sexual abuse he experienced at the hands of his father. During one particularly memorable meeting, Mike came in looking very distraught. He then explained that he needed to sell his car as he just couldn't afford it anymore. In the back of my mind, I must admit some judgment flashed: "Let's get to the real counselling, what's the big deal with selling a car?" Fortunately, I was able to shift my posture toward curiosity. I inquired into what the car meant to him.

Mike told me that as a youth he would spend Saturdays with his grandpa, and the two of them would work on the car together. These Saturdays were the one time during the week where he felt safety, security, and love. This car was not just a means to get around, but it was also an anchor to safety and security. Mike then spoke of his grandfather's death five years ago and spent much of the rest of the session sharing his favourite memories of his grandpa.

Mike taught me a valuable lesson that day. It's not the loss (such as selling a car) that is the real issue. It is the *meaning* given to the loss that creates the need to grieve. With curiosity, the uniqueness of the personal experience of grief becomes more accessible.

One helpful way to understand the numerous influences on how a person experiences grief is the context of their individual experiences, as well as their family, community, and society. Individual influences can include age, current stressors, mental health, gender expectations/assumptions, supports/coping skills, and previous losses. Family influences may consist of values/beliefs, routines and rituals, communication patterns, and intergenerational trauma. Community influences may include access to resources, the "isms" (such as racism and sexism), and community health. Broader societal influences can include cultural or religious beliefs and our country's history of colonialism and cultural genocide.

COUNSELLING STRATEGIES

As meaning is influenced by many factors, we need to explore the person's experience of grief, rather than make assumptions regarding impact and what *we think* is needed. In fact, the person's meaning may have more impact than the actual loss. A sensitive and curious posture can be the most significant way to help the individual explore their unique experience. Explore meaning with curiosity by asking curious questions like these:

➤ What influences in your life (such as previous losses, culture, assumptions) may affect your experience of this loss?

➤ What do you wish others understood about your experience?

➤ What did you value most about _____?

➤ What influence did _____ have on you?

➤ What parts of this relationship do you want to hold onto? To remember?

➤ What parts of this relationship do you wish to let go of?

➤ What was the worst part of _____?

➤ What do you need now? What might you need next week? Next month?

➤ How can I be a support with this?

Exploring meaning is important with any person, but it is especially important when supporting children or those that may experience cognitive difficulties; it's important not to assume that they understand loss in the same way others do. Rather, inquire directly on how they understand the loss. In addition, use clear and direct language and avoid using metaphors or "sugarcoating" (such as "Grandma has gone away" or "she has passed"), as this can confuse and complicate the understanding of the loss.

3) EXPLORE LIFE IN THE AFTERMATH OF LOSS

A key aspect of the grief process is the acknowledgement of the impacts of loss in different areas (including thoughts, emotions, and relationships). However, this may be difficult due to common patterns of avoidance, minimization, and denial. People may also experience fear and anxiety about exploring their losses due to beliefs that this may increase their sense of despair. As helpers, being able to explore, normalize, and anticipate the ebbs and flows of the impacts can assist with the grief process. However, this can also be overwhelming. As such, continued review of coping strategies will be important. We can help the bereaved explore their reactions on their own terms, allowing them to become their own experts of their grief.

CASE APPLICATION

THE BROWN FAMILY

I met the Brown family when I was working as a resource person for children with disabilities. Chris, the father, spoke about the joy he gets every day when he comes home from work and is met with his daughter Danielle's smiling face and her squeals of delight. After a bit of a pause, his manner of relating shifts, and his voice cracks somewhat as a tear rolls down his face. He tells me of his enduring love for his daughter but also talks of how reality does not fit with the hopes and dreams he had prior to her birth. He speaks of the profound loss of these dreams.

He notes he will never be able to teach her to drive, see her off to university, or dance at her wedding. He will not be a grandfather. He then speaks of the challenges that having a child with disabilities has created in his relationship with his partner, Michelle. They are not the couple they once were. Chris also talks about looking forward to an upcoming trip, Michelle's birthday party, and some much-needed respite where, as a couple, they have a weekend away.

At the close of the meeting, Chris tears up again and thanks me for listening. He tells me he has not been able to share like this with others.

Everyone will experience grief differently. For some, grief is sudden and unexpected, such as with an accident or suicide. For others it is gradual, such as a chronic illness or the dissolution of a relationship. The impacts may come and go, be delayed or be triggered by various reminders, such as holidays, anniversaries, places, or emotions. Although everyone will experience differences in grief and loss, common patterns do occur (Figure 9.3).

Common Behavioural Impacts	Common Cognitive Impacts
➤ Isolating or needing to be with others ➤ Decreasing interests and activities ➤ Numbing ➤ Changes in relationships	➤ Difficulty concentrating ➤ Preoccupation with the loss ➤ Questioning ➤ Worries
Common Emotional Impacts	Common Physical Impacts
➤ Sadness and despair ➤ Anger ➤ Numbness ➤ Mood swings	➤ Lack of energy ➤ Loss of appetite ➤ Difficulty sleeping (too much, broken, too little) ➤ Aches and pains (head, stomach, body in general, etc.)
Common Spiritual Impacts	
➤ Change in values or priorities ➤ Search for understanding – the "whys" ➤ Lack of meaning ➤ Disconnection from self and others	

Figure 9.3
Common patterns of the impacts from grief

COUNSELLING STRATEGIES

1) Explore the impacts of loss with curiosity

> ➤ There is a lot of judgment when it comes to grief. We see this in terms of assumptions made around timelines and our compelling need for others to "get over it." We judge which losses are most severe and how loss should or shouldn't impact people. Judgments around grief are further influenced by the fact that we have all experienced loss and grief – yet this may trick us into believing we understand a universal experience. Each experience of grief is different and unique. Do not assume anything. Rather approach each person with curiosity. Pose curious questions to explore the impact of the loss:
>
>   - What does grief look like for you?
>
>   - What has been lost, what has been changed, what remains?
>
>   - Which impacts are the hardest?
>
>   - Do these impacts shift and change with time? If so, how?
>
>   - What do you wish others knew about your experience?

4) RESPOND TO GRIEF

Inherent in any loss is a sense of disconnection. Given this, it would only make sense that strengthening connections should be an important element when working through loss. A key element of walking through grief is the support of others. Support means different things to different people and may shift with time. Whether we are friends, family, neighbours, co-workers, or professionals, we can and do have an important role in the grief process. We just need to have some understanding of grief along with intentionality in how we respond.

Here's the challenge – and it's a big one. Grief is uncomfortable, messy, and chaotic. Those around the person experiencing grief feel this and are often reminded of their own losses. They may also share in some of the feelings of hopelessness, helplessness, and powerlessness. This can lead to advice giving, which is a less effective reaction/response.

CASE APPLICATION

SARA

I met Sara in a small northern community in a workshop I was delivering on grief. The group was doing an exercise working with Play-Doh, where they were sculpting what grief looks like to them. Sara shared her sculpture of grief with the group. It consisted of an enclosed circular wall with a small opening in the top. Within the circular wall was a small round bit of Play-Doh, which represented herself, and on the outside of the wall was a number of other round bits of Play-Doh representing others in the community.

Sara noted that her grief kept her alone. She couldn't see out, and others couldn't see her. Sara then shared her story of loss. Sara's son David had been murdered a few years ago. She talked about how this shattered her life and left her feeling very much alone. The emotional walls around her were very high, and were both protective and isolating. Sara talked about how much courage it took to venture out from her protection and even to go for a walk around the neighbourhood. But on her walk, people avoided her. People literally crossed the street to avoid crossing her path. This made her feel even more alone.

KEVIN

Recently, I met with Kevin, whose son died at the age of one month. Life has never been the same for him. Kevin shared his experiences of people's acts of support, some of which he valued, and some that were profoundly unhelpful. He noted that many people tended to avoid him and his partner. Others offered words intended to be supportive, like "He is with the angels." or "You had one month together – treasure it always." or "You are young. You can have another child."

These responses angered Kevin. With time, he was able to look back on the good intentions in these responses, but, in the moment, they were not welcomed.

> *When we honestly ask ourselves which persons in our lives mean the most to us, we often find that it is those who, instead of giving advice, solutions, or cures, have chosen rather to share our pain and touch our wounds with a warm and tender hand. The friend who can be silent with us in a moment of despair or confusion, who can stay with us in an hour of grief and bereavement, who can tolerate not knowing, not curing, not healing and face with us the reality of our powerlessness, that is a friend who cares.*
>
> —Henri Nouwen in *Out of Solitude* (2004, p. 38)

All too often, people get caught up in trying to make things better with words and/or actions. Sometimes, the best support is just our silent, caring presence and being witness to the grief.

COUNSELLING STRATEGIES

In supporting others, whether it be in their grief or in other struggles, *who* we are and *how* we are with people is more important than what it is we *do*. Helping is an art, rather than a science. As such, the following qualities are foundational within the supportive relationship:

➤ Empathy

➤ Supportive listening

➤ Patience and a non-anxious presence

➤ Ability to shift judgment to curiosity

➤ Ability to hear difficult experiences

➤ Comfort with a wide range of emotions

➤ Reflection on own experiences with grief – having done one's own work

The first priority while supporting those experiencing grief is sitting with and bearing witness to their grief. Alongside this, offering practical supports is often welcomed. The following can be a helpful guide.

1) Ask permission and offer practical support

➤ All too often, we offer the support in terms of "Just let me know if there is anything to do." Although well-meaning in its intent, this places the initiation on the person who may be too overwhelmed to know what they need, may not want to impose, or is too tired to ask or care. It's better to ask permission and offer particular means of support, such as, "Is it okay if I stop by with a meal?" or "Can I help by picking up the kids after school?" or "Can I call you next week to see what you need for groceries?"

2) Share stories and favourite memories

➤ How and who we are shifts and changes depending on the context we are in. Friends, family members, and co-workers may have unique stories/experiences of the same loss. Through sharing stories, the richness of the person or thing lost becomes more alive and increases connections to that person as well as to others. If you do not have experience about the person/thing, ask for favourite memories, or experiences.

3) Practice double listening

➤ This practice holds both the story of loss and of the relationship valued. Being able to hear, hold, and draw out these two sides of grief can be an important aspect of supporting the grief process. Focusing too much on either of the stories does not do justice to the other. Rather, to hold each in balance is the art of support. For example, a client might say something like "I can't bear to be without him." A double listening response helps the client explore both aspects of grief, such as the loss story ("What do you miss most about him?") and the relationship ("Can you share a story that highlights this quality?").

4) Check in

➤ Pay attention to the rhythms of grief. Anticipate times, places, and situations where the impacts of grief may be more pronounced and support more appreciated. Examples may include: anniversaries, holidays, returning to work, and other memorable dates. Wonder with the person(s) ahead of time what these experiences might be like and strategize what supports may be needed (or not).

5) Help mobilize resources

➤ Grieving is a lonely process. As helpers, we can assist the bereaved in considering what they need in terms of support and how best to communicate these needs. In doing so, the following questions may be helpful:

  • What do you wish others knew about what you were going through?

  • What do you need from _____?

  • What don't you need from _____?

  • When do you need them the most? The least?

  • When do you prefer to be on your own?

  • How can you let them know this?

➤ Some people have found it helpful to draft a letter to others regarding their needs and preferences about support. Organizations affected by loss may also consider drafting a letter (with the consent and input of the primary bereaved person) regarding how others could be supportive.

➤ It can be helpful to consider what types of support various people may offer, creating a list of such resources:

- **Doers:** People who are helpful at getting things done and can offer practical supports such as help with transportation, repairs, or housework.

- **Listeners:** Those you can count on to be patient, supportive, and empathetic.

- **Organizers:** Those who can help create a plan of action when one feels too tired or overwhelmed.

- **Respite Supporters:** Those who can offer a needed break from grief and engage in activities of enjoyment, such as going to a movie or the gym.

➤ As helpers, we can help the bereaved create such a list and assist in how they may reach out to such supports. We can also help plan for how they may deal with negative or destructive people in their lives.

6) Be there for the long haul

➤ The experience of loss can bring out the best in people. Supports often come out of the woodwork. For some, this experience can be very welcoming, while for others it can be overwhelming. Unfortunately, many supports are short-lived. Grief can be a long process. Walking alongside the person for whatever time it takes is an important aspect of support.

7) Be cautious of ineffective responses

➤ Despite grief being a normal, natural, and regular part of life, we are often ill-prepared to face grief and loss. Discomfort and a sense of not wanting to make things worse can impede support and can lead to ineffective or avoidant responses.

➤ Common (but ineffective) themes in responding to grief and loss include

- not knowing what to say or do, so avoiding any action;

- mistaken attempts at relating ("I know what you are going through.");

- intellectualizing responses or clichés ("Things will get better," or "There will be other … ," or "She/he is no longer in pain," or "God gives you only what you can handle.");

- avoiding painful emotions ("Big boys and girls don't cry," or "You need to be strong in the face of … ," or "You need to keep it together for the kids.");

- medicalizing or pathologizing grief ("This is depression," or "This is PTSD."); or

- emphasizing faith ("Find comfort in God," or "She/he is with God now.").

5) UNDERSTAND GRIEF AS A PROCESS

There are numerous models of understanding grief, the most well known of which is based on Elisabeth Kübler-Ross' (1973) ideas around dying. Kübler-Ross described that, in coming to grips with death, people go through five stages: denial, anger, bargaining, depression, and acceptance. But grief is a journey without clear markers or maps, rather than stages. The process may contain elements of anger, denial, depression, and more, but rather than a linear progression, it is more of a chaotic process.

We are always in a state of *becoming*. Identity is not static but in a constant state of change. Loss is a part of this change. Integrating and learning from loss will be important aspects of becoming the person we want to be.

Part of the grieving process is the creation of a *new normal*, a new reality that is borne as a result of the loss. In moving towards this new reality or story, there is a back-and-forth dialogue between the event story (the loss) and the relational background story. Eventually, these stories merge into something new. This dialogue (and the fruit of this dialogue) will look very different for each person. It can be a difficult conversation, but it is an important one.

CASE APPLICATION

JOHN

One of my own personal grief stories occurred several years ago, after an international work opportunity disintegrated after only one year. My family and I had uprooted our lives to take on a massive adventure that we hoped would be a profound cross-cultural experience, while being professionally challenging for both my partner and me. When we returned to Canada sooner than we had expected, I vacillated between being sad, angry, resentful, and depressed. I was mourning the personal and professional opportunities we would now never have. Over time, as I worked through my feelings of grief in contrast with my assumptions, expectations, and hopes of this experience for me and my family, I was able to find a new equilibrium that allowed me to access and honour the joy of that one year we had spent abroad. While the process of building this internal dialogue was difficult, it has allowed me to integrate the great personal and professional learnings I gleaned from that experience while continuing to acknowledge my feelings of loss. I now use my insights from that year every day in my work.

COUNSELLING STRATEGIES

1) Name the process

   ➤ Providing support to those experiencing grief starts with helping them name their experience of loss. As people continue in their relationship, it too can be helpful to name this grief process. Terms such as "healing" or "recovery" at times sound too artificial or too clinical. Labelling the process gives a personal sense of ownership and control. For example, Mike called the process "getting on with it." Other clients have described their grief process as "the journey," or "picking up the pieces," and, simply put, "life."

2) Explore intentionality within the relationship

➤ All relationships shift and change with time. At times, relationships are closer or more intense. At other points, they may drift and become more distant. As a counsellor, I use the following questions to explore relationships:

- How are you in this relationship?

- How do you *want* to be?

- What do you need as you continue in this relationship?

I find these questions particularly helpful in assisting clients explore their relationships with grief, especially after the initial intensity of the loss has passed. When a person is more engaged with their grief, the above questions may spark interesting reflection. As with any relationship, there is danger of going on autopilot, of turning off, of being less intentional and involved. Within relationships, especially important ones, intentionality in the relationship is key. When we have a clearer picture of how we *want* to be in our relationship with grief, we are more likely to see it realized. This can allow a person to develop a plan for the next phase of their grief. *See page 307 in the Resources section for a description of this activity.*

6) REFLECT ON STORIES OF LOSS AND RESILIENCE

One of the things I love best about my job as a counsellor and trainer is that I have the opportunity to meet interesting and remarkable people from all over Canada and the United States. Their stories and experiences influence both my professional and personal life (in welcome and unwelcome ways).

For the past several decades, there has been greater awareness in the helping field about the drawbacks of intense helping work, which include compassion fatigue, vicarious trauma, and burnout. However, alongside the challenges that come with helping, there are clear benefits for us as helpers. One such benefit is the newer concept of vicarious resilience (Hernández,

Gangsei, & Engstrom, 2007). Not only do we have the potential to be negatively impacted by the work, but we also have the potential to learn, grow, and develop resilience alongside our clients. The stories of sadness and sorrow influence me, and, in the same way, I am influenced by the stories of overcoming and growth. I intentionally carry many stories that inspire me and provide me with hope and encouragement in the face of the despair this work sometimes brings.

CASE APPLICATION

OKI

I met Oki during one of my first visits to the Northwest Territories as a trainer. Having never been so far north before, I asked the group to educate me on the area. The following day, Oki approached me during one of the breaks and asked if I had a few minutes. Oki reached into his pocket and removed a small round badge on a string, declaring, "Identification Number #####". Oki then shared his experience of being forcibly removed from his home at a young age and sent to live in a very remote residential school. Oki shared what the experience stole from him, including his home, his family, his traditions, his fun, and his sense of safety.

After a brief pause, Oki placed the badge in his pocket and said, "This is part of me and I carry this experience with me everywhere I go. This is a reminder of what was, but look at me now. I am a father, a son, a partner, a coach, a friend, and a helper. I am strong, and I am good." Oki's story of looking loss in the eye, embracing grief, and walking with it continues to influence me in all aspects of my life.

MARY

I met Mary a few years back in a very remote community where I was leading a workshop. Mary was a soft-spoken woman, but when she spoke, the whole group would go silent and soak up her words. It was very clear that her wisdom was well respected. When she laughed, which she did often, it would fill and influence the room. Her laughter was a welcomed break from the heaviness of the topics we were exploring.

Over a lunch period, I asked Mary if she always had such laughter in her life. Mary shared briefly of a few of horrors she experienced as a child in residential school. The chaos and the aftermath of this experience led to the suicides and early deaths of family and friends. She spoke of accidents and illnesses that took her children and others close to her. To deal with the unbearable pain, she found relief in alcohol. Alcohol had been a friend and a comfort for many years but began to cause problems in its own right. Getting sober was a process that took time, effort, and many supports. Attending a treatment program and embracing her culture and traditions has helped along the way.

Mary shared that getting sober meant facing her grief in new ways. Rather than continuing to choose alcohol in her walk with grief, she embraced the elders in the community, her culture, and her traditions. Mary reflected on a profound personal change that came about in the process. Laughter, described as a long-absent friend, began to visit her more and more as a gift on her journey. When I met her, laughter was clearly no longer the absent friend but a constant companion.

COUNSELLING STRATEGIES

Working with grief can be both challenging and rewarding. Sometimes we need to put energy into warding off the downsides of helping and building our own resilience. Some ways I work at developing resilience as a helper include keeping my mind and heart focused on the powerful stories of people like Oki and Mary, whom I've met in my work. The following strategies can be tools to aid this process:

1) Keep a "rainy day" folder to look at and reflect on when feeling particularly overwhelmed or burdened. This can include stories, cards, art, or music that remind you of the transformative power of grief.

2) Share these powerful stories with others while always respecting your clients' confidentiality. As we vocalize such stories, their influence becomes richer and further influences others and us.

FINISHING THOUGHTS

In the end, it is important to simply acknowledge that love and loss are two sides of the same coin in relationships. Understanding the value in grief and helping others explore the meaning and impact of their losses can play a huge role in how a person grieves. This, in turn, can foster the continued growth of their love, even in the midst of their devastating loss.

ABOUT THE AUTHOR

John Koop Harder, MSW, RSW

John is a trainer and training development specialist with the Crisis & Trauma Resource Institute and has been working as a therapist for 20 years. He is a Registered Social Worker who holds a master's degree in social work. Much of John's career has centred on working with children, youth, adults, and families dealing with crisis and trauma. While he has a diverse practice, he has particular interest and specialized experience in working with individuals and families impacted by grief, mental health concerns, post-war trauma recovery, and sexual abuse recovery.

REFERENCES

Callner, M. (Producer & Director). (1998). *Jerry Seinfeld – I'm Telling You for the Last Time – Live on Broadway* [Motion Picture]. United States: HBO.

Hernández, P., Gangsei, D., & Engstrom, D. (2007). Vicarious resilience: A new concept in work with those who survive trauma. *Family Process, 46*(2), 229-241.

James, J. W., & Friedman, R. (2009). *The grief recovery handbook: The action program for moving beyond death, divorce, and other losses.* New York, NY: Harper Collins Publishers.

Kübler-Ross, E. (1973). *On death and dying.* New York, NY: Routledge.

Nouwen, H. (2004). *Out of solitude: Three meditations on Christian life.* Notre Dame, IN: Ave Maria Press.

CONCLUSION

THE STORIES AND STRATEGIES IN THIS BOOK REFLECT THE VULNERA-
bility and strength of both clients and helpers as they work together toward increased health and resilience. Helping people is complex work filled with varied emotions such as hope, worry, inspiration, and sometimes even surprise at the developments in people's lives.

Ultimately, each person seeking help needs to choose their own direction. In these pages, you have heard stories of many people charting their own path of change through diverse life circumstances. For each of these stories, there is a parallel storyline of how each counsellor is affected and changed from feeling and learning with their clients.

Sometimes helpers will have a lot of influence, and other times, we may feel like we're along for the ride with little control over the outcome. As we travel alongside another person on the path toward their goals, we will witness and feel many perspectives and emotions. This vicarious journey will ultimately also shape our own experience and understanding of life. In conversations with the authors of these chapters, I have heard expressions of heart-wrenching concern and awe-filled amazement at the strength and grit of people they worked with. Above all, the authors share a sense of gratitude for the privilege to witness such survival and transformation.

I am frequently asked how I persevere in a profession of listening and helping others who are suffering. The answer to this question is hard to articulate, and I have discussed with many colleagues and friends in this field about how they also come up with a response. A common theme in these conversations is the primary importance of taking true care of oneself as a helper, knowing what matters to *you* – what refuels and nurtures your passion for this work, and learning to find the right boundaries and support to anchor your care. This means staying grounded and open-hearted and remembering that we do not have the power or the right to change people. We have an opportunity to offer connection, skill development, empathy, and insights. If we do our job well, those we are supporting will make their own choices, and we won't be needed in the same way anymore.

The focus of this book has been to describe ideas of how to *be* with other people, and *ways to offer support* for a variety of life situations. Each chapter has been a conversation between helpers, hopefully bringing a sense of community to a role that can sometimes feel very isolating as we work with people on very private and intimate subjects. I want to encourage you to pay careful attention to your own insights and learn from your work with people. Attend to your own body, mind, and spirit. The most important tool in your toolbox is your own self and well-being.

I hope this book has offered you insights, inspirations, and validation for the work you do as a helper. Thank you for your time and dedication. When we each bring our most sincere efforts to this work, the tide rises and lifts us all up.

Be well.

Vicki Enns
Editor and Clinical Director, Crisis & Trauma Resource Institute

RESOURCES

The resources in this section will provide detailed guidance and examples for putting the ideas presented in this book into action. Each has been referenced in one of the preceding chapters.

Below is a list of the page on which each resource was referenced, so you can go back and re-read the section for further context.

The topics highlighted here follow the same order in which they were referenced in this book. Additionally, you will be able to find these resources as downloadable PDFs on our website at www.ctrinstitute.com.

PAGE 278   **Sensation Charades**

PAGE 280   **Identifying Sensations**

PAGE 282   **Pendulation Activity**

PAGE 283   **Resource Emotion List**

PAGE 284   **Feelings Walk**

PAGE 285   **Relaxation Breathing Script**

PAGE 286   **Progressive Muscle Relaxation**

PAGE 287   **Identifying Body Clues**

PAGE 288   **Making the Mind–Body Connection**

PAGE 290   **Distinguishing Depression from the Depressed**

PAGE 291   **Mapping out the Self-Injury Cycle**

PAGE 293   **Building a Coping Tool Kit**

PAGE 295   Informal Suicide Risk Assessment Checklist

PAGE 297   Safety and Wellness Plan

PAGE 298   Chain Analysis

PAGE 300   Goal Setting

PAGE 301   Managing Problematic Substance Use Thoughts

PAGE 302   Identifying Emotions

PAGE 303   Wall of Fame for Raising Awareness and Visibility for LGBT2SQ+

PAGE 304   Resource Library for Expanding Exposure and Integration

PAGE 305   Lifeline Exercise

PAGE 307   Grief Exercise: Packing for the Journey

SENSATION CHARADES

Referenced on page 17

Purpose

This is an activity that can be used to practice identifying and naming sensations in a playful way. It can be used to explore and deepen body awareness, to learn to notice the immediate experience of sensation, and as a stepping-stone skill toward discerning between sensations, emotions, thoughts, and behaviours.

Instructions

With a partner, each person will take a turn describing sensations, while the other person tries to guess what item or situation the person is referring to. It is more important that the person describing sensations is accurately reflecting their own experience, regardless of whether the other person can guess accurately or not. It can be fun to compare what the description evokes for each person, even if entirely different. Rather than guessing, each person can just take turns practicing identifying sensations.

Choose a word card and take a few moments to imagine and visualize this item in your mind. Really fill in the details, allowing your imagination to shape it in whatever way makes most sense to you. Use your senses to help you: what do you imagine you hear, see, smell, taste, and feel (with your sense of touch).

Using only descriptions of sensations, describe your word (without using the actual word) to your partner. Try not to get abstract describing metaphors or memories, just describe the sensations (taste, touch, inside feeling, quality of sound or smell). You can use a list of common sensation words to help with this. Use some of these beginning phrases to help you describe sensations:

➤ When I touch it, my fingers feel …

➤ When I smell it, my nose feels or senses …

➤ When I taste it, my tongue and mouth feel …

➤ When I visualize it, I can feel or sense _____ in my belly (or chest, or hands, or arms).

➤ When I imagine hearing it, the rest of my body responds by …

Sample Word Cards

Cotton ball	Campfire smoke	Toes pinched in too-small shoes
Chicken soup	A candied apple	Waking up from a good sleep
Sandpaper	Ginger ale	Ice skating
Black licorice	Snowflake	Holding a freshly caught fish in your hands

IDENTIFYING SENSATIONS

Referenced on page 17

Purpose

Learning to notice and identify sensations is helpful for learning to recognize and manage emotions. This capacity is also essential for working more directly with helping one's body shift from a stressed, dysregulated state to a resourced and regulated state. It is important to be able to notice and connect with sensations that are associated with both *stressed* states and *resourced* states. These word lists are just samples and may carry different meanings for each person. Some words fit in both lists; it will depend on the quality of it. Feel free to add your own words.

Sensation words often associated with more *stressed* and *dysregulated* states:

➤ Abrasive, Angular

➤ Barbed, Bendy, Bloated, Blunt, Bristly, Broken, Bulging, Bulky, Bumpy, Bushy

➤ Chafing, Chapped, Choppy, Chunky, Clammy, Coarse, Cold, Corrugated

➤ Dense, Dented, Dirty, Distended, Distorted, Dry, Dusty

➤ Edgy, Etched, Filmy, Flat, Flimsy, Fragile, Freezing, Frigid, Furry, Fuzzy

➤ Glassy, Glazed, Gnarled, Gooey, Grainy, Grating, Gravelly, Greasy, Gritty

➤ Hairy, Hard, Harsh, Hollow, Hot, Icy, Impenetrable, Inflated, Irregular, Itchy

➤ Jagged, Limp, Lumpy, Metallic, Narrow, Pointy, Prickly

➤ Ragged, Rasping, Razor-sharp, Ridged, Rigid, Rough, Rusty, Rutted

➤ Sandy, Saturated, Scalding, Scarred, Scored, Scraped, Scratched, Sculptured, Serrated, Shaggy, Sharp, Slimy, Soiled, Spiky, Spiny, Steely, Stubbly

- Stiff, Sticky, Sweaty, Tepid, Thick, Thin, Thorny, Throbbing
- Uncomfortable, Uneven, Vibrating, Viscous
- Waterlogged, Withered, Woollen, Wrinkled, Zigzag

Sensation words often associated with *resourced*, *solid*, and *regulated* states:

- Airy, Aerated
- Breathy, Bubbly, Calm, Circular, Clean, Cool, Cushioned
- Doughy, Downy, Earthy, Even
- Feathery, Firm, Fleecy, Flowing, Fluffy, Fluid, Frothy
- Gentle, Glossy, Grounded, Grooved, Hot
- Layered, Leathery, Level, Lined, Loose, Lukewarm
- Malleable, Moist, Moving, Mushy, Neat
- Oily, Open, Padded, Patterned, Pliable, Polished, Pulpy
- Quiet, Ribbed, Rock-solid, Rubbery, Rolling
- Sheer, Silky, Slick, Slippery, Smooth, Soaking, Soapy, Soft, Soggy, Solid
- Sparkly, Spongy, Springy, Stable, Steely, Syrupy
- Tepid, Thick, Thin, Tingly, Unbreakable, Unyielding
- Varnished, Velvety, Veneered, Vibrating
- Warm, Wavy, Well-oiled, Wet, Wide, Wiry, Woven
- Yielding, Zigzag

PENDULATION ACTIVITY

Referenced on page 37

Purpose

This activity can be used to encourage clients to notice how emotional responses manifest in the body. Clients may feel disconnected from their body, and this activity is a good introduction to the mind-body connection. This exercise can be grounding, promote an awareness of calm, and promote safety and self-soothing in a session.

Instructions

Ask your client to find a comfortable seated position with their feet on the ground. Speak slowly, using a calm voice. Listen for when you can direct your client to notice safety within their own body. Adapt the language to be consistent with your practice approach.

Sample Script

"Move into a comfortable position with your feet on the floor. Take a few breaths, just noticing how each inhale and exhale feels. (Pause). Take your awareness to your body, from the top of your head, all the way down to your toes. Notice any area of tension, tightness, or discomfort. (Pause).

"Continue to breathe, and bring your awareness back down your body from your head to your toes. Notice any area of calmness, lightness, or comfort. This can be as small of an area as your baby toe or earlobe. (Pause and check in with your client about their awareness of a calm place).

"Now, still breathing in and out, bring your awareness to the area of discomfort and imagine your awareness as a pendulum that swings back and forth. Swing your awareness from the area of discomfort to the area of calm in your body, back and forth, back and forth (slowly, pausing). Just notice your body and your breath. What are you noticing in your body now?"

Continue to do this until the client reports calmness in the previously tense area of their body. If the client reports no change, transition to a grounding exercise that focuses on breathing only.

RESOURCE EMOTION LIST

Referenced on pages 38 and 133

Purpose

This list is used as a psycho-educational activity to assist clients in identifying their emotional experience. At times, people can ruminate on the experience of an emotion without being able to identify it. This can cause distress and worry in our clients. The emotion list can be used to assist clients in naming their experiences to better understand and address them.

Mad	Sad	Happy	Fearful	Disgusted	Surprise
Bitter	Grief	Joyful	Scared	Awful	Startled
Angry	Pensiveness	Proud	Anxious	Hesitant	Amazed
Aggressive	Despair	Peaceful	Insecure	Revulsion	Confused
Frustrated	Abandoned	Positive	Avoidant	Repulsion	Excited
Distant	Guilty	Optimistic	Submissive	Disappointed	Jolted
Critical	Lonely	Accepted	Humiliated	Disapproval	Scared
Ridiculed	Bored	Powerful	Embarrassed	Judgmental	Shocked
Jealous	Depressed	Open	Worried	Detestable	Dismayed
Hostile	Remorseful	Playful	Overwhelmed	Loathing	Disillusioned
Annoyed	Ashamed	Loving	Rejected	Avoidance	Perplexed
Withdrawn	Ignored	Inspired	Terrified	Aversion	Awestruck
Violated	Victimized	Courageous	Inferior	Bored	Eager
Let down	Powerless	Confident	Insignificant	Contempt	Energetic
Humiliated	Vulnerable	Independent	Inadequate	Shame	Unsure
Rage	Inferior	Liberated	Ridiculed	Embarrassed	Unsettled
Insecure	Empty	Ecstatic	Disrespected	Worthless	Bewildered
Suspicious	Indifferent	Inquisitive	Worthless	Worried	Disturbed
Provoked	Abandoned	Amused	Alienated	Remorseful	Frustrated
Irritated	Isolated	Respected	Panic	Sorrowful	Ambivalent

FEELINGS WALK

Referenced on page 71

Purpose

This activity is designed to help clients become more aware, in an experiential way, of the physical sensations associated with different emotions. When clients are tense or feel keyed up, the feelings walk can be used to reduce tension and help shift them into a calmer state.

Instructions

➤ Ask the client to stand up and begin to walk around the room.

➤ Name a feeling and ask them to walk in a way that embodies that feeling in their body and face. For instance, "Walk sad … walk happy."

➤ Use contrasting feelings so the client can notice the difference in their body (happy-sad, anxious-relaxed, bored-excited).

➤ End the exercise with a calm feeling.

RELAXATION BREATHING SCRIPT

Referenced on pages 71 and 139

Purpose

Relaxation breathing is a strategy for helping to reduce intense anxiety. It can also be used as an anxiety-prevention tool. Clients can be encouraged to routinely practice relaxation breathing to prevent the buildup of stress and anxiety.

This relaxation breathing can be done anywhere and at any time. Many people find four-four-eight is a comfortable count to slow down and regulate their breathing, while for others the count may be too long or short and will need to be adjusted. The exhale should be about twice as long as the inhale. The long, slow breath out triggers the relaxation response. If clients are able, encourage inhaling through the nose and exhaling through the mouth.

Instructions

➤ Get into a comfortable position.

➤ Notice your breathing.

➤ Breathe in to the count of four.

➤ Hold the breath for a count of four.

➤ Breathe out to the count of eight.

➤ Repeat five times, inhaling through your nose and exhaling through your mouth.

PROGRESSIVE MUSCLE RELAXATION

Referenced on pages 71 and 139

Purpose

Intentionally tensing and releasing muscles reduces tension and relaxes the body. Focusing on specific muscle groups helps clients become more aware of their bodies and the presence or absence of tension.

Instructions

Progressive muscle relaxation involves the tensing and releasing of muscles in the body to initiate the relaxation response. Clients should be encouraged to do relaxation breathing after each muscle group is tensed and released.

Short, targeted format:

➤ Get into a comfortable position.

➤ Clench your hands (or any tense area of the body) and hold them tightly while keeping the rest of your body relaxed.

➤ Hold for 10 seconds. "One, two, three … hold it tight … eight, nine, ten, and release."

➤ Notice how your hands feel loose and relaxed.

➤ Breathe in slowly.

➤ Exhale slowly, imagining the tension leaving your body.

➤ Repeat.

Full body format:

Using the tense and release procedure from the short format, start with the feet and move up the body, tensing and releasing major muscle groups or tense areas of the body, ending with muscles in the face. Do each area once and take five slow breaths after each tense and release, imagining tension leaving the body on the exhale. This practice is helpful at night to induce relaxation and sleep.

IDENTIFYING BODY CLUES

Referenced on page 71

Purpose

Using this activity in a group or one-on-one with your client can be effective in normalizing the physical symptoms associated with anxiety and helping your client develop awareness and understanding of their anxiety experience.

Instructions

➤ Use the outline provided or draw an outline of a body on flipchart paper.

➤ Identify the physical symptoms/body clues experienced when feeling anxious or worried.

➤ Draw a line from each body clue to the part of the body where the symptom occurs.

- Example:

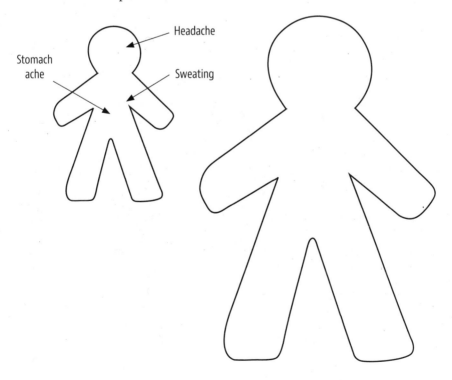

MAKING THE MIND–BODY CONNECTION
Referenced on page 95

Purpose
Exploring patterns in physical health can aid in raising awareness about the direct connection between body and mind. This allows a person to make more informed and healthy choices.

Instructions: Part 1
Have clients document basic information regarding their physical, nutritional, sleep, and hygiene habits for seven to 14 days. Explore the findings with your clients and work together to identify areas that can be aggravating and/or mitigating their depression-related symptoms. Build an action plan that works to strengthen helpful patterns and modify or eliminate problematic patterns.

Item	MON (example)	TUES	WED	THUR	FRI	SAT	SUN
Water Intake	3 glasses						
Eating & Snacking Times	11:44 am 4:40 pm 10:15 pm 4:00 am						
Hours of Sleep	5.5 hours						
Minutes/ Type of Exercise	30 min – 5-km run						
Alcohol Intake	Glass of wine @ 10:15pm						
Hygiene Activity	Shower						
Physical Discomfort	Back pain						

Instructions: Part 2

Have clients document basic information regarding their emotional, psychological, spiritual, and financial health for a period of seven to 14 days. Explore the findings with your clients and work together to identify areas that can be aggravating and/or mitigating their depression-related symptoms. Build an action plan that works to strengthen helpful patterns and modify or eliminate problematic patterns.

Item	MON (example)	TUES	WED	THUR	ETC.
Activities that brought me joy	Lunch with an old college roommate				
People/pets who brought me joy	Brad – my old college roommate				
Sense of my financial status	Okay – payday was just on Friday				
Time spent outdoors	None				
Things I am proud of	Made it to work on time				
Things I did well	Can't think of any				
Stress items	Son recently diagnosed with autism – met with school today				

DISTINGUISHING DEPRESSION FROM THE DEPRESSED

Referenced on page 100

Purpose

Paying attention to the status of key depression indicators is important for establishing, implementing, and modifying a client-centred action plan. Assessing the indicators in a consistent way keeps the counsellor in the know regarding where things started, how things are progressing, or how things are digressing. This allows planning for the right interventions at the right time and knowing when more support is needed or when light challenges would be more useful.

Areas of Concern	Week 1 (example)	Week 2	Week 3	Week 4
Ability to Interact with Counsellor	· Limited · Difficulty communicating hopes or desired outcomes for seeking counselling · Difficulty making eye contact			
Appearance and Hygiene	· First time meeting · Today appears tired · No notable hygiene difficulties			
Daily Functioning	· Reports an inability to go to work or interact with others · Sleeping 12-14 hours			
Suicide Assessment Findings	Medium Risk			
ACTION PLAN	· Client to connect with family doctor · Release of Information signed · Follow-up appointment scheduled			

MAPPING OUT THE SELF-INJURY CYCLE

Referenced on page 129

Purpose

One of the most important tasks is increasing awareness of the connection between self-injury behaviour and a person's emotions, thoughts, and behaviours.

Instructions

The following questions provide a guide to helping the person discover their experience of the self-injury cycle:

1) Finding triggers

   ➤ What kinds of situations cause you to feel stressed out?

   ➤ When do you notice yourself becoming angry? Scared? Sad?

   ➤ What overwhelms you?

   ➤ How do you handle conflict?

2) Discovering what continues the escalation

   ➤ What do you notice in your thoughts when you are angry?

   ➤ What do you say to yourself when you experience other strong emotions?

   ➤ Do you consider yourself to be a perfectionist?

   ➤ What kind of self-talk do you use when you are upset?

3) Prior to the self-injury behaviour

   ➤ What do you notice usually happens right before you cut/burn/scratch/hit?

   ➤ Do you feel an impending sense of dread or panic?

   ➤ Do you feel numb, unfeeling, or dissociated?

4) Self-injury behaviour and the immediate impact

➤ What happens after you cut/burn/scratch/hit?

➤ Describe how you feel immediately after the self-injury behaviour.

➤ How do you think the self-injury behaviour helps you?

➤ Do you feel better after? If so, tell me how.

5) The aftermath

➤ How long do you feel better? When do you notice that start to change?

➤ How do you feel after a few hours?

➤ Do you experience a sense of guilt or shame?

5. Aftermath
Reaction of Anger,
Shame or Guilt

1. Trigger
(Trauma, Negative
Beliefs About Self,
Negative Emotions)

4. Self-Injury
Action and
De-Escalation: Calm

2. Increased
Emotional Tension
and Distorted
Thinking

3. Overwhelm
Leading to:
a) Panic or
b) Shutdown

BUILDING A COPING TOOL KIT

Referenced on pages 144 and 178

Purpose

This activity is designed to build resources to help clients move toward making healthier choices when they are coping with stress and adversity. The person can choose activities, objects, pictures, and quotes that will remind them about how to self-regulate, reach out for help, nurture themselves, or simply to help tolerate difficult experiences.

Instructions

If possible, provide access to some materials that could be incorporated into a small box or chest. Also, some reminders, such as quotes, photos, or websites, could be written on business cards that could be carried at all times. Materials used may include

- magazines;
- inspirational quotes;
- natural materials, such as feathers or stones;
- candies or chocolates;
- journals;
- art materials, like crayons, markers, or paint;
- helplines and crisis lines;
- websites that provide helpful information;
- clay or Play-Doh;
- fidget toys;
- names and photos of support people;
- pictures of pets, favourite places, or peaceful scenes;
- prompts for breathing exercises;
- music that is calming or uplifting;
- reminders of healthy activities they enjoy.

Building a Coping Tool Kit Example

photo of grandmother	picture of a campfire	fuzzy socks
favourite quote	Kids Help phone line	favourite book
ginger ale	breathing square	chicken soup
fuzzy peach candies	snowflake	my pet dog

INFORMAL SUICIDE RISK ASSESSMENT CHECKLIST

Referenced on page 157

Purpose

A risk assessment document can be a helpful guide to refer to when determining how many high-risk chronic and current risk factors are present for someone who is experiencing suicidality. The following assessment can assist helpers to ensure that they have explored a variety of individual, family, and systems-related risk factors, as well as protective factors and identified reasons for living. While documents like this should never be used as a substitute for an in-depth clinical assessment, they can act as a guide for both the assessment and documentation process.

See Informal Suicide Risk Assessment Checklist on Next Page.

Informal Suicide Risk Assessment Checklist

Agency/ Program:		Client:		DOB:	
Screen Completed by:		Date:		Time:	

☐ Client Denies Suicidal Thinking   ☐ Client Confirms Suicidal Thinking

RISK FACTORS

	Chronic:		Acute:
	Previous Suicide Attempt		Current Suicidal Thoughts
	History of Suicidal Thoughts/ Behaviour		Current Suicidal Plan
	History of Mental Health Issues		Recent Suicidal Thoughts/ Behaviour
	History of Psychosis		Access to Suicidal Methods
	Impulsive/ Aggressive Tendencies		High Lethality of Suicide Methods
	History of Non-suicidal Self Injury		Increased Non-suicidal Self Injury
	Chronic Illness and Pain		Current Mental Health Issues
	Family History of Mental Health Issues		Current Psychosis
	Family History of Suicide		Agitation or Anxiety
	History of Family Loss		Current Substance Use
	History of Abuse, Neglect, Trauma		Feelings of Hopelessness
	Cultural Risk Group		Recent Loss or Major Life Change
	Male Gender		Recent Suicide(s) in Family/Community
	LGBT2SQ+		Minimal Social Supports
	Other:		Minimal Professional Supports
			Minimal Support from Caregiver
			Unresponsive to Supports
			Other:

Assess Reasons for Living:		Assess Protective Factors:	
• What has been keeping you safe now? In the past?		Family and community connectedness	
• Is there anything that gives you hope or helps you think more about living?		Skills in coping, problem solving and conflict resolution	
		Hope for the future	
• Do these things help you feel better, even briefly?		Opportunities for contribution and sense of meaning	
		Cultural and spiritual beliefs that increase hopefulness/ support self-preservation	
Suicide Risk Estimation:		Willingness to access supports	
		Willingness to work together to stay safe	
☐ Low ☐ Medium ☐ High			

Next Steps: _____

_____

Note: This tool should never be used alone or as a substitute for a thorough clinical assessment. Assessing risk needs to be collaborative, developmentally appropriate, and include collateral information.

SAFETY AND WELLNESS PLAN

Referenced on pages 102 and 158

Purpose

Safety plans should be used as a resource for clients to highlight what they are willing to do in order to increase their use of external and internal resources and stay safe from suicide. The following plan is a guide that can be used both during a suicide intervention and throughout the span of one's work with someone who struggles with ongoing suicidal ideation.

Name: Date:

If I am unable to keep myself safe from suicide, I will:

- ➤ Call 911 or my 24-hour crisis line _____
- ➤ Go to the emergency room
- ➤ Ask for help from a supportive adult _____
- ➤ Not use drugs or alcohol

PEOPLE WHO CAN SUPPORT MY PLAN

	Name:	Contact information:
Caregiver		
Counsellor		
Social Worker		
Teacher		
Doctor		
Spiritual Support		
Other		

I COMMIT TO PURSUE WELLNESS IN THE FOLLOWING WAYS:

Notice My Warning Signs:

- _____
- _____
- _____

Use My Coping Tools:

- _____
- _____
- _____

Remember My Reasons for Living:

- _____
- _____
- _____

Next Steps: _____

CHAIN ANALYSIS

Referenced on page 176

Purpose

A chain analysis can be used to assist an individual to become more aware of how their thoughts, emotions, and behaviours can contribute to problem responses. Using this process with clients can assist them in both developing more self-awareness and in feeling more in control of future responses. A key component of this process is reviewing possible points of change following the identification of the chain of events, so that one can determine areas of change and potential skill development.

Instructions

1) Identify areas of current vulnerability (environmental stress, physical illness, injury, pain, fatigue, hunger, drug use, emotions).

2) Identify prompting event/trigger.

3) Identify response: P – Physical; T – Thoughts; E – Emotions; A – Actions; B – Beliefs.

4) Identify outcome/consequences.

5) Identify possible points of change.

6) Identify ways to help and prevent response next time.

7) Identify skills to be further developed.

Chain Analysis Example with Client

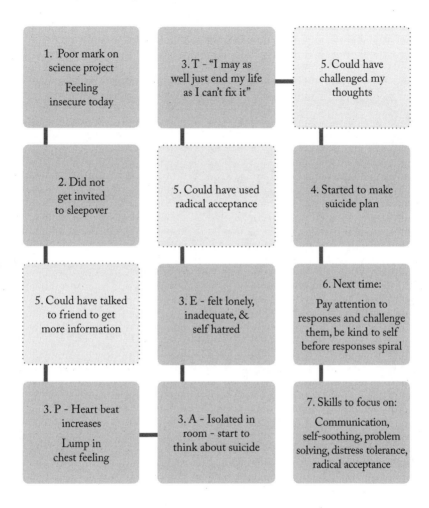

1. Poor mark on science project

   Feeling insecure today

2. Did not get invited to sleepover

5. Could have talked to friend to get more information

3. P - Heart beat increases

   Lump in chest feeling

3. T - "I may as well just end my life as I can't fix it"

5. Could have used radical acceptance

3. E - felt lonely, inadequate, & self hatred

3. A - Isolated in room - start to think about suicide

5. Could have challenged my thoughts

4. Started to make suicide plan

6. Next time:

   Pay attention to responses and challenge them, be kind to self before responses spiral

7. Skills to focus on:

   Communication, self-soothing, problem solving, distress tolerance, radical acceptance

GOAL SETTING

Referenced on pages 194 and 200

Purpose

This goal-setting worksheet can be used to help direct counselling by clarifying for the counsellor and the client the goals they are working to achieve. It assists in breaking down the large goal into manageable chunks and allows for small successes along the way.

GOAL SETTING	

Substance Use Goal   Abstinence ☐   Harm Reduction ☐

Long-Term Goal (What kind of use by what date – be as specific as possible)	Short-Term Strategies to Achieve Goal (Concrete plans, tasks, or strategies that will help achieve long-term goal)
	1) 2) 3)

Life Domain Impacted (Physical health, emotional regulation, financial, workplace, family relationships, spirituality)	Long-Term Goal (Be as specific as possible)	Short-Term Strategies to Achieve Goal (Concrete plans, tasks, or strategies that will help achieve long-term goal)
		1) 2)
		1) 2)

MANAGING PROBLEMATIC SUBSTANCE USE THOUGHTS

Referenced on page 203

Purpose

This worksheet can be used to help the counsellor and client identify and manage thoughts that lead to problematic substance use and then generate alternate thoughts. The client should practice thinking about these alternative thoughts in their own time. The counsellor and client should collaborate to generate thoughts that support refusal of problematic substance use patterns.

MANAGING PROBLEMATIC SUBSTANCE USE THOUGHTS

How to use this worksheet: Identify the triggering thoughts that lead to cravings and urges to use. Develop alternative thoughts that would be helpful to think about the situation. The thoughts can be used as coping statements when the trigger thought comes to mind.

Tips for Identifying Problematic Substance Use Thoughts
- Read the statements below and see if the client relates.
- Ask the client to think about the thoughts that come to mind right before they use.
- Ask the client to keep a record of the thoughts they had when they had cravings.

Tips for Creating Alternate Thoughts
- Acknowledge the thought. (For example, Ben acknowledging his thought: "I am thinking about getting drunk before my date.")
- Generate a positive coping statement. It could be helpful to think about the consequence of using or using a positive affirmation. (For example, Ben might use a positive coping statement such as "If I get drunk before my date, this girl is not going to be interested in me. I choose not to drink before this date. I've got this.")
- Use assertive language. Pick language that a person who believed they could reduce their use or quit their problematic use would use. Try assertive words like "no" or "choose" when thinking about the craving or urge. (For example, Ben's assertive language could be "No, sneaking-drinking thought, I cannot have just one. I end up wasted, and the girls don't like that. I choose to be sober for my date tonight, so I can date a girl who is nice and smart.")

Problematic Substance Use Thought	Alternative Thought
No one will ever know if I have this one _____.	
I'm going to do an experiment and see if I can have _____.	
I won't be able to socialize if I don't have a _____.	
I deserve a reward. I've had a hard day.	
Other:	
Other:	

IDENTIFYING EMOTIONS
Referenced on page 207

Purpose

This worksheet can be used to help the client understand that emotions are part of the human experience. The client can use it to identify what their emotions are and to generate ideas about what they could do to cope with their emotions without engaging in problematic substance use.

IDENTIFY EMOTIONS WORKSHEET

How to use: Look at the word list and select the emotions that are triggering and lead to problematic use.

Happy	Shame	Humiliated
Sad	Remorse	Disgust
Joy	Love	Enraged
Fear	Lonely	Other:
Anxious	Embarrassed	Other:
Scared	Grateful	Other:
Guilt	Hurt	Other:

PROBLEM SOLVING	
Emotion	**Coping Strategy**

WALL OF FAME FOR RAISING AWARENESS AND VISIBILITY FOR LGBT2SQ+

Referenced on page 232

Purpose

This is an activity and an outcome that builds the visibility of well-known people who identify as lesbian, gay, bisexual, trans, Two-Spirit, queer, questioning, and intersex. Developing a Wall of Fame in one's workplace is a concrete step toward increasing queer-friendly workplace culture, as well as communicating to people coming into the workplace that this environment recognizes and celebrates the rainbow community.

Instructions

Place a suggestion box in the reception area with a sign inviting anyone coming in to deposit the name of a public personage who is out as lesbian, gay, bisexual, trans, Two-Spirit, queer, questioning, or intersex.

Choose a location in the workplace that is a central gathering place and easily viewable. The front entryway is preferred, because it is a well-established location for invitation and welcome. Find current, clear, and high-quality images of the people identified and erect a permanent, expandable display. This could be a material, tangible testament of printed photographs, or a digital version with a rotating slideshow of images.

RESOURCE LIBRARY FOR EXPANDING EXPOSURE AND INTEGRATION

Referenced on page 234

Purpose

A resource library communicates many messages. The contents can be of use to participants in an agency's programs and available for loan. Its existence demonstrates an investment in the learning, entertainment, and/or practical usage for staff, as well as clients. It can also grow to be a resource for community members and students, which helps to establish the credibility and relevance of the agency within the community. A resource library focused on LGBT2SQ+ people, interests, and issues also signifies a clear commitment to expanding exposure and integration among all people.

Instructions

Advocate for a budget item for a resource library based on the purpose noted above combined with the agency mandate to provide services of support to people in need. Find a location in your agency that allows space for browsing and display of a range of collection items. Strike up an agency committee or seek volunteers to find movies, documentaries, music, novels, magazines, and biographies related to people, interests, and issues that identify with LGBT2SQ+. Classify the materials in a manner that allows for easy tracking and additions and develop a borrowing system. Then promote your new resource library and keep it relevant and up-to-date with regular additions.

LIFELINE EXERCISE
Referenced on page 255

Purpose
Doing a personal lifeline or inventory of joys and challenges can be insightful as part of getting to know grief. When loss occurs, it often brings up memories of other losses. Reflecting back on the history, impacts, intensity, learnings, and others' responses to the losses can give new understanding into the current loss and the lingering impacts of previous losses. Such an inventory not only brings new awareness into the current situation, but also prepares for future losses.

Caution and Consideration
Doing such an exercise can be helpful, but caution ought to be used, as this can become very overwhelming. Prior to doing the exercise, it is important to review readiness and coping strategies. This exercise is most suited for those further along in their grief journeys.

Instructions
1) Draw a line across the page.
2) Label one side zero (indicating your birth), the far side your current age, and the middle half your age.
3) Now draw a vertical axis and label the axis -5 to +5 to indicate level of intensity.
4) Place your joys and losses in sequence on the timeline.
5) Indicate the impact, influence, and intensity of each of the experiences of joy and loss in relation to the vertical intensity.
6) Make brief notes (words, phrases, drawings) that come to mind with each experience.
7) Reflect/debrief using the following as possible prompters:

   ➤ What was it like doing this?

   ➤ What themes do you notice?

   ➤ Which losses were easier or harder to face? Why is this?

➤ What influence has loss had on your life?

➤ How have the losses influenced the joys?

➤ How have the joys influenced the losses?

➤ What will you take from this experience?

➤ If you were to share this with another person, who would this be?

➤ What would you hope they would gain from seeing this?

GRIEF EXERCISE: PACKING FOR THE JOURNEY
Referenced on page 269

Purpose

To reflect on the current grief journey or prepare for the next experience of loss. Some losses we see coming, while others happen out of the blue. Regardless, we all have and all will make a journey with grief. Like all travels, it is helpful if we can bring things with us to assist along the way. For some of the losses, we can prepare what we "pack." For others, we are thrust into the voyage with little to no preparation and are forced to consider picking up "items" along the way.

Instructions

Consider what might be helpful for the process of working through grief using the metaphor of being on a journey.

As we walk through grief, it is helpful to "pack" and consider the following:

➤ A notebook/guidebook: This represents lessons learned and notes made from previous experiences of grief. These lessons may be your own or have been observed or passed on from others.

➤ Compass: This represents the values and beliefs that you want to hold on to and guide you.

➤ Snacks: What may nourish you along the way?

➤ First aid kit: Bumps and bruises occur. What are the things that may help with the pain(s) on this journey that you want to intentionally employ?

➤ Toiletries bag: What are the rituals and routines that you want to continue (daily, weekly, and so on)?

➤ Souvenirs: What reminders of this journey do you want to hold on to and why?

Additional Considerations

➤ Companions: Some trips are best made alone, while others welcome company.

  • Who do you wish to accompany you?

  • On what parts of the journey would you welcome others, and on what parts might you prefer to be on your own?

  • Who are people that you have met along the way that have been helpful?

➤ Pit stops: What are some of the experiences that may provide a break and respite along the way?

GLOSSARY

Abstinence
To deliberately refrain from, or deny oneself, an action or practice, which often requires conscious effort. In the process of addiction recovery, it is the commitment to completely stop using a particular substance or behaviour pattern to break its hold on the person.

Acceptance and Commitment Therapy (ACT)
A form of mindfulness-based therapy at the core of which is the belief that well-being comes from overcoming negative thoughts and feelings. ACT addresses an individual's commitment to change and assists in reducing avoidant coping.

Amygdala
A brain structure that is part of the limbic system, it receives sensory information directly from the outside world through our senses and integrates thoughts from the prefrontal cortex. It then engages with other brain structures to form an emotional response and form associations that result in memories to guide future emotional responses. The most studied feature is the amygdala's role in organizing a fear response.

Asexuality
A sexual orientation where an individual does not experience sexual attraction.

Autonomic Nervous System (ANS)
A part of the nervous system that regulates involuntary bodily functions, such as breathing, heart function, and the digestive system. The ANS has two branches: the sympathetic and parasympathetic. The sympathetic system sets off survival responses known as fight, flight, or freeze, while the parasympathetic system relaxes the body and slows down high-energy functions.

Biosocial Theory
A perspective exploring how individual biological, genetic factors interact with social factors and environmental influences. In therapeutic models, it is used to form interventions that combine building positive social connections with developing skills for regulating and managing one's own emotional responses. This term is often used interchangeably with biopsychosocial.

Circular Questioning

A family or couple therapy technique that both gathers and introduces information. Each person in the session takes turns answering questions and expressing their views on the relationships and emotional processes in the family system. This form of questioning helps develop a perspective of the interactive and circular nature of family interactions, rather than an individual perspective.

Cisgender

When a person's gender identity and expression match their biological sex.

Cisnormativity

A combination of the assumption that people are cisgender (meaning their gender identity matches their assigned sex at birth) and all the cultural practices that serve to uphold this assumption.

Clinical Depression

Commonly referred to as major depressive disorder or major depression, it is a more severe form of depression where the symptoms cause noticeable problems in personal relationships, as well as causing a disruption to day-to-day functioning. Symptoms persist over a sustained period of time and are not attributed to psychological effects or other medical conditions. Clinical depression can affect people of any age. Symptoms of clinical depression can improve with psychological counselling, medication, or a combination of both.

Cognitive Behavioural Therapy (CBT)

A talk therapy (psychotherapy) approach that is short term and goal oriented. CBT focuses on identifying and changing problematic patterns in thoughts and beliefs, often called cognitive distortions. The assumptions and meanings that a person attaches to situations are examined to give the person more choice to learn to adopt more reasoned and flexible perspectives.

Cognitive Distortions

Ingrained patterns of thinking about the self and the world around us that are based on negative emotion or meaning. These inaccurate patterns of thought are rigid and contribute to negative emotional and behavioural patterns.

Developmental Trauma

Traumatic impact that occurs during the early and vulnerable developmental stages of life. Often these experiences are repetitive and include an interpersonal element, such as abuse, neglect, or maltreatment. Developmental trauma sets the stage for a person to be more vulnerable to subsequent stressors in life, often resulting in layers of symptomology and mental health concerns.

Dialectical Behavioural Therapy (DBT)

A form of cognitive behavioural therapy that is based on the biosocial model. It emphasizes the psychosocial importance of building positive relationships and developing skills for emotional regulation.

Disordered Anxiety

Characterized by unexpected or unhelpful persistent anxiety that seriously interferes with daily life, including how a person thinks, feels, and acts. Caused by an overestimation of threat and underestimation of one's ability to manage or cope, leading to intense and irrational fear, and avoidance of normal life situations.

Dissociation

Separation of an individual's consciousness, identity, memory, or actions from their regular behaviour. In the context of a traumatic event, dissociation can be an adaptive response to allow a person to "step out of themselves" or separate from the current situation in order to better survive it. Dissociation can occur to different degrees: on one end, everyday daydreaming is a form of dissociation, and, on the other end, dissociation can be associated with very high stress and be part of a traumatic freeze response to escape the present threat.

DSM-5

Diagnostic and Statistical Manual of Mental Disorders, currently in its fifth edition. The manual defines and classifies mental disorders in order to improve diagnoses, treatment, and research.

Emotional Dysregulation

The inability to regulate, control, and manage one's emotional response to provocative stimuli. Emotional dysregulation leads to an exaggerated response to environmental and interpersonal challenges.

Emotional Intelligence

The ability to understand, appraise and manage one's emotions and the emotions of others. To be able to use emotions to guide one's thinking, use emotional knowledge effectively, and to regulate emotions to promote both emotional and intellectual growth.

Emotional Regulation

The processes, both conscious and nonconscious, that an individual takes to monitor, evaluate, and modify their emotional response to a provocative stimulus.

Eye Movement Desensitization and Reprocessing (EMDR)

An evidence-based integrative psychotherapy approach using a standardized set of protocols to aid in the completion of formerly incomplete or maladaptive processing of traumatic or disturbing life experiences. The treatment is structured to use alternating bilateral visual, auditory, and/or tactile stimulation to activate the components of a disturbing memory and further an adaptive processing and integration of this memory into a person's larger life experience.

Genogram

A form of visual mapping that is typically an intergenerational diagram outlining the history of a family (marriages, births, divorces, etc.) as well as ongoing patterns. The map can be used to visually represent relationship qualities (closeness, distance, conflict), as well as diverse family structures (foster family, adoptive family, blended family, chosen family, etc.). Any information can be symbolically tracked across generations and relationships, such as physical or mental health, struggles, and strengths.

Harm Reduction

A set of practical strategies and ideas aimed at reducing the negative consequences associated with a particular behaviour (drug use, self-injury), without necessarily reducing or stopping the behaviour.

Heteronormativity

A combination of the assumption that people are heterosexual (they experience sexual attraction and that attraction is directed at a member of the opposite sex) and all the cultural practices that serve to uphold this assumption.

Heterosexism

The prevailing ideology and culturally sanctioned systems that together institutionalize a preference for and assumption of heterosexuality.

Holistic

Characterized by the analysis of the whole, rather than the individual components. In a counselling context, it is an integration of physical sensations (body), emotions, thoughts, perceptions (mind), connection and relationships with others (social), and one's broader sense of meaning, purpose, and culture (spiritual).

Homophobia

The fear of, aversion to, and discrimination against gay and lesbian people; also related to biphobia, which is the fear of, aversion to, and discrimination against bisexual people.

Imaginal Exposure

A client is asked to imagine and describe feared images or situations with the intent to expand their capacity to tolerate and manage their response, ultimately extinguishing the fear. The description should be done in present tense and include details about external (sound, sight, smell) and internal (emotion, thought) cues. Generally approached in a step-by-step graduated way to ensure a safe process that builds capacity and is improving one's quality of life.

LGBT2SQ+

An acronym used to specifically name lesbian, gay, bisexual, transgender, Two-Spirit, and queer identities, with the "+" intended to signify an inclusion of a full range of gender identity and sexual orientation expressions and experiences, including intersex, asexual, pangender, and questioning. The acronym may be used in different variations to intentionally increase the visibility of distinct communities. LGBT2SQ+ has been chosen here to highlight the growing societal recognition of the LGBT2SQ+ community generally and the important emerging recognition of the layered invisibility of Two-Spirit people within the colonized history of Indigenous peoples.

Limbic System
Group of brain structures centrally located, including the hippocampus, amygdala, and hypothalamus in addition to links with other brain regions. This system is considered the centre for emotional responsiveness, motivation, formation, and encoding of memory, and generating responses in promotion of survival instincts. Due to its central location, this system plays a crucial integrative role by connecting various brain regions.

Microaggression
The casual degradation or dismissal of a person or group of people that has a cumulative effect of creating a culture that privileges some and weighs down others. Comments or behaviours that carry an assumption or negative connotation, often minimized by the person doing the commenting or acting.

Narrative Therapy
A collaborative and non-pathologizing approach in which the individual is the expert on their own life. By transforming personal experiences into stories, the individual can learn about their identity, as well as their personal goals and purpose. This method separates the person from the problems they are experiencing and encourages individuals to rely on their personal skills to resolve and minimize the issues.

Open Questions
Questions that require more than a single-word or single-phrase answer. Open questions require the responder to think and reflect on their opinions and feelings. Typically, these questions begin with *what, when, who, or how.*

Outpatient
A patient who receives treatment without being admitted into a hospital.

Pansexuality
Sexual attraction or desire that is open and fluid to people of all genders.

Parasympathetic Nervous System
A branch of the autonomic nervous system that becomes activated after a stress response, to return body systems back to a calmer resting state. It slows down heart rate and increases gland and digestive activity to allow body systems to rest and recuperate.

Post-Traumatic Stress Disorder (PTSD)
A mental health condition that's triggered by a single or a series of traumatic events, either experienced or witnessed by the individual. Symptoms can include intrusive imagery, thoughts or memories of the event, anxiety and flooded emotions, withdrawal and avoidance of reminders of the event, and disconnection from oneself and from others. For a diagnosis, a person needs to experience multiple symptoms for a prolonged period of time that are disruptive to the day-to-day functioning of the individual.

Prefrontal Cortex
Located in the top and front of the brain (frontal lobe), the prefrontal cortex is involved in many integrative functions processing information from various sensory modalities. Key functions include forming and recalling memories, interpreting perceptions, generating responses to situations, and many other diverse cognitive processes.

Radical Acceptance

Letting go of the preconceived notions of how oneself and the world should be and accepting life as it is. This includes letting go of judgments and avoiding attempts to fight against or change things outside of one's control. This state can assist to decrease one's suffering as one experiences greater inner peace.

Residential Schools

Government-sponsored schools that were administered through churches. They were established to assimilate Indigenous children into Euro-Canadian or Euro-American culture. The residential school system operated from the 1880s into the latter part of the 20th century. The system forcibly separated children from their families for extended periods of time and forbade them to acknowledge their Indigenous heritage and culture or to speak their own languages.

Self-Regulate

The action of monitoring and managing one's own emotions, thoughts, and behaviours. Being able to adapt to the demands of a given situation.

Situational Depression

This is an informal term that does not represent a clinical diagnosis. Situational depression is a short-term form of depression that occurs when an individual has not adapted to changes brought about by a particular, sometimes traumatic, event. People may experience recurring episodes of situational depression, which can deepen its impact.

Situational Trauma

Traumatic experiences that are single incidences, typically sudden and with a clear ending of the situation. Also known as Type I trauma.

Social Contagion

Also called behavioural contagion, this term refers to the spread of behaviours, ideas, or attitudes through a group of people.

Subjective Units of Distress Scale (SUDS)

A measurement tool used by clinicians and healthcare professionals to determine the level of distress an individual is experiencing. Typically verbalized as a scale from zero (no distress) to 10 (highest distress).

Sympathetic Nervous System

A branch of the autonomic nervous system that becomes activated in response to stress, threat, and fear. Systems in the body are activated to prepare to flee from or fight off a threat, such as blood pressure and heart rate increasing, breath quickening, and adrenaline and glucose pumping through the bloodstream to provide energy to respond.

Therapeutic Alliance

The bond, founded on trust, between a helper and their client. Identified as a common factor for successful counselling, this bond is an active process that involves a helper's empathy, active listening and intuitive guiding of the process. It is also built by the client's active engagement and willingness to risk and trust the process.

Transgender

An individual whose gender identity differs from the biological sex they were assigned at birth. This may mean they identify with a different gender, such as FTM (female to male), someone who has female biology but identifies as male, or MTF (male to female), someone who has male biology but identifies as female. This term may also represent someone whose gender identity lies beyond the binary of male or female. This could include people who identify as gender fluid (identity moves along the male-to-female spectrum), Two-Spirit (an English word representing Indigenous identities that encompass all genders), or gender queer (someone who does not feel they fit within any of the established gender descriptions or identifies with a combination of them).

Transitioning

When an individual begins the process of outwardly expressing their gender identity, which may differ from their biological sex assigned at birth. This can include changing their clothing, hairstyle, asking people to use a chosen name or specific gender pronouns, taking hormones, or choosing to undergo surgery.

Transphobia

The fear of, aversion to, and discrimination against transgender and non-binary people.

Two-Spirit (2S)

A term developed by Indigenous activists in 1990. The term is a translation of the Anishinaabemowin term *niizh manidoowag*, which means "two spirits." It is sometimes used to distinguish Indigenous people within LGBT2SQ+ communities, and it refers to a multitude of cultural traditions that recognize the roles of people who have both masculine and feminine energies. The term may be used to name sexual, gender, and/or spiritual identities. It is only appropriately used by an Indigenous person to describe their own identity.

ACKNOWLEDGEMENTS

I am deeply thankful for the many people who have assisted in bringing this book to completion. This has truly been a project of many hands.

In particular, I want to thank the contributors to this book; they provided the knowledge and expertise without which this book would not be possible. Thank you John Koop Harder, Tricia Klassen, Michelle Gibson, Amber McKenzie, Trish Harper, Sheri Coburn, AnnMarie Churchill, and Marion Brown. Special acknowledgement goes to Wendy Loewen, who first read and provided feedback on the manuscript, helping me give the authors guidance. Thank you to Randy Grieser, Heidi Grieser, Wilma Schroeder, Tricia Klassen, Ana Speranza, Tyler Voth, Micah Zerbe, and Chantel Runtz who took the time to read, review, and provide feedback on the manuscript. I'm grateful for the skill and input of Anastasia Chipelski and Tim Runtz, who helped edit the book, for the care and watchful eyes of copy editor Danielle Doiron, and proofreaders Jessica Antony and Ardell Stauffer.

A big thank-you to Lisa Friesen. Her creativity resulted in a wonderful book cover and interior design.

Finally, I can't express my gratitude fully enough for the clients who have opened their lives over many years to all the authors in this book. It is because of this unique privilege as counsellors to enter the lives of others that we can hope to share something of use to others.

Vicki

SPEAKING AND TRAINING

Our trainers are not only specialists in their fields, but also dynamic speakers who deliver content-oriented presentations that are both engaging and informative. You can choose from over 40 workshop topics in the areas of counselling, mental health, and violence prevention, and you can access training three different ways:

Public Workshops

We offer workshops throughout the year in various locations that are open to anyone who wants to attend. Visit our website to find out what workshops are being offered near you.

On-site Training

Training offered on location – right where you are. If you have a group of people to train, on-site training is often the most cost-effective and convenient way to obtain training. Our workshops can be customized and tailored to meet your specific needs.

Webinars & Live Streaming

No matter where you live, you can easily access one-hour webinars, and full-day live streaming workshops right from your desk.

For more information:
Crisis & Trauma Resource Institute
www.ctrinstitute.com
info@ctrinstitute.com
877-353-3205